WILHELM DILTHEY
A HERMENEUTIC APPROACH TO THE STUDY OF HISTORY AND CULTURE

MARTINUS NIJHOFF PHILOSOPHY LIBRARY

VOLUME 2

WILHELM DILTHEY

A HERMENEUTIC APPROACH
TO THE STUDY OF HISTORY
AND CULTURE

by

ILSE N. BULHOF

1980

MARTINUS NIJHOFF PUBLISHERS
THE HAGUE / BOSTON / LONDON

Distributors:

for the United States and Canada

Kluwer Boston, Inc.
160 Old Derby Street
Hingham, MA 02043
USA

for all other countries

Kluwer Academic Publishers Group
Distribution Center
P.O. Box 322
3300 AH Dordrecht
The Netherlands

Library of Congress Cataloging in Publication Data CIP

Bulhof, Ilse Nina.
    Wilhelm Dilthey, a hermeneutic approach to the study of history and culture.

    (Martinus Nijhoff Philosophy Library; v. 2)
    Bibliography: p.
    1. Dilthey, Wilhelm, 1833-1911. 2. History - Philosophy. I. Title.
    II. Series.
    B3216.D84B84   901   80-12499

ISBN 90-247-2360-4 (this volume)
ISBN 90-247-2344-2 (series)

PRINTED IN THE NETHERLANDS

CONTENTS

ACKNOWLEDGMENTS

I am much indebted to Georg G. Iggers, Bernard Delfgaauw, Richard Kieckhefer and Lucy Gerritson Selby for their careful reading of the manuscript and stimulating remarks. Jim Kaufmann read an earlier version; without his encouragement this book might not have reached the publication stage. The hospitality of the Division of General and Comparative Studies of the University of Texas at Austin which he headed has been of great help to me. Walter Wetzels offered helpful comments on the translation of some German passages. The many conversations with B. J. Warnock Fernea on topics dealt with in this study have been very pleasant and profitable to me. I owe a special debt to Palmer Wright whose feeling for interpretation matters and language problems has greatly helped me in formulating my thoughts.

I am grateful for the grant awarded to me by the Netherlands Organization for the Advancement of Pure Research (Z.W.O.) for the publication of this book.

I also want to thank my husband Frans and my children Roger, Justin and Hanno for their understanding and patience with occasional spells of absent-mindedness on my part while writing this book. The interest of my relatives, Jan Rutgers, Miep Rowaan-Palm and Ina Kalff-Francken in my work has been very valuable to me.

Wir verstehen das Leben nur in einer
beständigen Annäherung; und zwar liegt
es in der Natur des Verstehens und in der
Natur des Lebens, dass das Selbe auf den
verschiedenen Standpunkten, in welchem
sein Zeitverlauf aufgefasst wird, ganz
                verschiedene Seiten uns zeigt.

We understand life only in a continuous
approximation; it is in the nature of
understanding and in the nature of life
that life, according to the various points
in time from which it is understood
discloses to us very different aspects of
                                        itself.

CHAPTER ONE

INTRODUCTION

Philosophy originates in man's amazement over the richness and complexity of reality. It attempts to articulate in words and concepts what reality is. Starting from the recognition that this reality is experienced by all humans but experienced in many different ways, the philosopher tries to find reality's heart, its center, its hidden treasure — the tree in the middle connecting heaven and earth, the central point from which the stupendous intricacy of experience begins to make sense and from which order can become visible. To ask "what is reality?" is, indeed, to recognize that we have entered a maze.

The hermeneutic philosophy of Wilhelm Dilthey (1833-1911) is the fruit of his own wanderings in this maze. Like many intellectuals of his age, he had lost faith in the Christian religion in which he was raised. In his college years, he turned from theology to philosophy, in particular, the history of philosophy and of human thought in general — wondering about the origin and value of the astounding variety of past belief systems. At the center of reality's maze he found the insight that reality as faced by man is comparable to a literary text: it "means" something to us. Reality is not a mute object, but an autonomous source of meaning, an act of self-disclosure; knowledge of reality is therefore not the product of actions performed by an active subject upon a passive object, but a communicative interaction between two subjects. What is known — reality at large or an aspect of it — is never a world out there, existing independently from the observer; reality speaks to us and gives itself to our understanding. Life styles and cultures are lived interpretations of this self-disclosing reality. The meaning of human existence is found by "reading" the meaning of reality's grand text, and to actualize in concrete existence one's interpretations of it.

Some philosophers, after having found what they thought to be reality's guiding principle, have transformed this maze into a French garden and have presented it as a well-organized picture, static and docile. Dilthey is different. His philosophical thoughts never completely coalesce into one formal system. In this sense, his writings present a puzzle to the reader, a second maze through which the reader must find his own way. Perhaps Dilthey failed to reach the center of his own thought; perhaps he could not think through in any precise way the discoveries he made; perhaps he cautiously refrained from arbitrary reductions of the elusive processes he saw disclosing themselves. In Dilthey's defense, however, we can recognize that philosophy at times does need to be heuristic — provisional — when faced with new emergent possibilities.

Dilthey belongs to those philosophers who enlarge the agenda of legitimate philosophical concerns: their works are rich, often repetitive, congested — full of promise; they are seminal resources of thinkers, more systematic, but less imaginative. Such seminal philosophers need the collaborative assistance of a scrupulous critical commentary, which this study hopes to provide.

In exploring the maze of Dilthey's writings, the twists and contradictions of his thought become apparent. We come to see the architect as a thinker torn apart by the conflicting tendencies of his thought. Dilthey was a thinker who as a positivist rejected metaphysical speculation, but who as an idealist continued to yearn for it. He wanted to be a scientist but he realized that the positivistic ideal of scientific objectivity cannot always be applied to subjects like history. For this reason he devised a hermeneutic science with a special kind of objectivity, but he nevertheless modeled his conception of objectivity after that of the natural sciences. He wanted to use for the understanding of the human world the hermeneutic understanding used in the interpretation of literary texts, but he could not explain in what respect texts, and works of art in general, differ from ordinary objects; while he attempted to do justice to the intrinsic validity of man's interpretations of reality as translated into personal life styles and cultural patterns — as the Historical School had first stressed — he could not free himself from the conception of a temporally coherent history to which these interpretations are subordinated. Dilthey seemed overwhelmed by the richness his imaginative mind perceived.

I intend to show that Dilthey's insight, however gropingly formulated, that reality discloses itself like a text, is the most promising aspect of his thought, and anticipates much current discussion of a hermeneutic approach to the study of man. Dilthey is interesting because on the one hand he adhered to the Enlightenment tradition of increasing man's domination over reality through science, while on the other hand he realized the human mind's historical and cultural conditionedness. This latter insight gives Dilthey his startling modernity.

The purpose of this study is to guide the readers through the intricacies of his labyrinth and then to show the relevance of some of his insights to the contemporary study of history and culture.

However, to find the center, or guiding principle, of any system of thought (whether it be a maze such as Dilthey's or a French garden such as Hegel's), and to enjoy the fruits of the tree growing at its center — the tree of knowledge — is not enough. Understanding its underlying pattern is therefore only the first part of the challenge presented by Dilthey's maze. After having found the center of the labyrinth, the wanderer has to find his way out again — a part of the task as perilous, if not more so, than the first one, as every reader of the story of Theseus, the Minotauros and Ariadne knows. Indeed, after having found the guiding principle that creates order the explorer has to return home to his own world. The new insights gained during the adventure have to be made fruitful for his own life; they have to be integrated in his own existence, and be acted upon. For this reason in this study I will distinguish between Dilthey's personal assessment of his work and my own evaluation of it — between Dilthey's consciously stated intentions and the promise of his thought.

The relevance of Dilthey's thought to the study of culture may surprise those who are familiar with his historical orientation. But as in his approach the past's periods are being transformed into the past's cultures, I feel justified to extrapolate from his writing a general hermeneutic philosophy of culture that is of equal importance to history and cultural anthropology.

Dilthey considered cultural products as expressions of meaning comparable to literary texts — texts written in a variety of scripts such as behavior, artifacts and social structures. As expressions of meaning, these "texts" have to be interpreted. Consequently, the discipline of interpreting literary texts, or hermeneutics, became relevant to Dilthey in his study of cultural products. The word hermeneutics is associated with the Greek god Hermes, messenger of the gods who functioned as the mediator between gods and men. Hermes transmuted what was beyond the limited understanding of man into a form mortals could understand.

At the time, the dominant approach to text interpretation was the philological. The philological approach developed in connection with the study of classical antiquity, focused on the literal meaning of texts. The philologist established the text in its original form, and made a close study of the period in which it was written. This enabled him to know the exact meaning of words. The philologist studied the text in the context of its time, that is to say, he studied it "historically."

Another hermeneutic approach, by contrast, developed in connection with the study of the Bible focused on the existential meaning of texts – its message. Because this theological hermeneutic approach to text interpretation sees the text primarily as communicating a message, it has three aspects. First, the interpretation is seen as a form of translation by which the unintelligible and alien is rendered in an intelligible and familiar idiom. Second, the text is approached as relevant to its readers; the interpretation is therefore done in such a way as to personally affect its readers. Third, the text is considered as a voice coming from an alien world – as disclosing insights the readers could not have acquired by their own efforts alone.

The novelty of Dilthey's approach to the study of the human world lies in his application of this latter hermeneutic model of text interpretation to the study of cultural products in general and in his intimation of a hermeneutic approach to human existence. Dilthey's philosophy of world-views (*Weltanschauungslehre*), a hermeneutic philosophy of existence, considers reality itself as a text to be interpreted by man, and concrete human existence as a lived interpretation of reality's text.

This view enabled Dilthey, in a remarkable reversal of the then prevalent Enlightenment and historicist conceptions of man and history, to accept the intrinsic validity of past and present cultures, however strange they might seem, and to consider the others of those alien cultures as equals.

Dilthey simultaneously considered human life from two perspectives. He employed the familiar outsider's perspective of reflective thought, which looks back upon history or anticipates its future course, establishing its past structure and meaning and projecting plans for the future. This has been the dominant perspective on history since the Enlightenment. Dilthey also used, however, a novel insider's perspective: that of lived experience. Approached from this angle, history appears as a synchronic structure of which the living person represents the center. This latter perspective provided Dilthey with the foundation for his philosphy of world-views, which articulates the life experience of a subject who finds himself in the midst of life and history, and who is unable to emancipate himself from his historical conditions in order to direct sovereignly the course of history. By linking man's inability to emancipate himself from history with the notion that reality is comparable to a literary text, Dilthey suggested that cultures are lived interpretations of reality, and as such intrinsically valid. Thus, the periods of history or the steps of historical development are transformed into the cultures of the past. Dilthey's philosophy of world-views offers thereby a model of history as an aggregate of cultures rather than a line of progressive achievements — a model which harmonizes well with the comtemporary trend toward an "anthropologization" of history.

Any study discussing Dilthey's work would be unfair if it only treated his hermeneutic approach. For in attempting to construct an appropriate methodology for the study of man, Dilthey came up with many other suggestions besides that of a hermeneutic study of culture and a hermeneutic philosophy of existence — suggestions which are of great interest to contemporary social science and philosophy.

As far as the social sciences are concerned, he saw philosophies, religions, and the arts as rooted in human consciousness; consequently, instead of writing what is called today "intellectual history," he envisioned a history of consciousness (*Bewusztseinsein-stellungen*). He proposed a structural theory of human psychological development, according to which the human personality is gradually formed in a process of interaction with the natural and cultural environment. He suggested a similar structural theory of historical development, seeing it as analogous to personal development. He drew attention to the structural relationships between cultural phenomena. His study of cultural and social structures led him to an understanding of the function of social phenomena. He thus became a precursor of contemporary structural functionalism in sociology and cultural anthropology. He proposed a theory of historical significance that deserves to be explored further. He suggested that human culture represents a kind of language, thereby anticipating a major element of Lévi-Strauss' cultural anthropology. His notion that understanding the human world is interpretation of meaning has much influenced Max Weber's conception of sociology as a *verstehende Wissenschaft*.

In Dilthey, the social scientist and philosopher are combined. His reflections on the temporal structuredness of human existence furnished a point of departure for Martin Heidegger's philosophy of human existence and of being. Jean-Paul Sartre, on the other hand, was diametrically opposed to Dilthey's ideas on history and time, ideas that functioned negatively as a springboard to initiate a philosophy of his own.

In this study I have frequently compared Dilthey with Nietzsche. For although Dilthey's scholarly temperament was nearly the opposite of Nietzsche's daring style of life and thought, their goal was the same: to understand and value human life "as it is," that is, without appeals to a transcendent reality. Dilthey and Nietzsche both realized that new understanding of "time" was crucial to such an effort.

Contemporary philosophers such as Hans-Georg Gadamer and Jürgen Habermas have revived the interest in Dilthey's thought. Gadamer's own hermeneutics, however, is decidedly past-oriented, stressing the "power" of the past and the value of tradition, while that of Habermas is future-oriented, stressing the power of man and his capacity to overcome tradition – man's social-historical "self" – by creating new responses to life. The aspect of Dilthey's hermeneutic philosophy emphasized in this study differs from these approaches: its concern is Dilthey's foundation of the intrinsic validity of cultures – past and present, and his hermeneutic approach to the study of man and his products.

In the English-speaking world, Dilthey's contributions to social science and philosophy have not been sufficiently appreciated so far. Among historians and social scientists of the English-speaking world Dilthey is known almost exclusively for his advocacy of the theory of intuitive understanding of the world of man (*Verstehen*), presented in his *Introduction to the Human Sciences*. English-speaking philosophers have hardly heard Dilthey's name at all.

A combination of several factors has kept scholars from exploring Dilthey's work adequately. First, in the beginning Dilthey's theory of *Verstehen* was misunderstood as an empathy with actors of the past, with what they had thought and done; thus, Dilthey was accused of a simplistic psychologism. That the British philosopher Robin George Collingwood took up Dilthey's theory of *Verstehen,* turned out to be a mixed blessing for Dilthey's reputation; in Collingwood's hands, *Verstehen* was limited to an understanding of the conscious decisions of the past's actors, and was, moreover, linked to an extremely subjectivist interpretation of historical knowledge. But even more important, Dilthey's thought is usually classified as belonging to the tradition of historicism, which has become increasingly suspect in the eyes of Anglo-American scholars. In particular German historicism is often seen as an expression of that irrationalism that eventually resulted in Nazi politics, or that, at best, undermined the ability of the German people to resist the Nazis. Today, we can look, however, at Dilthey's work afresh.

The precipitating concern behind this study is the challenge posed by the plurality of world cultures. After World War II, the United States and the countries of western Europe seemed to resume the world leadership they had exercised for so long. But the rise of Marxism in various parts of the world and the nationalistic drive for political and cultural independence on the part of Third World countries challenged this Western world political and cultural hegemony. The stubborn persistence of nondemocratic and non-Western cultures has destroyed any illusion that all cultures will eventually merge into one world-wide civilization resembling existing Western culture.

So this present political situation has caused a renewed interest in Dilthey's hermeneutic reflections. Having lost its naive belief in the exclusive validity of Western civilization, our age has finally become open again to the puzzling richness of the variety of world cultures. As a result, we are ready to explore Dilthey's imaginative attempt: to embrace the historicity of human existence without becoming defensive about, or losing faith in, our own culture.

The present discussion of Dilthey's work is organized around eight themes, each treated in a separate chapter. Each theme represents, as it were, a separate walk in Dilthey's maze.

The theme to be discussed in the next chapter is that of the human sciences and Dilthey's early response to positivism and historicism — the two intellectual avenues by which his thought was shaped. At this stage of his development, Dilthey attempted to defeat positivism by separating the human from the natural world, thus making room in the first for man's creative mind. He attempted to defeat historicism by devising a study of the mind-created human world that was as empirical and as objective as natural science.

Dilthey became increasingly aware of the fact that a study of the human world could not attain the same kind of objectivity as natural science. The third chapter's theme is Dilthey's attempt to found the objectivity of historical knowledge on the similarity between history and memory.

As he realized, however, that this solution to the problem of objective historical knowledge did not lead to its goal, he elaborated his novel hermeneutic approach to history. This approach sees the concrete historical world as a text inviting various interpretations.

The theme of the next — fourth — chapter is Dilthey's further venture into hermeneutics: his philosophy of world-views. In this philosophy Dilthey extended the hermeneutic approach from historical evidence to reality as a whole. He considered human behavior and its products as interpretations of the grand text of reality as it is encountered by man.

Dilthey was, however, too close to the Enlightenment conception of history to accept a conception of history that did not have a meaningful temporal order between its periods. Chapter V has as its theme Dilthey's reflections on the problem of history's temporal coherence, or "meaning." Considering history from the perspective of its mind-created temporal coherence, Dilthey saw history as a literary text being written by mankind — a text in which the author himself, mankind — figures as the hero. Although at first he had resisted the interpretation of history as a progress in civilization, he ultimately described history's course in progressive terms.

Chapter VI deals with the conception of man that underlies Dilthey's philosophy of culture and, as we will see in chapter VII, of history as well. He considered man as a psycho-physical organism with limited freedom. Although conditioned by nature and by previous experience, man has a capacity for personal, creative action because he can remember and anticipate events. Dilthey's view of man accounts for the historicity of human existence — man's conditionedness by natural and cultural factors, and his freedom toward them.

Dilthey applied the model of personality development to historical development. This view of the course of history is the theme of chapter VII.

The translations of Dilthey's texts are mine, unless otherwise indicated. As each language orders differently the world of experience — each expressing in its own words and syntax a different world, as it were — translating is a hazardous enterprise. One example of many is the problem of how to translate the German word *Geist* which can be translated as "mind" or "spirit." In most cases I have opted for the translation *mind* which I think Dilthey would have preferred, as mind has fewer mystical overtones for the English reader than spirit. In cases in which a German word seemed particularly suggestive I have added the German words between brackets. In pondering how much freedom I could allow myself in translating Dilthey, I took my lead from Hermes who not accidentally was the God of interpreters and travelers. This caused me to consider the passages to be translated as stepping-stones leading the reader from a world seen through the glasses of his familiar English language to the world as seen by Dilthey's at the turn of the century. Consequently I have aimed at a compromise between a literal translation which is too close to Dilthey's German, and a free translation which has lost too many of its moorings in the original.

The organization of this study as outlined above does not present the chronological development of Dilthey's thought. Instead, it represents one itinerary through the maze of his thought — a trail chosen in the hope that its exploration will stimulate the reader to undertake his own study of Dilthey's writings, and eventually to find his own way to a hermeneutic study of history and culture.

CHAPTER TWO

THE HUMAN SCIENCES (*GEISTESWISSENSCHAFTEN*)

The goal of this chapter is threefold: first, to examine Dilthey's social background and the ideological aspects of his work; second, to describe the combined challenge that positivism and historicism posed to his thought and; third, to analyze Dilthey's first response to this double challenge. I will begin the chapter with examining his environment. This will provide us with a background for the interpretation of his work.

Wilhelm Christian Ludwig Dilthey was a typical representative of the class of public officials which for centuries had played a prominent role in the bureaucratic Prussian monarchy. He was born in 1833 in Biebrich on the Rhine in the Duchy of Nassau. His father was the chaplain of the Duke of Nassau. The ministry was also a profession common in his mother's family.

Dilthey graduated in 1852 from the Gymnasium in Wiesbaden, and following the family tradition, enrolled at the University of Heidelberg to study theology. Three semesters later he transferred to the University of Berlin. But Dilthey did not like the dogmatism of the theologians, and he became more interested in philosophy. He passed the examination in theology at Wiesbaden in 1856 to please his parents, but he graduated at Berlin at the same time in philosophy.

For a few years as a secondary school teacher, Dilthey could not combine his studies with the requirements of teaching. He then became a free-lance writer, publishing short articles and reviews under a pseudonym. In 1861, he went back to the university, enrolling in the faculty of philosophy, where he worked under the supervision of Friedrich Adolf Trendelenburg, whose main interest was the history of philosophy. Dilthey also took courses and seminars from Leopold von Ranke, the leader of the Historical School, who impressed him deeply. In 1864, he received his doctoral degree in philosophy, with a dissertation on the theologian David Friedrich Schleiermacher. In that same year he was admitted as a university teacher after writing an essay on ethics.[1] From 1866 till 1882, Dilthey taught philosophy at several German and Swiss universities: Basel (1866), Kiel (1868) and Breslau (1871). In 1882 he received a call from the prestigious University of Berlin, the intellectual and administrative center of the recently created German Empire. Dilthey occupied the chair of philosophy till 1905. After that date he devoted himself exclusively to his writing, his main philosophical interests being the history of philosophy and of consciousness, and the epistemology of history. He died in 1911.[2]

The period of his life he spent at Berlin coincided with an era of great social and economic change in Germany. In 1883, when Dilthey published the work for which he is most widely known, *Introduction to the Human Sciences (Einleitung in die Geisteswissenschaften)*, Bismarck dominated the political arena, and industrialization the economic sphere. This setting is significant. In Germany, the 1850s and 1860s were decades of rapid industrialization: in relatively few years, Germany developed from an economically backward country into one of the great industrial powers of Europe. As a result, the shopkeepers and public officials who during the 1840s dominated the German middle class became overshadowed by a new entrepreneurial bourgeoisie. Whereas this older middle class, to which Dilthey belonged, had been oriented toward the public good and liberal politics, the new middle class gave up such idealistic principles for profit making; much to Dilthey's dismay, the new capitalists were interested in immediate gains such as competitive selling and the accumulation of capital.[3]

By moving to Berlin, he entered the traditionally most prestigious social circle of the country. In the nineteenth century, the public officials of Prussia, and later of the Empire, the gymnasium teachers, university professors and government officials, had become the nonentrepreneurial ruling class of the country, an aristocracy of the mind, who with their classical education and long university training considered themselves the bearers of culture.

In accordance with the general outlook of his class, Dilthey was deeply concerned about the rampant economic materialism of his age. In mid-century, the problem had marked social overtones. Till far into the nineteenth century the public officials had virtually no contacts with the industrial elite. The latter had not received the standard education, nor did it occupy itself with politics. In the years 1850-1870, however, this situation changed. The industrial elite now began to send its offspring to the gymnasia and universities, thus acquiring the certificates which were the official entry into public life. As a result, the style of the political discourse changed: the cultivated elite of officials had appealed to timeless universal ideals of moral and political legality, national greatness, and cultural creativity; its style had been idealistic. In the second half of the century a realistic style in politics emerged, in which power conflicts, bargaining, and competition played an important role.[4]

Given these circumstances, it is not surprising that Dilthey increasingly lamented the lack of faith and idealism in his time. He firmly believed in the importance of such values as individuality, loyalty, and community. As a professional historian of philosophy, he focused on the "life of the mind." He was more interested in the cultural aspects of history than in the economic and political ones.

University professors in particular formed a highly prestigious and well-salaried segment of the German officialdom. Like most intellectuals, they had generally speaking, been liberals. Their liberalism, however, was oriented more toward government by law than by consent — playing down such ideas as voting rights, parliamentary government, and civil rights. The German liberals were mostly interested in a cultural, more-or-less apolitical liberalism; they advocated freedom of thought, learning and expression. The events of 1848 and 1849 had created reservations toward democratic ideas and popular pressure: the liberals began to assume a more defensive position and to compromise with the monarchic-bureaucratic powers. This inclination became especially strong after 1870. The liberals tended to lean more and more toward an unquestioning support for the existing regime. They became a "vaguely conservative and decidedly official establishment."[5]

Dilthey was no exception. His political sympathies lay with the right rather than the left.[6] He adhered to the well-known Burckean conservative notion that the left typically strove to recreate society according to abstract ideas, and thereby ignored the unique character of German society: "It is clear to the historical sense that the historical ethos of a people . . . should not be hurt and dissolved by the intervention of a radical theory . . ." (*Gesammelte Schriften* [hereafter abbreviated as GS], vol. VI, 82). Dilthey's view of the French Revolution is similarly indicative of his conservative political position. He maintained that the Revolution had failed because of an inadequate understanding of human life. Trusting human reason, it had ignored the nonrational power of the will (GS, vol. X, 50).

After 1848, the traditional German ruling elite saw its culture and values threatened not only by the acquisitive temper of the younger, capitalistic generation, but also by the rising demands of the working classes. Socialism was much feared.

Dilthey attacked the Socialists by dismissing their hopes for a better world as a Utopian vision. He saw mankind as saddled with invincible instincts, such as the drive for power and the instinct of aggression, which would never be changed. The Socialist vision of a classless society he considered unrealistic. "These [namely human] instincts and the [political and social] relationships [*Verhältnisse*] that originate from them, will, in spite of all dreams, vanish only with mankind itself" (GS, vol. V, 210). He did not believe in the ability of Socialism to shape the future in a creative way. The poets of his own age did not find grace in his eyes either: they embraced such "silly" ideals as Socialism, individualism and irrationalism. Comparing his own age with that of the Renaissance, Dilthey exclaimed:

How much more fortunate were Cervantes, Erasmus, Rabelais, when they attacked the feudal-aristocratic society. They did this in the name of healthy bourgeois reason. They had the feeling of the future victory of their cause. Sovereign humor radiates as a result from their works. Our bourgeois dramas have no heroes. The sharp pictures of existing society that we create do not display the feeling that even in social crisis human nature disposes over secret victorious forces, and that man can shake off all the nonsense that plagues us today. Now our writers are impressed by the romantic ideal of the destruction of the family and property in favor of tyranny by the State, then by the backward Scandinavian cult of the law of the individual divorced from social ties, then again by the Slavic stirrings of those parts of man where the barbaric animal resides (GS, vol. VI, 287–287).

Dilthey had little confidence in the lower classes. We can infer his antidemocratic position from a remark made in the introductory part of the 1887 essay *The Imagination of the Poet: Elements for a Poetics (Die Einbildungskraft des Dichters. Bausteine für eine Poetik)*. He stated that the function of art and literature is to remind man of the "ideal goals" which are constantly threatened by the "lower instincts of human nature." In order to fulfill their functions, artists need institutional support to combat the masses, which are ruled by their instincts.

The arts definitely require a training of the artists and an education of the public by means of esthetic reflection, if their higher character is to be formed, appreciated and defended against the lower instincts of the masses. Has not the grand style of our literature been maintained by the royal power of our two poets who resided at Weimar?[7] By means of an all-compassing esthetic process of manipulation directed from Weimar supported by available journals not without the terrorism of the *Xenien*,[8] they [the poets] have kept Kotzebue, Iffland, Nicolai Albay, and have uplifted the good German public and have confirmed it in its belief in *Hermann and Dorothea*[9] and *The Bride of Messina*.[10] This belief has not come naturally to it (GS, vol. VI, 106-107).

Dilthey was a patriot, deeply committed to the Prussian monarchy, later to the Empire, and generally, to the ideals and values of German culture. Dilthey concluded, for instance, in the passage just quoted on the "silly" ideals of contemporary writers, that "only from the profundities of Germanic nature can the poets acquire an aware-

ness of what life is about and what society should be, [an aware-
ness] that answers better the needs of the present age" (GS, vol. VI,
286).

In a letter from Basel in 1867, he told his father that he did not
understand the pessimism of his colleague Jacob Burckhardt, and
suspected that it stemmed from provincialism and a lack of knowledge: if Burckhardt had lived in Berlin, he would not have enter-
tained such negative ideas about his age![11]

In contrast to many of his colleagues in history, Dilthey never
succumbed to a narrow nationalism. In a letter to Heinrich von
Treitschke, professor of history at the University of Berlin, Dilthey
in 1870 agreed with Treitschke that Prussia should remain a military
state with a strong monarchy, holding that the war of 1870 was
a necessity for Prussia. But he expressed reservations about
Treitschke's idea that war is good in general: it seemed to him "evil"
(*frevelhaft*) "to declare such an immense quantity of terrible pains
to be suffered by others as necessary for the moral development of
the human race."[12] Although he made special study of German
culture history, his orientation was cosmopolitan. He was, to use
Nietzsche's expression, a "good European." There is no trace of
racism in Dilthey's love of German culture.

In the correspondence with his friend the Count Paul Yorck von
Wartenburg, Dilthey expressed negative feelings about his time. He
was alarmed by the rootlessness of modern city life. He claimed
that only agricultural occupations with their firm ties to the soil
could guarantee "steadiness of character."[13]

In contrast to his political and social views, intellectually Dilthey
was more innovating. In the *Introduction to the Human Sciences* he
attacked the prevailing positivism and historicism. He was in the
vanguard of the thinkers who turned away from the one-sided
mechanistic image of man associated with positivism and scientism.[14]
But he was not alone in this respect. In the early 1870s, the philosopher Friedrich Wilhelm Nietzsche had launched the attack
against positivism and historicism in his *Untimely Meditations*, but
had received little response.

Almost thirty years later, Edmund Husserl published his *Logical
Investigations* (1900-1901), a work which joined Nietzsche's and
Dilthey's attack, and which Dilthey immediately recognized as
important.

In biology another protest against the mechanistic interpretation
of life was initiated somewhat later by Hans Driesch, who in 1903
published his *The Soul as an Elementary Factor in Nature*. In France,
Henri Bergson published his book on conscience, *Essay on the*

Immediate Data of Conscience. In the field of literature, Marcel Proust, among others, focused in his novels on his inner life, describing in great detail the movements of his psyche. In psychology, several authors drew attention to the importance of consciousness and will in human life; in England, for instance, the philosopher James Ward.[15] In the United States, William James worked in the same direction. In Austria, Sigmund Freud demonstrated from the 1890s onward the importance of unconscious factors in human behavior. However varied the interests of these scholars and writers were, they shared the concern of re-establishing the importance of the creative activities of the mind that were ignored by the positivistic scientists. Although the idealist reaction was a general phenomenon in Western civilization, it was especially strong in Germany. The negative attitude toward modern quantifying science and mechanism was typical for the German tradition of natural and social science thought.[16] Their attitude had been articulated with particular clarity in response to Cartesian rationalism by Gottfried Wilhelm Leibnitz, who may be considered as the founder of the German tradition. Johann Gottfried von Herder and Wilhelm von Humboldt applied Leibnitz' normechanistic conception of the universe to the study of man and history. Dilthey's philosophical efforts continued this German tradition, now directed, however, at its nineteenth-century adversary, scientific positivism.

Dilthey's concern for the recognition of the mind's creativity expresses both a moralistic concern for spirituality and also the concern of the older middle class that was replaced by a new, more materialistically inclined generation of capitalists. It also expressed their class' resistance against Socialism. This idealism was also used as a weapon against Socialism. Indeed, in the second half of the nineteenth century, idealist reaction against positivism acquired political overtones. For the positivism Dilthey combatted was not only the positivism of the liberals, but also that dominating Socialist thought of the time. For the modern reader, the identification of Marxism with positivism may sound surprising. But it should be remembered that at this point the young Marx and his humanism had not yet been discovered. Marxists and Socialists saw in positivist science their best weapon against the ruling classes, and against the ideologies employed by these classes to keep the lower classes at bay. By the same token, middle class thinkers saw in the idealist approach to the world of man with its emphasis on the power of mind, the most convincing defense against Marxism and Socialism. Dilthey was one of them: in his case antipositivism is clearly connected with his conservative political stand.

Though Dilthey was a member of the ruling elite, and his philosophy can be seen as an expression of the frustrations and aspirations of this class,[17] the significance of his work lies in his imaginative approach to the study of man. After all, the contrast between a teleological-descriptive and a causal-mechanistic approach to human reality — which is the basis of the contrast between idealism and positivism — transcends that between nineteenth-century political parties. It has a long ancestry: it goes back to Leibnitz, to medieval realist philosophy, to Plato and Aristotle, and even beyond. Such a long history of a difference in philosophical orientation should make us hesitate to reduce all such philosophical differences to a reflection of political orientations. The ideological connections between theory and praxis that have occurred in the past are not necessary ones,[18] just as positivist philosophy or science is not a necessary precondition for a politics that deals with the problem of social injustice.[19] Indeed, it would be ludicrous to explain such a long-standing divergence in terms of the modern opposition between political conservatives and progressives. However, at the end of the nineteenth century, specific historical circumstances caused thinkers with conservative instincts to turn to humanism, progressive thinkers to embrace positivism. Having said this, it is important to keep in mind that Dilthey was less concerned with social than with intellectual problems.

As a theological student, Dilthey quickly perceived that the theology taught at the universities had lost its relevance for contemporary life. Thus, the Christian faith in which he had been raised so piously came to represent in his eyes a useless survival in the modern world from an age in which religion had played a vital function in people's life. Although he was of the opinion that the Christian faith had nothing to offer to modern man, Dilthey felt that the emotional and intellectual needs formerly answered by it still persisted, but were neglected in the contemporary agnostic and science-minded age. This neglect led to a shallow mode of life. Dilthey was deeply concerned about the age's materialism and lack of interest in the life of the mind. Thus, he set himself the task of restoring the former interest in the deeper questions of life — but in a form appropriate to an age which had turned away from nonempirical theological and philosophical assumptions.

In setting himself this task, Dilthey faced the combined challenge of positivism and historicism. The challenge posed by positivism was its suspicion of everything reminiscent of metaphysics, such as conceptions of a soul, or of the Hegelian mind. In response, Dilthey wanted to elaborate a conception of man that recognized the importance of mind in human life, without, however, falling back upon the notion of a substantive soul.

The challenge posed by historicism was its conception of time as an eroding force invalidating past and present reflection. In response, Dilthey wanted to elaborate a philosophy that took seriously the historicity of human existence without, however, losing faith in its own statements.

Before analyzing the human sciences, Dilthey's first response to positivism and historicism, we must take a closer look at these movements, and at Dilthey's attitude toward them.

Nineteenth-century positivism may be described as both a general philosophy of reality, and as a theory of science. As a general philosophy, positivism — first formulated by Auguste Comte in his *Course of Positive Philosophy* (1830-1842) — denies the existence of a transcendent reality behind the perceptible world; consequently, it rejects the validity of theological and metaphysical speculations. It sticks to the reality of experience. It adores natural science. Thus, nineteenth-century positivists studied reality, including man and his products, "scientifically." "Scientific" in the context of nineteenth-century positivism means empirical. Moreover, nineteenth-century positivists, assuming that everything in reality occurs according to laws, explain all phenomena, including the phenomena of individual life and human history, on the basis of causal connections.

As a theory, positivism has had both negative and positive results in regard to philosophical conceptions. On the negative side, positivism has led in the latter half of the century to a mechanistic conception of human behavior from which mentalistic conceptions were banned. On the positive side, in recognizing the reality of the outside world, and its independence from man, positivism kept open possibilities for seeing the concrete world as more than a reflection of human thought.

Although Dilthey's thought benefited greatly from exposure to positivism, he considered it a mechanistic science. It seemed to Dilthey strangely inappropriate for the study of man. For if man is not a being gifted with the theologian's soul, he certainly is a being gifted with such attributes as consciousness, reason, and a moral awareness — attributes of which no trace is found in the rest of organic or inorganic nature.

Dilthey was appalled by the positivists' neglect of man's moral nature, by their belief that moral values are merely the result of adaptive social processes, mere tools for survival in the struggle for life. For him, Darwinism in particular was "the mass grave of contemporary scientists."[20] He refused to believe that egoism and adaptive behavior could ever lead to a sense of justice.

Dilthey considered that other standard-bearer of positivism in the study of man, John Stuart Mill, as naive to think that all citizens of a modern society are rational, responsible persons with a capacity for independent judgment. He felt that Mill overestimated the role of reason in human behavior.[21] Dilthey had no more sympathy for Thomas Buckle's attempt to write a "scientific" history of England based on historical laws. He called *The History of Civilization in England* "a dead book."[22] The utilitarianism of such positivists as Herbert Spencer and Jeremy Bentham was no better.[23] Dilthey saw British "lucidity" as superficial,[24] lacking in "mystical profundity."[25] For Dilthey, there was more to man than the banal drive for survival. He felt that man has a heroic and religious nature that often prompts him to sacrifice himself, often without any hope for compensation.

Now, we must consider historicism and Dilthey's reaction to it. Nineteenth-century historicism is, like positivism, both a general philosophy of reality and a theory of the study of history. In this study, the common usage of the word will be followed according to which historicism means the non-nomological individualizing approach to history.[26] It was first used by Johann Gottfried von Herder (1744-1803), and remained especially strong in Germany. Historicism as a general philosophy may be described as the view that everything pertaining to the human world is part of the stream of time — that is, part of history. Like positivism, historicism denies the existence of eternal values and the Enlightenment conception of natural law. Instead, it maintains that all cultural phenomena, including values and laws, traditionally believed to be "eternal and immutable," are products of a this-worldly creative force which could be nature, history or life. As history's creative force is constantly on the move, each historical age has a value system of its own. Historicism stresses that human behavior is conscious activity, and maintains that because history is — to a large extent — created consciously by free minds, it cannot be considerd a lawful mechanical process. It maintains that every age has a distinct individuality, and that historical phenomena cannot be understood or judged by means of universal principles. It rejects the view of history as a teleological process.

As a theory of history, historicism explained the phenomena of the human world on the basis of their historical context, stressing the uniqueness of each.[27]

As a general philosophy, historicism has both negative and positive consequences. On the negative side, historicism has always been followed by two persistent shadows: moral scepticism and its opposite, the idolatry of history. The realization of the transitoriness of all value systems made it difficult for many people to feel a firm commitment to the values of their society. What was the justification for the value systems they were asked to uphold? Why that particular system and not any other? Thus, historicism undermined faith in reason's ability to know any truth, and easily led to moral scepticism.

Historicism's second shadow is the opposite of the first: the idolatry of history. Historicists sometimes tended to romanticize history, transforming it into a creative force in its own right. They saw history as the manifestation of some creative force – the human mind, or time, or nature, or life. Some historicists concluded therefore that the history of their own society must be a movement toward the inherently good. Their critical attitude toward their own society was undermined by this blind faith in the historical process.

Historicism also has, however, its positive side. To its credit, it has evidenced a deep respect for the different ways in which man has shaped his world in the course of history. Historicists evaluated the variety of past and present cultures positively as the specific manifestations of the creativity of the particular force that they saw as giving birth to history. They contended that the individual belongs to his contemporary environment and that human behavior should be judged only according to the value systems operative at the time.

The fact that the epithet "historicist" commonly is reserved for writers who have fallen prey to moral scepticism or the idolatry of history indicates a negative attitude toward historicism.[28] This one-sided focus on historicism's dangers, however, causes students to overlook its most interesting aspect: its affirmative attitude toward past and present alien cultures. Dilthey was well aware of the dangers of historicism. As he saw it, philosophy had been defeated by history – reason had been defeated by time. An almost overwhelming amount of facts about the past had been flooding the present, and had given so much information concerning past belief-systems that nobody could still believe in the "eternal" value of any one of them. As a result of the modern historical awareness, all belief systems seemed somehow faulty and untrue. If in the long history of mankind nobody had been able to find the truth about life, it was unlikely that reason would discover this truth in the future.

All his life Dilthey was haunted by what he saw as the failure of philosophy – and thus the failure of reason – to find the truth about life. As late as 1911, in his essay "The Types of World-views and Their Elaboration in Metaphysical Systems" Dilthey described the disturbing anarchy of systems resulting from reason's failure:

We look back upon endless ruins of religious traditions, metaphysical statements, demonstrated systems. For many centuries, the human mind has attempted and tried out possibilities of all kinds to find a scientific basis for the coherence of things, to depict it in poetry or to proclaim it by means of religion. Methodical and critical historical research investigates every piece, every relic of this long labor of our race. Each of these systems excludes the other; one contradicts the other; none can prove itself (GS, vol. VIII, 76).

He commented that philosophy was a mere "lifeless shadow" of its former self, for it could obviously no longer provide "a fixed [feste] position for the feeling of life [Lebensgefühl] and a certain goal for action" (GS, vol VIII, 6). Philosophical systems were merely expressions of the inherent tendency of every living religion and philosophy toward "fixity, effectiveness, power, universality" (GS, vol. VIII, 86). He ascribed to belief systems what Nietzsche called a "will to power," a tendency to expand and acquire power over men's minds: metaphysics is "the will to ... subjugate [unterwerfen] the coherence of the universe and of life itself" (GS, vol. VIII, 97). Thus, the fact that a philosophical system has commanded respect and has attracted followers testified to its vigor, not to its rational truth. Far from being the products of a pure and sovereign reason, philosophical systems were historically conditioned products of the human mind. And as "what is conditioned by historical circumstances is relative in value" (GS, vol. VIII, 6), philosophies could not contain the objective or scientific truth about reality.

He felt that attempts of contemporary philosophers like Mill to overcome scepticism and to restore philosophy to the status of a scientific discipline had failed. Mill's empiricism had been destroyed. Nor did he find the older Cartesian rationalism credible: "the superb religious-metaphysical background" upon which it was based was "no longer self-evident"; the "religious coherence between creator and creation" was consequently no longer "an inescapable fact." The capacity of reason to grasp and conquer reality in thought had consequently become a mere hypothesis (GS, vol. V, 88).

Dilthey personally suffered from the rootlessness the increase in modern historical awareness had brought — from the historical malady, as Nietzsche called it. In his later writing he referred to the loss of certainties historians had brought as "the wound brought about by the knife of historical relativism"; he wrote about the "destructiveness" of historical consciousness (GS, vol. VIII, 121, 234). In another essay also written in his later years, "The Essence of Philosophy" (1907), Dilthey described how historical awareness conflicted with philosophical creativity and undermined the philosopher's self-confidence.

Seen historically, every philosophical solution belongs, to some present, and a position in it. Man, this creature of time, has — as long as he works with it — the certainty [*Sicherheit*] of his existence in that his creation is not immersed in the stream of time, that it is something lasting. In this illusion, he creates more confidently and forcefully. Here lies the eternal contradiction between creative mind and the historical consciousness. It is natural to the first to want to forget the past and to ignore the potentialities of the future; the latter, however, lives in the knowledge of overall time; it sees in the creation of any one work the relativity and transitoriness common to all. This contradiction is the quietly suffered pain of contemporary philosophy. For the present philosopher's creative thinking has to confront historical consciousness for without the latter, his philosophy would embrace only part of reality (GS, vol. V, 364).

The tone of despair of these utterances indicates the pressing existential problem that the failure of reason, resulting in moral scepticism, created for Dilthey. Thus, upset by the negative effects of positivism and historicism on his contemporaries' morale, Dilthey launched a counterattack, a strategy of combining history and philosophy which he called the human sciences (*Geisteswissenschaften*).

The project for the human sciences went back to the years 1859 and 1860, although Dilthey remembered that he first had an inkling of combining philosophy and history while a student at the gymnasium.[29]

In a reflection of 1859, recorded in his journal, Dilthey noted that it might be better to turn from a speculative discipline as is philosophy to the empirical study of history, though a new kind of history. The history he had in mind would provide insights "from the totality of human development" concerning philosophical questions such as the end toward which the earth had been made, and the goals toward which society had been moving in the previous fifty years. "The historian with a special interest in the forms of human existence, [and] the laws which condition it, has an equally authentic insight into that part of the truth which man is allowed to see as the philosopher."[30]

On the same day in which he envisioned this new kind of history, Dilthey in his diary mentioned also the other interest that would occupy him during his lifetime: the necessity for a new "critique of reason." He indicated the following points of departure for such a critique:

1) [it has to study] the psychological laws and drives from which art, religion and science equally originate

2) it has to analyze systems as products of nature — as crystallizations, of which models [*Schemata*] are the original form — models which follow from the basic features of (1)

3) it does not result in scepticism; it has as its basis those necessary and universal ways of operating of the human mind [which require], like all sensory perception, scientific treatment.[31]

A few days later, Dilthey indicated the focus he had found for his philosophical thought: no longer should the philosopher devote his efforts to a study of reality "out there"; this is beyond his grasp. He should study man, because man is the origin of all philosophical systems of past and present. Dilthey traced the history of philosophy to "the nature of man." He rejected the notion of any independent development of philosophical thought that follows its own laws. The human origin of philosophy, however, does not make its history arbitrary: the ideas created by man develop from a given kernel according to universal laws.[32]

So far we have seen the emergence of two topics that would occupy Dilthey's attention in later years: history, and the "critique of reason." A third lifelong interest surfaced during these years: his fascination with structures. Dilthey compared a philosophical system with a melody, and also with a crystal. He stated that a system of thought has a structure as its basis as do melodies and crystals. By seeing its basic design, a philosophical system can be simplified, and this, Dilthey commented, is the best proof that one understands it.[33]

About a year later, in 1860, Dilthey expressed an interest in what he would later call the history of consciousness (*Bewusstseinstellungen*) (GS, vol. I, 416): he planned to write "a history of the Christian world-view in the Western World," a project he intended to combine with a psychologically based "critical investigation of the philosophizing and religious mind on the basis of a historical understanding of the genesis of systems and system-building."[34]

In a remark of November 14, 1860, Dilthey announced triumphantly that he had found the goal of his life: "to understand the importance of religious life in history, and to present it in its [living] movement of these our times, which are moved exclusively by state and science."[35]

In spite of his feeling that religion does no longer present a satisfying world-view, Dilthey realized the overriding importance of Christianity in the past. Deeply influenced by Schleiermacher, he saw the essence of Christianity not in the content of its dogmas but in the religious feeling they expressed and the religious life they embodied. The Christian faith was rooted in the emotional needs of the human mind. Changes in religion correspond to changes in the human mind, in man's consciousness of reality. If one wanted to understand religion, one had therefore to study human nature, not "ultimate reality" or "God." The contemporary study of religion and of religious history had to focus on the psychological conditions under which religious beliefs originated.

Dilthey also maintained that if one wanted to understand the nature of man, one had to study religion. He believed that mankind had not outgrown its religious needs as such, only the specific ways in which they had been expressed in Christian theology.

Dilthey was already aware of his opposition to the positivistic world-view. He wanted to bring home to his contemporaries that the "mind" was of overriding importance in human life and history, and that they themselves were also "spiritual" or religious beings. He wanted to make his contemporaries aware of the essence, the real nature, of philosophy and religion from which they were alienated; the essence of religion was not its intellectual content but its emotionality and idealism. People had to realize again the importance of the life of the mind — with its emotions and will — so alarmingly neglected and despised at that time. Dilthey complained that in the contemporary age everybody pursued political and social goals, that nobody reflected any more, not even in traditionally religious Germany. Indeed, he reported that many thought that it had taken the Germans too long to forget their speculations (*Grüblerei*), and that they had only at the last possible minute switched instead to happy activity in the service of progress. Still a minister at heart (and also a future public official), Dilthey warned that "no people can flee itself," that the worst way to progress "is by simply breaking with the achievements of a laborious past." He preached that the stern awareness of duty, the earnestness of religious reflection were the best basis for free constitutions" (GS, vol. XI, 69).

Dilthey intended thus to revive the life of the mind. He planned to formulate for his own time the "religious-philosophical world-view," now "buried under the ruins of our theology and philosophy."[36] Such a world-view should not be yet another philosophical system, however, for "a glance at the past of speculation" makes clear that such an enterprise is impossible.[37] But what was the new philosophy to look like?

Dilthey sought a solution by assuming that there is partial truth in each system. Anticipating his later hermeneutic doctrine of world-views, Dilthey wrote in 1861 that philosophical systems were "one-sided, but nevertheless honest [*aufrichtige*] disclosures of human nature." Whoever understands these systems, understands man.[38]

Thus, we find in Dilthey's writings of the early 1860s many elements that went into his later philosophy: the curious mixture of positivism — in the form of empiricism — and idealism — in the form of a commitment to man's creative mind — the idea of a history of human thought as a whole, the tranformation of philosophy into an empirical historical science, the notion of the structuredness of mental phenomena, the necessity for a new critique of reason, and the hermeneutic notion of a partial disclosure of truth of philosophical and religious systems.

Dilthey doubted at this point, however, whether his forces would be sufficient to carry out such a gigantic task, for it would be necessary, first, to clarify the phenomenon of historical conditioning of the human mind; this would have to be done by developing "a new critique of pure reason on the basis of our historical-philosophical world-view."[39] The problem of form would be a second difficulty in writing the history of philosophy and religion he planned to undertake, Dilthey indicated. Whereas political history has a "poetic form," the "history of the mind" is still "formless"; only in biographies has a form in which to present historical material been found. Dilthey asked himself whether it would be possible to write the history of the mind in a similar way.[40]

His plan for the human sciences represented an attempt to combine all of these demands. As he said in his inaugural address given at the University of Basel in 1867, entitled "The Literary and Philosophical Movement in Germany 1770-1800," philosophy has to become a "science based on experience," "focused on the lawful coherence of phenomena" (GS, vol V, 12-13). As the progress of the study of the human world has so far been less successful than that achieved in the natural sciences, he saw it as the special task of his generation to give the science of man a new basis — to found "an empirical science of mental [*geistige*] phenomena" (GS, vol. V, 13).

Thus, Dilthey appeared to advocate positivism in philosophy. But he warned his hearers at the same time not to ignore the speculative generation of thinkers that had succeeded Kant. In defending Hegel, Schelling and Fichte, he argued that their appeal lay not in the intellectual constructions they built, but in the emotional power they radiated. They offered a world-image (*Weltansicht*) that satisfied a need of the German mind of the time, a worldview which for the first time since the Greeks gave people again a sense of coherence and meaning concerning the totality of facts (GS, vol. V, 14). He argued that the character and the success of the Idealist movement was "determined by the continuing historical conditions under which they emerged," conditions which demanded systems that could arouse enthusiasm. In the address, Dilthey undertook to explain "the feeling of life" (*Lebensgefühl*), "the spirit of the epoch" (*Geist der Epoche*), and the "ideal of life" (*Lebensideal*) of those romantic generations. He showed that philosophy in general has a "lawful (*gesetzmäszig*) relationship to the sciences, art and society," and that philosophy is an integral aspect of the life of any given period. But he argued that "the task of philosophy is different in each period" (GS, vol. V, 27). During the years 1770-1800 the task of philosophy had been the formation of grandiose systems. Today, he said, the task is "to continue on Kant's critical road, to found an empirical science of the human mind in cooperation with researchers of other disciplines; [and] to discover the laws which condition the social, intellectual and moral phenomena" (GS, vol. V, 27).

Such a philosophical study is important for practical life, Dilthey maintained, because it gives man "power over mental phenomena," just as the natural sciences give man power over external nature. Dilthey felt that if philosophy could be transformed into an empirical science, it would regain the important position that it had, for the time being, lost to the natural sciences.[41] To upgrade philosophy was, to Dilthey, to work for the supremacy of the mind. Idealism might at the moment be a phenomenon of the past, but Dilthey felt that its spirit should be revived in the present. Whilst his announced empirical methods were those of a nineteenth-century positivist, his sympathies lay with the idealists.

Although at the time Dilthey gave this address, he had little direct knowledge of the natural sciences, during the years which followed he became deeply involved with natural science research. He worked closely with colleagues in physiology and psychology. He was especially friendly with the physiologist Wilhelm His and followed his classes and laboratory sessions. He studied works on physiology, psychology, and biology. In particular, he was interested in the evolution of species.[42] Dilthey took the student of nature, carefully analyzing the laws and structures of the natural world, as his model for the human scientist analyzing the laws and structures of the human world.

Finally, in 1883, Dilthey published the *Introduction to the Human Sciences,* in which he laid the foundation for the study of man as an autonomous field of research with a methodology of its own — a field he called the human sciences or *Geisteswissenschaften*. This plan for the human sciences represents Dilthey's first response to the challenge of positivism and historicism, although he treated the problem posed by historicism as creative thought in later writings. He hoped that by means of a "positivistic" study of man, that is, a study as rigorously empirical or "scientific" as that of nature, the essence and basic goal of human life could be objectively established. By declaring at the same time the existence of a fundamental separation between the world of man and of nature, Dilthey made it possible that in this study of man the life of the spirit could be fully appreciated.

The theme of Dilthey's study, as announced in its introduction, is the necessity to understand human life "on its own terms," now that religious and philosophical systems, with their claims of absolute validity, have collapsed. To that end, human life has to be understood by empirical means, by studying the experience man has collected of life in past and present. The emphasis of the introduction is on the methodology of the empirical study of human life.

The writers of the German Historical School had emancipated the study of society and history from metaphysics, but had not developed a theoretical framework which could be brought to bear on the empirical study of history. They had neglected to think about the theory of knowledge and the subjective, or "psychological" factors involved in knowledge of the human world in general, and of history in particular. Dilthey's *Introduction* was intended to fill that gap.

Dilthey proposed that a foundation for the study of man and his world could be found in the central phenomenon that characterizes human beings: the human "mind" manifested itself in will, in responsibility, and in reason. Dilthey felt that in the world of nature, everything works mechanically. The world of man, by contrast, is one of freedom and creativity. The unique development of each individual human person and of mankind is the consequence of this specifically human freedom (GS, vol. I, 6), stemming from the human mind. The human-historical world man has created is a "mental" (*geistige*) world, because it is created by persons conscious of their goals; it is also a historical (*geschichtliche*) world, because it changes with man's consciousness of the world.

By stressing the unique nature of the human person and the world he has made, Dilthey attempted to protect the study of man against attempts of the natural scientists to apply their methods and their mechanistic concepts to the study of man. He tried to build a fence, as it were, around the human world, a barrier carrying the sign "positivists, keep out." Within the fence would be an area in which the life of the mind was allowed to flourish freely – an area, moreover, in which Dilthey himself could experiment in developing his own research methods and concepts.

Following in the footsteps of other German thinkers about history, notably Wilhelm von Humboldt, Johann Gustav Droysen and Leopold von Ranke, Dilthey rejected the natural science approach as inadequate. Instead of the causal explanation by which the natural scientists made nature intelligible, he suggested making the world of man intelligible by means of "understanding" (*Verstehen*). Nature has no consciousness, no volition, reason, or emotion. It can only be explained in purely mechanical terms of cause and effect. Human beings, on the other hand, are goal-oriented. Man and his products — such as the social worlds he has built in past and present, his works of art, literature, science and religion — have to be understood "from the inside."[43] One way to understand the inner reasons that prompted an actor or group of actors to act as they did in creating would be by means of "re-experiencing" (*nachempfinden*). Dilthey suggested that re-experiencing (through empathy) would clarify the actors' behavior.

Dilthey did not think, however, that simple acts of re-experiencing were enough to explain the human world. His conception of the mind was, indeed, more complex. Like Freud, he saw the mind's operations as coherent over time. Human memory links present thought with past experience for the individual and for the society. The events and thoughts of a person's life make a coherent pattern which the human scientist must seek to understand. Similarly, the historical events and products of a particular society form a coherent pattern. *Verstehen* is the process of discovering this underlying pattern — which can be done by recognizing that relationships exist among mental acts, and between mental and physical acts. *Verstehen* is therefore not so much the investigation of motives, but the discovery of these coherences existing among mental events.[44]

Dilthey suggested that in view of the complexity of the human mind a number of specialized disciplines should study human life from various points of view. Just as it had been necessary to divide the study of nature among several natural sciences, so there had to be likewise an array of human sciences. These included psychology, anthropology, political economy, history, law, philology, literature and the arts, and philosophy. Dilthey introduced the word *Geisteswissenschaften* for these disciplines.[45]

The source material for the human scientists would include the life-experiences of the researcher and those of others. Dilthey argued that man's awareness of life stems from his total life-experience, not just from scientific experiments or logical thinking (GS,

vol. I, 38). Man's understanding of life is best expressed in a variety
of cultural products, such as religious, philosophical, social and
political writings, works of science, and works of art. As
the existing notions of life are the outcome of a long developmental
history of man's experience with life, the study of languages and
of history are important for the knowledge of human life. Thus,
the source material for the human sciences consists of the present
and past cultural products in which man expressed his understanding of life, as well as the researcher's personal experience.[46]

In summary: the human sciences as formulated in the *Introduction
to the Human Sciences* are the fruit of Dilthey's transformation of
philosophy into an empirical or "scientific" enterprise. The human
sciences are "philosophy" in a form appropriate to modern times:
the speculative philosophy of former times had become the array
of empirical sciences studying human life as it has been lived through
the ages. The knowledge gained, Dilthey felt, would enable man to
project his goals effectively, that is, in accordance with the inner
tendencies of human life and history. Dilthey always rejected an
esoteric philosophy – the philosophy of professors of philosophy,
cathedra philosophy as he called it – that has no influence on
practical life. Knowledge, and first of all philosophical knowledge,
should be useful to man.

In view of the practical benefits Dilthey expected from his
"philosophy," the human sciences, it is not surprising to discover
that "the age of reason" figures as a kind of lost paradise in Dilthey's
thought. At that time people still had confidence in reason and
philosophy.[47] Dilthey wrote in the *Introduction to the Human
Sciences* that during the eighteenth century, man had finally
succeeded in seeing the history of mankind from a "natural" point
of view: the human past was then for the first time interpreted as a
steady growth in rational thinking and in civilization. At that time,
it had seemed so easy to continue to progress in the same civilizational direction society was already heading. And indeed, Immanuel
Kant could still hope that the discovery of the laws of nature in
history would soon enable man to control social life.[48] After the
discovery of the laws of social life, Kant had hoped, the students of
man and his world would join the natural scientists in guiding
mankind toward a happy future.

But while the natural sciences had proved quite successful in
gaining power over nature, the students of society by the end of the
nineteenth century had not all succeeded in formulating laws that
would give man similar power over society. They consequently were
failing to provide the kind of intellectual leadership for mankind's

march into the future. The task of guiding man's lives had passed by default to the natural sciences.

Dilthey expected that in its new form of the human sciences, philosophy would again be able to fulfill its task of leading mankind into the future, by discovering the general principles that underlie human life — a task, he felt, the Historical School had sadly neglected:[49]

The approach of the Historical School which wanted only to describe, and which excluded rational guidance by scientific principles, is finished for us. Fortunately! For life needs guidance through reflection . . . (GS, vol. VI, 189).

Now philosophy had to become once more "a power that could determine human action and thinking" (GS, vol. V, 89). By being able to manipulate history on the basis of a knowledge of human nature, man would no longer be subjected to a history that was senselessly, purposelessly developing by itself. In this way, reason would conquer time.

Nietzsche and Marx expressed similar hopes for man's future control of history. They hoped that by freeing man from the past, as it continued to exist in the present in traditional dogmatic beliefs, he would become free to devise his own future.

Dilthey considered the human sciences also to possess an emancipatory power. He wrote that, generally speaking, philosophizing has always been "a personal property, a kind of character to which had been ascribed at all times [the ability] to free the mind [*Gemüt*] from tradition, dogmas, prejudices, from the power of instinctive affects, even of the power [*Herrschaft*] of that which limits us from the outside" (GS vol. VIII, 32). By freeing the human mind from its former dependencies, philosophy in the form of the human sciences would encourage the growth of independent and autonomous individuals and societies.

Because of his desire to restore the mind to its rightful place in human life, Dilthey neglected to pay attention to the material factors operating in history. He considered that a free mind was enough to shape history into a desired direction. This one-sided idealism is, however, tempered as we will see later by Dilthey's insight into the restrictions put on finite minds by natural and historical circumstances.

It is interesting to compare Dilthey's project to the thought of Pierre Bayle and David Hume. These thinkers wanted also to base philosophy on an empirical study of history. Like Dilthey, Bayle was interested in the nature of man. His method was to question the philosophers of the Western political tradition on this topic, reasoning that ultimately he would find some common ground in the philosophers' thoughts on man, and he believed that those shared insights would represent universally valid knowledge. However, Bayle discovered that all the philosophers he studied contradicted each other on just about every point; he became a sceptic, concluding that the nature of man could never be known, and that reason does not lead man to truth.[50] In contrast, Dilthey accepted the contradictions expressed in the sources as evidence of the richness of human life. What for Bayle constituted partial and therefore invalid understanding, represented to Dilthey a wealth of information.

History and philosophy had been combined also by Hume. His *History of England* illustrates his views concerning political philosophy, while his historical knowledge in turn supported his political views. Hume's historical and philosophical interests are complementary aspects of his philosophical scepticism, according to which complete certainty regarding the essential nature of things is beyond the grasp of human reason. But Hume's scepticism was mitigated, because it allowed for an adequate level of certainty with regard to appearances, the phenomena of daily experience. Thus, Hume undertook to establish a "science of man" that would be useful for private and public life. The similarities between Hume's science of man and Dilthey's human sciences are obvious. But there were also differences: Hume ascribed predictive power to his science of man, while Dilthey did not. And whereas Hume felt that it was a relatively easy task to establish the laws and uniformities of human life, Dilthey felt that the structures of human life were hidden and had to be searched for.[51]

Dilthey felt, unlike Bayle and in agreement with Hume, that their search would be rewarded by valid knowledge. The problem for Dilthey, then, was how the objectivity of the human sciences would be established.

The *Introduction* represented only a beginning of Dilthey's struggle against positivism and historicism. In order to refute the moral scepticism encouraged by historicism, objectivity in the study of man was an absolute requirement, for nobody would be convinced of the value system to guide the proper conduct of human life if he were not sure that such a system corresponded to human life's true nature.

In the natural sciences, he felt, objective knowledge mirrors reality; it is "pure," untainted by distorting subjective factors, the fruit of "pure," or scientific abstract reason. Kant had studied the limitations of this scientific reason, drawing its boundaries around the domain of natural science. But what kind of objective reason was to be employed in the human sciences? The problem here was that knowledge of the nature of the human world coincides with the knower's consciousness of himself as a human being, and cannot be abstracted from the life of the knower. His reason, then, is an integral part of his total life, his personal history and the history of his society, hence, Dilthey's designation of it as "historical" reason.

Dilthey had planned a second volume to follow his *Introduction*. Its topic would be the critique of historical reason. He described this as the philosophical elucidation of "man's capacity to know himself, and the society and history he has created" (GS, vol. I, 116). He tentatively indicated that this historical reason – we might also say, this finite reason – is not only conditioned by "external" factors – or, as we would say historical factors, but also by "internal" and "psycho-physical factors" (GS, vol. I, 119). He would begin the book with a historical investigation of the relationship between "the modern scientific consciousness" and the human sciences (GS, vol. I, 407). Here, he would show that metaphysics was only slowly defeated, that the epistemological consequences of the collapse of metaphysics, caused by the insight into the conditionedness of the knowledge of the human world, were being drawn only little by little, and that the process was not yet quite completed.

This introductory historical part of volume II would smoothly lead to the substantive part of the book in which Dilthey would explain what he called the "psychological" point of view, which "attempts to solve the problem of knowledge, not on the basis of the abstraction of an isolated reason, but from "the totality of the facts of mind" (GS, vol. I, 408), that is to say, on the basis of concrete, finite or historical reason.

But the path leading to his "psychological" point of view was not as smooth as Dilthey had hoped. He never wrote the planned sequel to the *Introduction*. Two reasons may be cited for this, one external, and one internal.

The external reason was the discouraging lack of support for his human sciences on the part of his colleagues. During the 1880s and 1890s, Dilthey's view of the special nature of the human historical world, and of the specific methods appropriate for knowing it were attacked by Wilhelm Windelband and Heinrich Rickert. In an 1894 address, *History and Natural Science,* Windelband stated that the reality studied by the historian and the natural scientist are the same, but that their interest and approach differ. In his book *The Limits of Concept Formation in the Natural Sciences: A*

Logical Introduction to the Historical Sciences (1896-1902), Rickert reaffirmed the notion of transhistorical values.[52] Although he was educating a generation of new scholars at the University of Berlin, Dilthey was deeply affected by these signs that his basic ideas were not being accepted by other philosophers.[53]

However, his disappointment with the reception of his ideas on the human sciences was not the major reason he was unable to finish the second volume. The real barrier was instead provided by Dilthey himself, through his own conflicting understanding of history and historical reason. On the one hand, as a thinker following the Enlightenment tradition, Dilthey embraced the Enlightenment hope that history could be mastered by objective knowledge; on the other hand, as an empirical historicist historian, Dilthey was aware that the historian himself is part of the stream of history and that therefore his knowledge of history must be in some sense subjective and consequently incapable of mastering history. The central challenge to Dilthey, then, was to solve the problem posed by his Enlightenment conception of history and his historicist under-standing that all knowledge is historically conditioned. His attempts to meet this challenge form the subject matter of the next three chapters.

As we will see, Dilthey did not explore one, but two strategies simultaneously in the hope of reaching the goal of objective histori-cal knowledge of the human world. The first strategy he tried was the self-oriented approach; here, knowledge of the human world is seen as a form of knowing oneself. The second strategy was the hermeneutic approach, in which human reality is considered as a text to be interpreted. His progress along these trails was outlined in several shorter studies intended to serve as preparations for the planned critique of historical reason. One of these was the 1890 essay "Contributions to the Solution of the Question concerning the Origin of the Belief in the Reality of the External World, and its Justification"; another the 1894 essay "Ideas for a Descriptive and an Analytic Psychology." Later, he wrote two studies, "The Structure of the Historical World in the Human Sciences" (1910), and "The Types of Worldview and their Elaboration in Metaphysical Systems" (1911).[54] These later writings will provide most of the material for the next chapters.

CHAPTER THREE

HISTORY AS MANKIND'S MEMORY

Dilthey's interest in the study of history was motivated by his continuing search for guiding principles for human conduct. But how to find these principles? Historical study had shown him that human life had varied considerably during the ages. Thus, he realized that it did not make sense to search for human life's timeless structure. Moreover, because of the variability of life, he realized that no timeless principles existed upon which to base such a study. Dilthey therefore believed that the best way to understand life was to discover history's overall structure. For history, in Dilthey's eyes man's most significant product, could be expected to reveal something about its creator, man. But how, he wondered, could he, being himself a human being, know man's history objectively? How could historical knowledge, being a form of self-knowledge, be objective? The difficulty of knowing historical structures is, indeed, that their shapes cannot be directly perceived. A history is not given the way a material thing is given to visual perception: ready to be inspected from all sides. Histories have first to be recomposed as coherent structures by the historian. As Dilthey emphasized, in this process the historian has to decide which among the many facts constitutes a part of a history and which not. Facing the question how the historian can ever be sure that his reconstruction of the past's general structure is right, Dilthey found Hegel's thought on historical knowledge helpful.

In his earlier and middle years Dilthey had no sympathy for Hegel's speculative philosophy. In the *Introduction to the Human Sciences*, he praised only Hegel's historical sense and his awareness of the dynamic nature of history. But at the end of his life, after having studied Hegel's earlier works, and having written a work entitled *The Young Hegel (Die Jugendgeschichte Hegels)* (1905), Dilthey developed more sympathy for Hegel's thought. In particular, Hegel's identification of historical knowledge with memory seemed to offer a means of guaranteeing the objective knowledge of historical structures. Concerned about the apparent fruitlessness of the ups and downs of world history, Hegel affirmed in his philosophy of mind that history is the dialectical development of mind. In this development the achievements of earlier periods will never be totally lost: the "essential" elements of the past, those elements that had contributed to the development of mind's self-consciousness of itself, remain part of mind in the final stage of history, when it has reached absolute knowledge. Mind, having completed its work, retains in memory those aspects of its journey that are intrinsic or "essential" elements of its development. Because mind can easily recognize the essential elements of its development in its self-consciousness, it has no difficulty in establishing its own "essential development," that is, the basic structure of universal history. As a form of direct self-knowledge, mind's knowledge of its past is absolutely certain, that is, "objective." In Hegel's philosophy historical knowledge is a form of mind's memory of its own historically grown essence. The creator of history – mind – and the history it creates, or subject and object, are identical.

Dilthey felt, however, that by the identification of reality with rational mind Hegel had missed totally the fullness of historical existence as lived by man. Dilthey substituted therefore his concept of spontaneous nonrational life for Hegel's notion of rational mind.

In *The Structure of the Historical World in the Human Sciences* and its sequel, the *Project for a Continuation (der Aufbau der Geschichtlichen Welt in den Geisteswissenschaften* and *Plan zum Fortsetzung der Aufbau der geschichtlichen Welt in den Geisteswissenschaften)*, Dilthey designated life as the creator of history. Like Hegel, he thus equaled history's subject and object. As the life of history is "localized" so to speak, in man "life knows life" in studying history. That is to say, that in studying the past, man studies himself (GS, vol. VII, 136). Indeed, in *Verstehen* in general and in historical knowledge in particular, "man knows himself" (GS, vol. VII, 250).

Understanding [*Verstehen*] is a rediscovery [*Wiederfinden*] of the I in the Thou; the mind finds itself again in ever higher stages of coherence; the sameness of the mind in the I, in the Thou, in every subject of a community, in every system of culture, finally in the totality of the mind and universal history makes the cooperation between the various achievements in the human sciences possible. The subject of knowledge is here one with its object, and this [object] is the same on all levels of its objectifications (GS, vol. VII, 191).

Dilthey had, however, to adjust Hegel's theory of historical knowledge to this conception of nonrational life. How, he wondered, can one conceptualize a science of the nonrational? How can reason know what is not rational? (GS, vol. VII, 151, 191). In his words, "because life in its totality — experience, understanding, coherence of historical life, power of the nonrational in it — takes the place of Hegel's absolute reason, the problem arises as to how a science of history might be possible" (GS, vol. VII, 151; see also vol. VII, 191). Because he assumed that individual and collective, that is, historical, human life share the same type of structure, Dilthey sought the key to the scientific study of history's temporal structures, and of history's structure as a whole, in the empirical analysis of the temporal structure of an individual's life. Thus, in the *Project for a Continuation of the Structure of the Historical World in the Human Sciences* he investigated the possibility of objective autobiographical knowledge of an individual's life history. He called the auto-biography "the highest and most instructive form, in which the understanding of life presents itself to us" (GS, vol. VII, 191). After all, he felt, the observer best equipped to know the events of a person's life and to evaluate their true significance in the context of his life's coherent structure is the actor himself; the actor has in self-reflection (which is a form of direct self-experience), a direct means to know the basic structure of his past. Because the person who writes the story of his own life is identical with the person who has lived it, a special "intimacy of understanding" exists. With this approach Dilthey hoped to answer the question how a history — a coherent succession of events — can be known with any degree of objectivity or certainty.

First of all, Dilthey stated that there is such a thing as a coherent personal life history — that an individual's history forms a diachronic structure. He explained the temporal unity of a person's life by referring to the goal oriented nature of human behavior. Human beings do not live from moment to moment. They pursue goals which are projected on the basis of values. Because a person antici-pates the future, and moves from project to project, an individual's life receives some kind of unified structure. In Dilthey's words:

The same person who searches for the coherence in the history of his life has in everything which he felt to be the values of his life, the goals realized in it, the plan designed for it, [in everything] which he in retrospect conceived as his development, looking into the future as the design of his life and its highest good — in all of this he has already pre-established a coherence for his life from various points of view in which he realizes goals conceived on the basis of what he experiences as valuable in his life (GS, vol. VII, 200).

The problem with knowing the structure of one's life is, however, that it cannot be known immediately; a person has to have arrived at the end of his life before he can perceive it with some clarity. For while a person is engaged in the act of living, the full significance of his acts and of the events he experiences are not clear to him. Only future events, unforeseeable at the present, can bring out the true meaning of past and present events. Dilthey maintained that the future corrects the "deceptions of the moment" by clarifying in hindsight the true significance of each moment (GS, vol. VII, 200). Only in his attempts post factum to see his life as a whole does a person become fully conscious of its structure.

Thus, only at life's end can he write an autobiography that can claim objectivity.

In order to write his life story, a person needs to strain his memory to its utmost limits. A simple backward glance is not enough, that gives only a skeleton of the personal past. "I approximate a view of its totality only by taking it up in memory, so that all coherent moments have a place in it. Understanding thus becomes an intellectual process requiring the greatest efforts . . ." (GS, vol. VII, 227).

An autobiography is therefore a statement in which a person enlightened by hindsight expresses the true structure of his life. To a certain extent this structure has always been present, Dilthey felt, but it had remained unknown to the actor as long as his attention was absorbed by momentary experiences, and as long as he lacked full overview of his life. But the structure or "truth" of a life can be visible only at its end, when no future is left to correct or clarify any more elements of past meaning: "Only at the last moment of life can its meaning be determined, and thus meaning can properly speaking emerge only for a moment, at the end of life (GS, vol. VII, 237). It can emerge also for a complete outsider, another person who re-experiences this life.

An autobiographer's knowledge of his own life is not a "literal" reproduction of all occurrences that have happened. It involves perception of its basic structure, or interpretation. Such interpretation is, however, not arbitrary, for a person's life has concretely, visibly happened in certain definite ways. The visibilities of a person's life, such as birth, marriage, illness, death, as well-established events are the autobiography's fixed points.

Among [the] experiences there are some which have a special dignity in themselves and with regard to the coherence of life; these are stored in memory and rise above the endless stream of past and forgotten occurrences; and a coherence is formed within life itself. . . . Life itself has consequently accomplished half of the historical presentation (GS, vol. VII, 200).

Having indicated that the structure of personal life can be objectively known, Dilthey proceeded to the investigation of history's diachronic structure. He assumed a unified life-force which can be considered the creator of history, the way an individual can be considered the creator of his own life. He saw therefore a coherence between a society's vanished historical past, its anticipated future and its visible present similar to that found in the life of an individual.

Dilthey saw another analogy between individual and historical life in the continuing presence of the past in both personal and in historical memory. In an individual's life, the past is gone, it is absent; but it still has a presence of its own because it exists in memory (GS, vol. VII, 195). Granted that there are personal pasts about which in later years nothing is known. Having been experienced by the subject, these are *forgotten* pasts − but because of the interconnection between past, present and future in human life, these pasts are somehow still latently present. Dilthey wrote that the historical past is similarly present − embodied in objects surrounding us in the present: "As time progresses, we become surrounded by Roman ruins, cathedrals, and castles of the mighty" (GS, vol. VII, 147).

But whereas the meaning of personally gathered objects and personal souvenirs is clear to their collector, the meaning of the remains of a society's past is not: these remains "lie there as something whose connection with us has been destroyed" (GS, vol. VII, 225). Here, the historian has to step upon the scene. With his interpretative activity, he restores the lost connection between the objects that seem so alien to the present. According to Dilthey, the historian restores the social memory of communities and nations, and, ultimately, the memory of mankind itself. Thus, he facilitates their selfawareness. The historian's role is in this respect comparable to that of the Freudian psychoanalyst, who restores to consciousness his client's forgotten personal memories.

As a result of the historian's activity, nations, communities, and mankind itself know not what they *were*, because of the interconnection between past, present and future, but what they *are*; they are made conscious by the historian of the basic structure of their life, of their identity. Knowing who they are, they can act in full consciousness of their needs and ideals.

History has, thus, the same vital function in collective life (of a society or of mankind) as memory has in the life of an individual (GS, vol. VII, 279): "Think of a person who has no memory of his own past, but who thinks and acts only on the basis of what the past effected in him, [yet] without being aware of it."

Having lost his memory, a person would not be able to know what to do, to act consistently, to carry out plans, to fulfill his responsibilities. He would be at the mercy of the moment.

This would be the situation of nations, communities, of mankind itself, if we would not succeed in completing the remains, in interpreting the expression [left behind by the past], and in bringing the stories of what has been done out of their isolation and back into the context amid which they originated (GS, vol. VII, 279-280).

This identification of historiography with a society's collective memory drew Dilthey's attention to the social function of history. A society's study of its past articulates its memory. This memory is "productive for the social life of mankind": it causes a feeling of solidarity, a sense of shared values and a commitment to common goals which in turn inspires its cultural leaders — its hereos, political founders and religious leader (GS, vol. VII, 264).

This view of the historian as the facilitator of a society's memory, helping its members to become aware of their society's identity, and "historical" place in the world — and hence of the individual's task within his society — explains why Dilthey advocated an important place for the study of history in public education (GS, vol. IX, 10). Dilthey intended, after all, as we have seen in chapter II, his study of history to alert contemporaries to what he considered their "real," but at the time ignored, "spiritual" nature by reminding them of a past in which religion and philosophy played such an important role. By thus restoring the memory of the German people, and the people of Western civilization in general of their past, and by thus reminding them of their true nature, Dilthey hoped to reawaken in the present this "higher" nature.

Another similarity between the life of an individual and collective historical life, is that both have a coherent structure, because both are lived consciously and are goal oriented. The societies of history develop social value systems on the basis of their experiences, and they establish goals in conformity with these values. So collective, like individual, history occurs in a structured fashion. The individual, in writing his autobiography, has to state the truth of his life by sketching this structure, or essence; similarly, the historian finds, and expresses, the true structure, or essence, of the history of his nation, and of the human race.

Just as the "truth" of a person's life could be clear only at its end, so one would have to wait for the end of history "before one could possess the complete material needed for the establishment of its meaning" (GS, vol. V, 233).

But the life of history will, in contrast to that of a person, never end; the further history progresses, however, the better the past can be interpreted. The diachronic structure and meaning of life's past history can always be searched for. But as life never ends, history can never be known with total clarity by the historian; nor can it ever be remembered in its totality. It therefore can never become totally transparent. Thus, the Hegelian equation of history with memory failed to provide a basis for the study of history's structures.[1]

There was a second reason why Dilthey could not establish the possibility of objective historical knowledge: life's nonrationality. He realized that even a person's life — let alone history with its complicated structure — could never, not even at its very end, be interpreted in all its details. There are always events that cannot be forced into any meaningful interpretation, events that simply do not make sense:

[An autobiography] is an interpretation of life in its mysterious combination of chance, fate and character. Wherever we look, our consciousness works, toward the mastery of life. We suffer from our fates as well as from our nature; they thus force us to accommodate ourselves. The past invites [us] mysteriously to get to know the network formed by the meaning of its moments. But our interpretation remains nevertheless unsatisfactory. We never master what we call chance: what has become meaningful for our life as being marvelous or frightful, always seems to enter through the door of chance (GS, vol. VII, 74).

Nietzsche had pictured the Overman[2] as the master of his own fate; Dilthey had no such illusions. Not only is the individual not the author of his own life, but life itself has no rational structure. History coheres because historical subjects as nations anticipate the future and carry out plans. But not only did this coherence seem unknowable to Dilthey, at times it even seemed nonexistent. Dilthey often felt threatened by the arbitrariness of a life that cannot be mastered by reason; he was often close to experiencing life as an alien and almost hostile force. He admitted at one point having been overwhelmed by the immensurality of the impenetrability of the universe (GS, vol. VIII, 224). With such chilling realizations we are, indeed, not far from Sartre's experience, so poignantly expressed in *Nausea*, of the absurdity of life and of the futility of attempts to look for an objectively existing structure in personal life and history.

A third reason why Dilthey had to admit that history written by historians is less objective than a person's autobiography was the nonidenitity between the historian and his object of study. In writing history the historian is, after all, not describing the life he knows from personal experience. Dilthey saw in autobiographies fixed points of reference, because the individual knows from direct personal experience which events had been especially important to him. In historiography, however, no such fixed points exist: "The fixed relationships of the autobiography disappear. We leave the river, that is, the course of a life, and the endless ocean engulfs us" (GS, vol. VII, 252).

Dilthey maintained that there are means by which man can orient himself in travelling the ocean of history. He suggested that we take with us on "this wide ocean" certain "means of orientation" emerging from man's personal experiences with life, and his study of biographies. He listed several such "means of orientation," categories for the understanding of life: structuredness, movement in structured time, individuality of life's separate parts, life's dual forces of enduring and striving, its joy in progressing, and structured change[3] (GS, vol. VII, 252-253). He stressed that these categories are "not applied to life as something alien to it," but that they are present "in the nature of life itself" (GS, vol. VII, 232). But in the end he had to acknowledge that though life itself evidences those features, and thereby provides man with the proper tools to understand it, past life or history could inevitably by interpreted in different ways. The act of knowing the past cannot be compared with the processing of raw materials in industry; the latter is processed in one efficient, logical way. But, in treating the raw materials of history – the historian's sources – no such linear procedure exists in which one operation logically follows another, because the acts of knowing carried out on the historical data results from the observers' personal, and inevitably haphazard, experiences of life (GS, vol. VII, 160).

Reluctantly, Dilthey concluded that nothing can ever be proved in any final way in history; historical knowledge is forever vulnerable to scepticism. If documents are available, the actual events of the past can, from an external point of view as it were, be reconstructed with a high degree of probability; but the motives of past actors – the inner connections – can never be objectively ascertained. In *The Structure of the Historical World in the Human Sciences* he wrote that contemporary scholars "are still in the middle of solving [the] problem" of knowing historical coherences (GS, vol. VII, 106).

That memory does not lead to an objective knowledge of history seems hardly surprising to us. Since Freud's discovery of the unconscious, we know that a subject's memory is not a sovereign faculty able to perceive his past as it really is, but the humble servant of his unconscious needs. Memory sees only what its subject's unconscious needs allow it to see. The contemporary philosopher of history argues therefore that, to the extent that historiography can be likened to memory, it is, indeed, subjective.[4]

Dilthey, by contrast, still conceived of memory as a sovereign power linked to reason, a faculty which objectively can observe a subject's past. As a subject's objective observation of itself, memory was to Dilthey the counterpart of the natural scientist's observation of nature. As the natural scientist could master nature by his knowledge of it, so would the human scientist master history by his knowledge of mankind's past.

Dilthey's reflections on the self-oriented approach to the problem of objective historical knowledge are interesting because they are representative of the typical Enlightenment conception of man and history that has dominated the nineteenth century, and a large part of the twentieth century as well. They also show the weakness of this conception because of the impossibility for man to be objective about himself, and the need for a different conception of man and history.

In order to understand, first, what attracted Dilthey in this self-oriented model of historical knowledge, and, second, what its failure to provide objective historical knowledge meant to him, we turn to a description of its complex roots in the experience of life in the eighteenth and nineteenth centuries, and in the ways this experience was interpreted.

For the eighteenth-century thinker, history was neither self-oriented nor comparable to a subject's knowledge of his past. Before the nineteenth century "history" did not primarily focus on the actions and experiences of a subject such as mankind or a nation recollecting, in the person of the historian, its past.[5] History described actions performed and experiences not of one's own people, but simply of human beings, including the world's other peoples and cultures — actions and experiences that had occurred on the vast world's unchanging, timeless stage.

From classical antiquity until the nineteenth century, the writing of history was an act of *commemoration* of exemplary actions performed by others — worthy to be commemorated for that reason — rather than an act of remembering carried out by a collective self. Similarly, the word "memory" did not refer primarily to the past. Instead of meaning knowledge of what the subject remembers about himself or itself, memory simply meant memorized knowledge.[6]

The events of history were thus not primarily past events, but were facts that required memorization because it was believed that knowing them would be useful for later generations. These facts belonged to the timeless world of human affairs — timeless because they were unchanging in any fundamental way. The unchanging human world, the classical and premodern historian's object of study, was outside of the accidental confines of the small world of personal experience; the historian learned therefore about this world's past as he learned about nature. This type of historical knowledge, the memorized knowledge of things past, is what we might call "outer memory," "inner memory" being knowledge in which the past is known by means of experience, either personal or collective.

The inner world — the world of personal experience — and the outer world — the world of experiences undergone by others — had, in fact, not yet become differentiated in the eighteenth century. The prenineteenth century historian could freely move from one world to the other. He studied the deeds of others, but considering the past agents as not very different from himself, he experienced little difficulty in understanding them. Communication between ages or cultures had not yet become a problem.

Historiography before the nineteenth century was therefore potentially cosmopolitan; it included the experiences of mankind. Thus, the realm of the past was enormous; it extended over the whole world. Moreover, the whole past was useful. Because human life was basically the same at all times and places, knowledge about the whole of mankind was of practical value. An example from the writings of Lord Bolingbroke illustrates the cosmopolitan orientation of prenineteenth century historiography.

Bolingbroke considered the study of history an important source for the understanding of human life, that is, for the understanding of the species man, and of ourselves as members of the human race. He maintained that we not only learn from history by studying our own, but also by studying that of non-Western peoples:

Man is the subject of every history; and to know him well, we must see him and consider him, as history alone can present him to us, in every age, in every country, in every state, in life and death. History, therefore, of all kinds of civilized and uncivilized, of ancient and modern nations, in short, all history that descends to a sufficient detail of human actions and characters [of Western nations, Peruvians, Mexicans, Chinese, Tartars, Muscovites or Negroes], is useful to bring us acquaintance with our species, nay, with ourselves.[7]

Bolingbroke contended that "the school of example . . . is the world: and the masters of this school are history and experience." History was the treasure trove in which the universal human experience of life is preserved. He compared the history of all times and peoples with one large country: "History is a collection of the journals of those who have travelled through the same country, and been exposed to the same accidents."[8] How far this notion of history is removed from "inner" memory is indicated by the fact that Bolingbroke explicitly contrasted historical knowledge to memory and experience; he preferred historical knowledge, because, as he stated, the range of history is so much larger:

The advantage on the side of the former [history] is double. In ancient history . . . the examples are complete, which are incomplete in the course of experience. The beginning, the progression, and the end appear not of particular reigns, much less of particular enterprises, or systems of policy alone, but of governments, of nations, of empires, and of all the various systems that have succeeded one another in the course of their duration. In modern history, the examples may be, and sometimes are, incomplete. . . . Experience is doubly defective; we are born too late to see the beginning, and we die too soon to see the end of many things.[9]

How can we explain the transformation of historiography as broad-minded cosmopolitan outer memory into the modern Europe-oriented conception of historiography as inner memory that we encountered in Dilthey? Several factors, all resulting from the modern experience of time and life as creative forces, are of importance in this context: the belief in historical progress, the fragmentation of human time and space in periods and cultures, the interpretation of historical movement as the mind's development, and the novel function of memory and historiography as means to protect the personal and the social identity against the power of destructive time.

As a result of the Western world's economic development, for the first time the earth — that "valley of tears" — was experienced as potentially a place for happiness, and time — that enemy of man — as a medium of growth and life. The writings of Herder and Hegel illustrate this momentous change in the experience of life and time.

For Herder, the world's temporality is no longer God's punishment for a fallen mankind. Time is, by contrast, the very dimension of God's creativity. "The history of mankind is ultimately a theatre of transformations, which He alone can review who animates all these figures, and feels and enjoys them all."[10] In Herder's view, time is the precondition of the marvelous variety of historical phenomena. Change is good, lack of change, or tradition, bad: where people cling to old customs, he wrote, "the revolving Globe hangs fixed, an idle ball of ice over the abyss."[11] Tradition "fetters the thinking faculty both in politics and education. It prevents all progress of the intellect, and all the improvement that new times and new circumstances demand." According to Herder, God has given man understanding which gives him the opportunity to consciously work for change; understanding is man's power to "raise himself with art" — to improve himself;[12] man is obliged to use it to combat injustice wherever it is encountered.

Herder used the images of winged time and of a streaming river to indicate time's creative and dynamic nature. In his perspective of creative time, the traditional sadness about the passing of things is more than compensated for by the joy of birth: the emergence of new phenomena.

Herder even went so far as to praise the much lamented transitoriness of the things of the world as the precondition for the emergence of new things. The wish that things might last forever would, if come true, destroy the infinite richness of history:

Unfortunate it would have been could the age that produced a Pericles and a Socrates have been prolonged a moment beyond the time which the chain of events prescribed for its duration: for Athens it would have been a perilous and insupportable period. Equally confined would be the wish that the mythology of Homer should have held eternal possession of the human mind, the gods of the Greeks have reigned to infinity, and their Demosthenes have thundered forever. Every plant in nature must fade; but the fading plant scatters abroad its seeds, and thus renovates the living creation. Shakespeare was no Sophocles, Milton no Homer, Bolingbroke no Pericles, yet, they were in their kind and in their situation what those were in theirs.[13]

Thus, time is a beneficent power; it opens up constantly new possibilities of existence; life is rich in beautiful creations of all sorts.

In Hegel, we find an even more positive evaluation of the world's temporality. In *The Philosophy of History*, he defended change as a positive good. Change and history are not evils characterizing the lowly status of the visible world. Certainly, he stated, it is sad to see "the decay of splendid and highly cultured national life." And one must agree with Hegel that, as long as the past's significant phenomena were believed to be degeneration and decline, it was, indeed, a disturbing thing to look at history.

But Hegel also saw that change, while bringing about dissolution, involves birth at the same time, the rise of a new life. While "death is the issue of life, life is also the issue of death."[14] Recognizing the suffering caused by the mutability of earthly life and the continuous rise and fall of empires, Hegel nevertheless looked upon history as something positive. History, for Hegel, has a purpose and a goal, which is the full realization of mind. In the end, this goal justifies the sacrifices made, and redeems temporality.

In the outline of concrete world history introducing the *Philosophy of History*, he paid significantly much more attention to growth and "life" — represented by the emergence of new empires out of the design of mind — than to the decline and fall that had long obsessed students of history. The fate of the Roman Empire had for centuries disturbed historians and statesmen; because if not even an empire as powerful as Rome could withstand the destructive power of time, what empire could hope to escape the fate of ultimate destruction? But the spectacle of the fall of Rome held nothing mysterious or terrifying for Hegel; he simply stated that the old had to make room for the new.

The new experience of time as a creative force caused Hegel to think that movement, even if it is for the worse, is better than stability. Not only did Hegel feel that partial historical decline was necessary for the overall progressive course of history, he even argued that the ability of an empire to decline was a mark of its greatness, that is, its "aliveness." He argued that "we must . . . banish from our minds the prejudice in favor of duration, as if it had any advantages as compared with transcience: the imperishable mountains are not superior to the quickly dismantled rose exhaling its life in fragrance."[15]

The positive experience of life and time as offering opportunities for progress brought with it the belief that history was not a movement of mere change, but one of progress.[16] It also brought with it the Promethean conception of man which we associate with the Enlightenment attitude toward life: the conception of man as the maker of history. It was now understood to be man's calling to effect the historical progress that was discovered to be possible. Not God, as more pious and less self-confident ages had believed, but man himself made history. Man-made history was a sign of man's emancipation from the supposedly repetitive movements of nature. As Turgot put it "The phenomena of nature, submitted to constant laws, are enclosed in a circle of perpetually the same revolutions. . . . The successions of man, by contrast, offer a spectacle that is always varied. Reason, passions, liberty produce constantly new events: all ages are interconnected by a series of causes and effects that tie the present state of the world to those preceding it."[17]

Man-made history was also a sign of man's independence from the past. Having reached maturity, man could take responsibility for his actions and feel himself in charge of his personal and historical life.

In summary: the positive experience of life and time caused people to conceive of history as progress, and of man as history's creator.

But the positive experience of time, the idea of historical progress and the Promethean conception of man did not as such cause the transition of historiography from cosmopolitan outer to self-oriented inner memory. Although these ideas led to a depreciation of the exemplary value of the past, they did not exclude the past's others from the historian's view. As long as it was felt that a great variety of peoples had contributed to the progress of history, the eighteenth-century historian, in describing this history, included them in his story as others, thus commemorating their contributions by means of outer memory. But these ideas helped to prepare the ground for the nineteenth-century exclusion of the people of the past in their otherness from history.

Another important factor was the fragmentation of human time in periods and cultures. In the eighteenth century the feeling that the present was a different, and in fact, a better age than those previous, naturally undermined the classical conception of historiography as "school teaching by examplars": the examples of other ages had lost their relevance and the knowledge of "exotic" peoples had lost its usefulness.

Even Bolingbroke in his *Letters on the Study and Use of History* commented on the relative lack of importance for practical life of the knowledge of early periods of history, compared to knowledge of the more modern period, starting with the end of the fifteenth century.

To continue the study of such different periods was to "misemploy our time": because "the causes then laid have spent themselves, the series of effects derived from them being over," they do no longer concern us. Bolingbroke stressed the importance of knowing the "new system of causes and effects, that subsists in our time, and whereof our conduct is to be a part.[18] He summed up his views by stating that "to be entirely ignorant about the ages that precede this era would be shameful. . . . But to be learned about them is a ridiculous affectation in any man who means to be useful to the present age."[19]

Voltaire also realized the different character of the modern period, and declared that ancient history related to modern history as old medals to modern coins: "the former are deposited in the cabinets of the curious, the latter circulate through the world for the use and convenience of mankind."[20] Herder did not share Voltaire's contemptuous attitude toward the past, but he was equally aware of the differences between the civilization of which he was a part, and those pertaining to the past and to other areas of the world. For Herder, too, the past had lost its practical importance – its usefulness in providing examplars. He urged an aesthetic enjoyment of the past in place of the traditional emphasis on practical usage.

Similarly, the non-Western cultures lost their practical political relevance and became of theoretical or scientific interest only. Savage man lost his function of representing an example of the good life for a degenerate Western world.[21] Each historical period came to represent a coherent diachronic system linked by the series of causes and effects and by the continuous flow of time. The formerly uniform past had become divided into two qualitatively different worlds: the own world of the historian, and the world of the past's and present's others; or, to put the matter differently, the past had become divided, as it were, into an inner world in which the historian is at home, and an outer world, to which he has no affinity, and which could consequently not be understood. The non-Western cultures and nonmodern historical periods were either put in history's developmental framework, or more frequently, entirely by-passed.

A third factor contributing to the decosmopolitization of history was the notion that the astounding historical progress represented the development of the human mind — a process which in the Western world had somehow reached its peak. We find this notion with particular clarity articulated by Hegel.

In order to explain history's progress as a movement from within this world, Hegel introduced a new principle: development. "Development" as Hegel sees it is neither static being nor mere change: it involves a state of evolving existence in which previous experiences and achievements are retained in each succeeding present in spite of its prior existence in past time. Development is based on an entity's capacity to retain its past in its present.

The developmental growth of purely natural things is short-lived, for after they have died, the same cycle starts all over again. So it is with the merely "natural" life of individuals, and of peoples who had not been elected by mind to make history. For Hegel, these "natural" peoples included the Oriental and African peoples, and those old peoples of the Western world like the Greeks whose time for historical creativity had passed. Non-Western peoples do not participate in the life of mind. They do not have real development — that is, not a "real" history.

The Eastern myth of the Phoenix stands for "a type of the life of Nature; eternally preparing for itself its funeral pile, and consuming itself upon it; but so that from its ashes is produced the new renovated, fresh life." In the East, mind was still the prisoner of nature. In the West, on the other hand, mind progressed to make history. Here, mind consumes "the envelope of its existence."

[It] does not merely pass into another envelope, nor rise rejuvenescent from the ashes of its previous form; it comes forth exalted, glorified, a purer spirit.

It certainly makes war upon itself — consumes its own existence; but in this very destruction it works up that existence into a new form, and each successive phase becomes in its turn a material, working on which it exalts itself to a new grade.[23]

Natural entities dissolve with their material embodiments.

Only mind can continue its development after its material in which it had embodied itself had disintegrated. Mind always retains if not the form, at least the essence of its past in its succeeding present. "Mere change" is a succession of unconscious states of existents which are connected to each other. In "real" change, in development, the successive states are stages of an existent's continued existence through time. Hegel called therefore the history of mind a "process of transcending its earlier stages."[24] It is a process of continued self-transcendence. The Western peoples had been elected by mind to be the means of its progressive self-realization.

Hegel's abstract mind was a typical philosopher's concept. Historians rejected this speculation of such a hazy mind. No abstract mind elected peoples to be the vessels of its progress. Mind was an attribute of concrete individuals and peoples. But this concretization of mind did not change the basic conception of its nature: the view that mind is able to retain the past in memory and to project goals. This ability remained the precondition of the mind's ability to progress, that is, to move beyond previous stages in a process of self-transcendence. Thus, mind had not elected the Western peoples to make history, these peoples themselves had strong enough minds to progress and make history. As in the Calvinist doctrine of predestination, Western man's ability to make history was seen as proof of his strong mind.

Progress and development had, however, a deeper significance than offering man who had lost his belief in paradise in heaven, hope for a paradise on earth. On a more fundamental level, historical progress represented man's victory over the time of mindless nature which threatened to devour its own creations, man and his history included.

We have seen that in the eighteenth and nineteenth centuries, time had become a creative force through which the human mind could achieve progress. The eighteenth century saw the introduction into the social world of the Newtonian view of uniform time as a flow of homogeneous moments into historiography. The Enlightenment *philosophers* used the model of "natural" accumulation of experience, as opposed to a miraculous history, to explain the "natural" progress of reason and civilization. Thus, they circumvented in their explanation of history the appeal to transmundane agencies. The concept of natural accumulation transformed the succession of the past's events into a purely natural developmental phenomenon.

This nonmiraculous "natural" development took place in the medium of a "natural" earthly time of homogeneous and continuously flowing moments. The concept of Newtonian time made intelligible the accumulation of experience and knowledge, hence the "natural" progress or growth in civilization. In the Romantic period, the Newtonian time of homogeneous moments became the medium of the human world's organic growth. The notion that history is man-made implied, however, for many people that God was a superfluous hypothesis. This implication was profoundly frightening: for it seemed to a generation that had believed in an eternal world that, if earthly life is all there is, the earth, in particular man, is totally at the mercy of destructive time. As Hans Meyerhoff has put it, "time became the great begetter and friend of man, or the great devourer."[25]

During the nineteenth century the specter of a destructive all-powerful time was exorcized on the intellectual level by mind. Mind was considered able to endure through time by retaining its past in memory, and by then using its remembered experiences in planning for its future, progressing beyond its previous stage.

We may put the nineteenth-century struggle against destructive time in more dramatic terms by stating that, around 1800, mind arose as the hero slaying the dragon of time let loose upon innocent people who had lost their foothold in the transcendental world. As mind was primarily localized in man, destructive time was, in fact, ultimately conquered by man — primarily in his historical progress.

Hegel described how the power of time was curbed for the first time in Greece as a result of the development of the arts and sciences:

It was first Chronos — Time — that ruled the Golden Age, without moral products; and what was produced — the offspring of the Chronos — was devoured by it. It was Jupiter — from whose head Minerva sprang, and to whose circle of divinities belong Apollo and the Muses — that first put a constraint upon Time, and set a bound to its principle of decadence.[26]

Jupiter put a "limit to the devouring agency of Time."[27]

The linear nature of the developmental history of mind in the Western world overcomes the mere passing of forms within the realm of nature by retaining the essence of its past in its successive presents. The concrete progressive history of the West is therefore the victory over destructive time. If "real" history, that is the developmental history of Western civilization, represents a triumph over time, memory becomes the indispensable faculty. As historical progress needs strong mind, it needs strong memory.

Thus it is not surprising that in Hegel, we see, for the first time, that historical knowledge operates inside of a temporal system as the inner memory of a subject: mind, of its development.[28] Because Hegel saw the past as organically linked to the present by an internal process of development, he was, in looking back in time, necessarily contemplating his *own* past as well, that is to say, the past of his own civilization. The knowledge of the past system to which the philosopher, in whom mind has reached its self-consciousness, belongs is therefore self-knowledge: knowledge of the determinate — and limited — self that the subject has become in the course of history, not of the general self one shares with all other humans. According to Hegel, historical knowledge is the mind's remembrance of those of its acts that in hindsight represent to it significant steps in the progress toward "Absolute Knowledge."[29]

This importance of memory was implied by Hegel, but forcefully stated by Nietzsche. Nietzsche's philosophical poem, *Thus Spoke Zarathustra*, rejects beliefs in Christian hereafters and in Platonic beyonds. Nietzsche preaches the enjoyment of this world, because there is nothing eternal. Earthly life with all its changes and impermanences is beautiful:

God is a thought that makes crooked all that is straight, and makes turn whatever stands. How? Should time be gone, and all that is impermanent a mere lie? . . . It is of time and becoming that the best parables should speak: let them be a praise and a justification of all impermanence.[30]

But, time is also the destructive force that takes away what man most dearly loves in life; it cuts short the existence of everything before it has a chance to become completed and becomes perfect. So, Nietzsche wants to break the power of time:

"It was" — that is the name of the will's gnashing of teeth and most secret melancholy. Powerless against what has been done, he is an angry spectator of all that is past. The will cannot will backwards; and that he cannot break time and times's covetousness, that is the will's loneliest melancholy.[31]

Nietzsche overcomes the power of time by *"amor fati"* — the love for life so strong that the individual wants to live life again and embraces the "eternal recurrence of the same." Only the Overman can achieve this triumph over time.[32]

Nietzsche was quite explicit in stating that forgetfulness and a strong memory are the prerequisites for the strong autonomous individual.

A strong and well-constituted man digests his experiences (his deeds and misdeeds included) as he digests his meals, even when he has to swallow some tough morsels. If he cannot get over an experience and have done with it, this kind of indigestion is as much physiological as is the other [namely physical indigestion]. . . .[33]

He described memory as "an active *desire* not to rid oneself, a desire for the continuation of something desired once, a real memory of the will: so that between the original 'I will,' 'I shall do this,' and the actual discharge of the will, its *act*, a world of strange new things, circumstances, even acts of will may be interposed without breaking the long chain of will."[34]

The possession of the memory faculty is what distinguishes men from beasts. An animal forgets, out of weakness, from moment to moment what it has felt and thought, and even what it is. Man is also an animal — but an animal who has bred a memory in itself. Here, Nietzsche begins to connect memory to history by saying that it took a long time for man to develop the memory faculty, which he describes as part of man's rationality:

To ordain the future in advance in this way, man must first have learned to distinguish necessary events from chance ones, to think causally, to see and anticipate distant eventualities as if they belonged to the present, to decide with certainty what the goal and what the means to it, and in general be able to calculate and compute. Man himself must first have become *calculable*, *regular, necessary,* even in his own image of himself, if he is able to stand security *for his own future*, which is what one who promises does.[35]

According to Nietzsche, memory is necessary for a strong will, able to maintain itself through time. Memory is victory over passing time and mindless nature. It is civilized victory over the momentary instinctual life of animals, and over the life of savages and other custom-bound peoples who have no way for consciously remembering things, no way to go beyond reaction passively and automatically to prescribed circumstances. To live without memory is to live without protracted will, without an identity that maintains itself through time. The absence of memory precludes the possibility of living authentically, with loyalty toward oneself. It thereby precludes creativity. For this reason, Nietzsche felt that only modern man could be an autonomous individual.

If we place ourselves at the end of this tremendous process, where the tree at last brings forth fruit, where society and the morality of custom at last reveal *what* they have simply been the means to: then we discover that the ripest fruit is the *sovereign individual*, like only to himself, liberated again from morality of custom, autonomous and supra-moral (for "autonomous" and "moral" are mutually exclusive) — in short, the man who has his own independent, protracted will and the *right to make promises*.[36]

In Freud's psychoanalysis memory fulfills an equally important function. Neurotic symptoms are caused by painful and therefore repressed memories. The symptoms disappear when these forgotten experiences are restored to consciousness, that is, remembered again. The mentally healthy, strong individual has a strong memory.

The theme of rescuing the personality from its dispersal in time pervades nineteenth- and twentieth-century literature.[37] The classic example is Marcel Proust's *In Search of Lost Time*. At the end of his quest — at the end of the novel — Proust has a total recall of his past, very much like Hegel's "Absolute Mind" after having reached the end of history. The same theme is found in the family novel, Alex Haley's *Roots*, being the most recent example.

The view of persons and nations as diachronic structures parallels that of things in general. In *The Order of Things*, for instance, Michael Foucault describes how linguistic entities, and the things of nature, are in the nineteenth century considered "from the inside" — from the point of view of their inner structure.[38] The same point can be made about material objects, the things of human history, and the human personality structure. All these things are seen as being drawn out over a period of time, as if they were accordions.

According to this new perception, all existents are conquests of and victories over time. With their origin in time and their center in themselves, they have their own will to be, will to exist, and will to be this or that through time. Their developmental history is a visible manifestation of their hidden underlying will-to-be. The coming-into-being of things is the formation of a new temporary power center, their ending its dissolution.

At this point we can see that personal and collective inner memory — personal memory and historiography — were the means by which nineteenth-century Western man neutralized his fear of destructive time. Memory and historiography, in the nineteenth century, became popular because they served a need experienced by everybody: the need to constitute the identity of individuals and societies. According to nineteenth-century thought, two ultimate expressions of the conscious will able to resist time's power are the autonomous individual and the "logical subjects" of history — abstract but nevertheless powerful subjects such as the state, or the nation. These realize on earth a form of existence that approximates the discarded eternity of existence of the absolute. Memory and historiography were also important because now the traditional belief-systems were no longer experienced as binding by the majority of people, the rules of conduct had to be found in the historical subjects themselves — individuals and social groups —

that is to say, in their historically grown selves. Thus, to know oneself or one's social group by means of memory and historiography was to know what oneself or one's society had to do in life. Inversely, if memory and historiography for some reason could not function properly, indecisiveness and rudderlessness would follow.

The last point leads us back to Dilthey who was forced to realize that historical memory does not lead to objective historical knowledge. Dilthey had hoped that memory would provide reliable or "objective" knowledge because only an individual knows for sure what he has done, and — if he does not lie — only he can tell us about it. This kind of indisputable knowledge, he felt, could be likened to the natural scientist's knowledge gained through observation of the natural world. As the natural scientist can objectively observe the exterior world because he is not part of it, the human scientist can objectively look at his own inner world at the end of his life — a time when he is no longer passionately entangled in life's struggles. Dilthey extended this idea to cover the historian's knowledge of history as well.

But by realizing the impossibility of objective historical knowledge, Dilthey was forced to question whether the optimistic Enlightenment assessment of man's powers as capable of mastering nature and history was a realistic one. The mere thought that it might not be scared him: for he felt that it would mean the meaningless of man's labors on earth. He strongly sensed that now the ideal future in heaven depicted by traditional religion was realized to be a childish fantasy, man would fall back into an animallike existence of pursuing egotistical pleasures and momentary enjoyments, thus giving up his moral calling, if he could no longer hope for a better future on earth for himself or his children. Just as the self-oriented model of historical knowledge seemed to promise a self-awareness, strength and a sense of purpose, its failure promised indecisiveness, rudderlessness and amorality. Thus Dilthey's dismay at the outcome of his reflections.

However, he was not so dismayed that he did not look for a better solution to the problem of objective historical knowledge.

Dilthey never doubted that there had been, and would be, progress toward the goal of objective historical knowledge in history. After all, he shared his age's positive experience of life and time. He also subscribed to the notion that the goal of an individual and of mankind was to emancipate himself or itself from nature and the past — to master nature and history. Painfully aware that in looking backward, he could not actually see history's course, being himself submerged in its stream, he searched for another method by which to know history. The present generation cannot actually remember a period such as the Middle Ages. But there are other ways of learning about the past. Mankind, he thought, can know its history by other means than by direct inner memory. The historian might use the physical evidence left behind by previous generations. He might try to "read " this evidence in order to reconstruct history's course. Previous generations have, consciously or unconsciously, communicated their experiences to us in the form of documents and other artifacts. The absence of the direct link with the past, Dilthey hoped, might therefore not present the obstacle it at first seemed to be.

CHAPTER FOUR

DILTHEY'S HERMENEUTIC APPROACH TO HISTORY

In the *Introduction to the Human Sciences*, Dilthey had indicated that *Verstehen* was the proper method by which to understand history. After 1883, Dilthey revised his conception of knowledge of the human world. He now felt that to know the human world is not an act of *Verstehen* of man's experiences, but an act of *interpretation* — a *"hermeneutic"* act — of products created by man and in which he has expressed his experiences. In the human sciences, life and experience themselves are beyond empirical investigation; but the expressions of life and experience are not. The products of human experience, said Dilthey, including architecture as well as systems of law, documents as well as musical compositions, may be regarded as texts to be interpreted.[1]

In order to realize what is involved in this shift from *verstehen* perspective to hermeneutic perspective, we must first, comprehend Dilthey's conception of the concrete historical world as "objectified mind," and as a literary text to be interpreted. Second, we must take a look at the discipline of interpretation, or hermeneutics, to which Dilthey turned.

For Dilthey, as we have seen, the phenomena produced by man "mean" something, for they have been created to fulfill a purpose. Human behavior and its products have intended meaning: they communicate — explicitly if they are created to convey a meaning, or implicitly if they simply express an inner state — experiences man has had with life. The communication contained in a human action or a product of human behavior is given in the form of a sign or symbol: a gesture, a word, a literary work, a social institution. What is meant can, therefore, never be directly known: its symbol has to be interpreted. The human sciences — in particular, history — are therefore similar in nature to literary criticism in focusing on the meaning of symbols. In his 1900 essay "The Origin of Hermeneutics" (*Die Entstehung der Hermeneutik*), Dilthey redefined *Verstehen* in hermeneutic terms as the activity "by which we understand a mental phenomenon (*ein Psychisches*) which is embodied in a materially given sign" (GS, vol. V, 318) — or again, as the activity

by which we understand "the inner on the basis of a sign that is
materially given in the outer world" (GS, vol. V, 318).

He conceived of the visible concrete cultural world in which man
lives as a product of an inner force, conscious life (GS, vol. VII,
148). Conscious life, or mind, expresses or "externalizes" (GS,
vol. VII, 146) itself in concrete forms, which together constitute
what Dilthey calls the "objective mind," defined as

the manifold forms in which the commonality [*Gemeinsamkeit*] existing
between individuals has objectified itself in the world of the senses. In this
objective mind the past has a lasting continuous presence for us. Its field
reaches from the style of life, the forms of [social] intercourse [developed]
in connection with goals set by the society, to custom, law, statecraft, religion,
art, the sciences and philosophy (GS, vol. VII, 208).

By "commonality" Dilthey means the sameness of human nature:
that everywhere the operations of reason are the same, that everywhere sympathy in emotional life is found, that everywhere there
are duties and rights connected with them (GS, vol. VII, 141).
The visible concrete cultural world he called the "external realm of
mind" (GS, vol. VII, 146). Mind has "deposited" itself in it (*hinein-
verlegt*). It has "objectified" itself. Thus, the entire concrete cultural
world becomes comparable to a text in which conscious life or
mind has expressed itself. As far as the world of the past is concerned, life is gone, leaving behind only the material objects, the
"texts," in which it has previously expressed its dynamic, human
experience:

Expression [*Ausdruck*] . . . is left, after life itself has passed: direct expression,
in which souls have articulated [*ausgesprochen*] what they were, and, beyond
that, stories of actions and situations, of individuals, of communities, of states.
And the historian stands in the midst of this debris, the remains of things past,
the expressions of souls – [preserved] in deeds, words, tones, images – souls
that long since have passed (GS, vol. VII, 279).

After life passes – after it "has become historical" – the true
meaning of the text it has written can be understood and "respected"
(*gewürdigt*) (GS, vol. VII, 249). Consequently the discipline of
reading and interpreting texts became relevant for Dilthey in
connection with the study of history. As indicated before, two
approaches to text interpretation existed at that time: philological
and theological. We must now take a closer look at the relationship
between these two.

The philological approach had been developed by humanist
scholars in connection with their study of the texts of classical
antiquity. It focused on the texts' correct meaning. Philologists
were not in the first place concerned with content – with the truth

or falsity of what the texts stated. Their interest was primarily aesthetic and grammatical, not philosophical or theological. During the Renaissance, the philologists worked to reconstruct the classical texts, mutilated by careless transmission during the Middle Ages, in its original form. During the eighteenth century, they began to study the historical milieu in which the text was written in order to understand the exact meaning of its words in the light of time and place of its genesis. A new philological interest emerging at that time was also the history of languages, their interrelatedness and their changes over time.[2] In this period, the philological approach began increasingly to be applied also to religious writing. Classical philology found a major spokesman in Friedrich August Wolf (1759-1824).

Theological hermeneutics had been developed by theologians for the study of the Bible. It focused on the text's meaning, its message. It had a practical intention, for it was concerned with the problem how the text's message could be applied to the praxis of life, how the message could be "appropriated." Since classical antiquity this type of hermeneutics had occupied itself also with the interpretation of two other kinds of works: works of art and jurisprudence. Till the middle of the eighteenth century, however, the interpretation methods of the Bible had been most intensively studied. Thus, theological hermeneutics dominated the discipline till the eighteenth century when philological hermeneutical methods gained ascendance for secular as well as for biblical writings. Theological hermeneutics came first to the fore in the Early Modern period in connection with the study of the Bible because the Reformers justified their opposition to the Roman Catholic Church on the supposed misunderstanding by the latter of the Holy Scriptures.[3]

Aware of the incommensurability of the divine word and the words of man, theological hermeneutics involved a process of translation and interpretation: translation because the texts had to be rendered in an idiom humans could understand and respond to; interpretation because the relevance of the texts' message had to be clarified, so that man could behave in ways that pleased God. The interpretation had to facilitate the process by which the texts' content could be "appropriated," that is, made part of the interpreter's own life.

It should be stressed, however, that although philological and theological hermeneutic approaches differed, they nevertheless were aspects of one interpretative enterprise: no philological hermeneuticist could hope to understand a text correctly without some

degree of interpretation of meaning, while no theological hermeneuticist could understand the text's message without proper philological training.[4]

The theologian Friedrich Ernst Daniel Schleiermacher (1768-
1834) was the heir of both traditions, philological and theological.
Schleiermacher applied the methods of philology to the biblical
writings, and the methods of theological hermeneutics to secular
texts. Whereas others, for instance Johann Salomon Semler (1715-
1791), also had used philology in studying the Bible, Schleiermacher's
application of theological hermeneutics to secular writings represented a new departure in hermeneutics. In a philologist's manner,
he was interested in the correct meaning of texts, but he felt at the
same time that the understanding of the message of any great text
has an important impact on the interpreter, in particular on the
way he perceives himself. Schleiermacher was indeed still keenly
aware of the traditional connection between hermeneutic interests
as practiced by the theologians, and religious or metaphysical
consciousness.[5] This secularization of hermeneutics by Schleiermacher, if we may call it that, did not alter the fundamental nature
of hermeneutic reading; hermeneutic reading continued to set in
motion the "Hermes process"[6] — the translation process by which
the alien world of the other is transmuted into a world the interpreter and his readers can understand and appropriate. In a way, all
literary texts were now considered holy — as disclosures of an
awesome reality; all texts, sacred and secular, spoke of another
world. Besides extending theological hermeneutics to literary texts
in general, Schleiermacher also introduced a new hermeneutic
principle that expressed his Romanticist approach to literature: the
interpretation of a text on the basis of its author's creative process.
Thus, texts began to say something about their human authors.

The attention of the next generation, as can be seen in the case
of Schleiermacher's pupil Philipp August Böckh (1785-1867) shifted
definitely toward the methods of philological interpretation. From
the 1840s till Dilthey took up the subject in 1883, the interpretation methods of theological hermeneutics virtually had eclipsed[7]
both with regard to the interpretation of religious as well as to
secular texts. This should be no surprise: firstly, to a great number of
modern men God no longer spoke at all, through the Bible or otherwise. Secondly, nobody believed anymore that "reality" — now in
the process of being conquered by science, or nature — was all that
mysterious, awesome or profound, it was not believed to hide or
express anything. Thus, with the decline of Christianity and of
German Idealism in the nineteenth century, the interpretation
methods developed in connection with biblical studies lost their
function.

Dilthey became interested in hermeneutical methods as a result of his conception of historical evidence as expressions of life, and of the cultural world as a "text" to be read. In his formative years, he had been exposed to theological hermeneutics: he had studied theology for a while and written a biography of Schleiermacher. Compared to his familiarity with theological hermeneutic principles, his knowledge of the methods of the philologically oriented studies of the Historical School, in particular of Ranke, was meager. The fact that Dilthey's training was in theology rather than in history accounts for the general nature of this hermeneutic approach, and the task he ascribed to it.

Dilthey's description of the nature and development of hermeneutics till his own time indicates his conception of this discipline. As a result of changing times, he wrote, the people of the Renaissance had become "separated" from classical and Christian antiquity (GS, vol. V, 323). Interpretation had from then on to deal with what had become alien. But the reader of the classical and biblical writings experienced an "unquenchable desire to complete his individuality" by "appropriating" (*aneignen*) "the great forces" (*große Kräfte*) of these texts (GS, vol. V, 324). The texts derived their forcefulness – their *Lebensmächtigkeit* – from the fact that in exemplary fashion they expressed the harmony of form and content. By contemplating others (Dilthey used the word *Anschauung*), the reader could make these forces his own (GS, vol. V, 328). Dilthey portrayed the philological interpreter of classical writings and the theological interpreter of the Scriptures as having developed during Early Modern times each in their own fields of study, useful but different ways of dealing with the texts they strove to understand. He then depicted Schleiermacher whom he admired so much as the great synthesizer of their efforts. Schleiermacher founded his hermeneutic approach on an analysis of the act of *Verstehen*. Maintaining that for a true understanding of texts it was not enough to philologically understand their language – their "outer" form – he stated that the interpreter also had to understand their "inner" form, their content or "message." For in great literary works "outer" and "inner" forms are inseparable. To truly understand a work it is necessary to understand its unity of form and content.

Schleiermacher demonstrated his hermeneutical method in his interpretation of Plato. Plato's philosophizing was rooted in actual life: the quest for truth was carried out in real conversations. This explains why Plato chose the form of dialogues to present his ideas (GS, vol. V, 328). At the same time, however, Plato's philosophizing

was highly systematic. The dialogues together form a logically connected whole. Real understanding of Plato ensues when the interpreter considers Plato's system of thought in connection with his
dialogical form of presentation (GS, vol. V, 329). As this unity of
form and content existed as such in Plato's mind when creating his
works, the interpreter could discover it by putting himself in
Plato's place and re-experiencing the creative process that had
taken place in the author's mind. Given their historical distance,
interpreter and author differ of course considerably as individuals.
This makes re-experiencing difficult. The interpreter can nevertheless
understand Plato by re-experiencing on the basis of their common
human nature (*allegemeine Menschennatur*) (GS, vol. V, 329). With
his own living and therefore flexible humanity (*Lebendigkeit*) the
interpreter descends into the past and probes the author's historical
environment. By then reinforcing some aspects of his own psychic
life and by allowing others to fade into the background, he is able
to repeat alien life in himself (Dilthey uses the word *nachbilden*)
(GS, vol. V, 330). In so doing the interpreter will experience himself
the interconnections of the author's thoughts among each other,
and their relationship to the form in which they are expressed.
Dilthey added that compared to this penetrating understanding of
the text's form and content, the establishment of the exact chronological order of the dialogues is a trivial matter (GS, vol. V, 331).
Although Dilthey did not say so in so many words, philological
hermeneutics — being an understanding from the "outside" — clearly
did not have his sympathy.

Two features of Schleiermacher's hermeneutical approach most
appealed to Dilthey: Schleiermacher's contention that form and
content form a unity, for this view reintroduced a concern for the
spiritual content, the "message" of the text; and his emphasis on
the existential impact of the act of interpretation on the interpreter.
Like Schleiermacher, Dilthey was more philosopher than philogist
in his dealings with historical texts; he was primarily interested in
understanding their philosophical meaning — the testimony they gave
of "the life of the mind," of man as a creature endowed with mind.
The originality of Dilthey's approach to the study of history lies in
his application of theological hermeneutics' methods as found in
Schleiermacher to historical evidence. We will first indicate how in
his approach to history the moment of appropriation surfaced again.

Dilthey stressed that the ultimate goal of understanding the past
is not disinterested and "historical" (as understood by the Historical
School) knowledge. The result of true historical understanding, he
felt, is an actual "appropriation" of past experience — an appropria-

tion that will have an effect on the interpreter's life. The achievement of hermeneutic re-experiencing is "our appropriation of the mental world" (GS, vol. VII, 215), specifically, the "appropriation of mental goods" (*geistiger Dinge*) (GS, vol. VII, 215) offered by historians and poets. In its "elementary" forms, which are the forms of understanding used in everyday life, hermeneutic understanding serves the process of inculturation; in its "higher" forms of understanding used in studying works of art and monuments of thought it widens our horizon, limited as it is by our personal experience:[8] "hermeneutic understanding opens a wide realm of possibilities, which are not present in [the interpreter's personal] life" (GS, vol. VII, 215). The life experience of any person, living briefly in some small corner of the earth, is restricted. But the limitations of human existence imposed by man's cultural and temporal finitude can be overcome by an expanded study of history that opens up the totality of life, at least as far as it has revealed itself up the present.

Dilthey viewed the understanding of historical actors and their products by means of "re-experiencing" (*nacherleben*) (GS, vol. VII, 213-216) or "putting oneself in somebody else's place" (*Sichhinein-versetzen*) (GS, vol. VII, 214), as a process of "appropriation." In Dilthey's words:

Let us have a look at the significant achievement of this re-experiencing for our appropriation of the world of the mind [*geistige Welt*]. It consists of two moments. Each time we call up the presence of an environment and of an external situation, we re-experience it. And fantasy is able to emphasize or decrease behavioral patterns, forces, feeling, desires, [and] ideas present in the coherence of our own life. In this way alien inner life [*Seelenleben*] is reproduced in us (VII, 215).

By means of such recreative processes "mental things [*geistiger Dinge*] provided by historians and poets" are acquired" (GS, vol. VII, 215). "Understanding offers a person a large realm of possibilities which in the determined situation of his life are not present" (GS, vol. VII, 215). Dilthey explained this process by stating that in studying the past, the scientist of humanity realizes, or activates, his own latent possibilities: "everything human becomes a document for us that represents one of the endless possibilities of our existence" (GS, vol. VII, 247). Each individual person is, as it were, a microcosm of man in general. Individual differences between people are only a matter of degree; each individual develops in the course of his life certain mental features that are potentially present in everybody. Although all persons are man-created objects, they speak, as it were, their own private idioms. The understanding of these idioms is possible because ultimately all languages are elaborations of the common ability of humans to speak and understand (GS, vol. V, 329). Thus, in the understanding of the past, the understanding of others reinforces the understanding of self. The knowledge gained by re-experiencing is not simply an external, mechanical repetition of other persons' experiences that can afterwards be forgotten — nor is it a total submersion, in which the person of the knower effaces himself. It is an active recreation of other persons' experiences — a process which leaves a profound impression on the mind of the knower. True historical understanding is a process of communication between two autonomous subjects who come to understand each other, be they living persons or their testimonies in symbols.

As a result of modern man's historical consciousness "all of man's history can be made present." Thus, he has access to the total experience of mankind so far. The historian "looks beyond all the barriers of his own age into the cultures of the past; he imbibes their power and enjoys their magic; and this results in a great increase in happiness for him" (GS, vol. V, 317). To study history is therefore an enriching experience of intellectual and emotional growth. The vicarious participation in different experiences enlarges the student's horizon. And the more he has experienced himself, the better he can unlock the past: "The more gifted a person is, the more possibilities exist in him. They have realized themselves in the course of his life; they are still present in his memory. The longer his life, the larger they become. [Think of] the total-understanding [All-Verstehen] of old age, the genius of understanding" (GS, vol. VII, 225).

Dilthey thus squarely rejected the merely contemplative understanding of past life advanced by Ranke. With his concern for the original past, the past as it had really been — the original "text" of the past as it were — Ranke was indeed much closer to the philological in interpreation methods than was Dilthey.

Dilthey felt that the re-creation of the author's creative process by means of re-experiencing was the most important part in interpretation, because it enabled one to see how the work fits into the oeuvre of the author and the context of its age. It should be noted at this point that Dilthey's use of re-experiencing does not imply that he was interested in individual psychological factors (see for instance GS, vol. VII, 205). Instead, he was interested in the cultural factors that influenced the author, and the author's general understanding of his own life and of human life in general. Dilthey maintained that the interpreter of a text can understand an author better than he had understood himself, because the interpreter is aware of mental, or "psychological", that is cultural, influences of which the author himself had not been conscious. Dilthey stressed throughout his writings that the individual and his works cannot be studied apart from the cultural and social structures to which he belongs. "The singular individual, in his individual existence resting in himself, is a historical being. He is determined by his place in the progression of time, his place in the interacting systems of culture and community" (GS, vol. VII, 135). Human beings evaluate, reason, pursue goals, accept responsibility and interpret life, but always in the context of their society. Thus, the study of an individual's motivations cannot be severed from a study of the subject's social organization and cultural values.[9]

Because of his emphasis on the impact of historical knowledge on the interpreter, we understand why Dilthey could claim that the human sciences achieve their highest significance through their effect (*Rückwirkung*) on life and society. He added hopefully that "this significance is increasing" (GS, vol. VII, 138). In his essay on world-views, too, Dilthey saw the practical usefulness of philosophical systems, which he considered as interpretations of reality, as being tested in the competitive struggle for life between them; he maintained that only those systems useful to man in this struggle survived (GS, vol. VIII, 85). Because of its relationship to life, Jürgen Habermas calls Dilthey's hermeneutic understanding "practical."[10]

It is, however, not easy to determine exactly what specific practical function Dilthey attributed to the hermeneutic understanding of human reality. Experience and understanding showed Dilthey what life is; but he did not want to draw any conclusions from this understanding about what it should be. Dilthey refrained from formulating political goals for social life. Basically content with his world, Dilthey felt that life "as it is" should run its course. The "liberation" resulting from the study of history was for him thus only an experience of *inner* freedom, a mental liberation from dominant belief systems and existing situations. It was not a preliminary step toward political action.

Dilthey stressed in particular the transforming effect on the historian of major historical figures — history's "heroes." He believed that "the best hope of understanding the powerful force [of such a hero], lies in his effect on our experience, in our being continuously nourished by him. Ranke's Luther, Goethe's Winkelmann, Thucydides' Pericles sprang from such a relationship to power radiating from the hero's life" (*Lebensmacht*) (GS, vol. V, 278). He wrote that to become acquainted with the Reformation opened up a world which expands our horizon in possibilities of human existence, which can become accessible to us only [through history]. Thus a person, determined from the inside [by his character] is able to live many existences in imagination. To a person limited by circumstances, the strange beauties of the world open up, including areas of life which he can never reach. In more general terms: man, tied to and determined by the reality of life, becomes free not only by means of art — as has often been stated — but also by means of history (GS, vol. VII, 216).

Besides the moment of appropriation, theological hermeneutics' conception of interpretation as a means to bridge the gap between the own familiar world and the alien world of the other by excellence, God, also surfaces in Dilthey's hermeneutics — be it that the divine other had become the human others of the past.

An interpretation [of the remains of the past] would be impossible if the expressions of life were totally alien. It would be unnecessary, on the other hand, if there were nothing alien about them. [The art of interpretation] is situated between these two extremes. It is required wherever something is alien that the art of understanding needs to appropriate (GS, vol. VII, 225).

Dilthey was very much aware of the cultural differences between periods. He realized that it takes much study and practice to truly familiarize oneself with past cultures and to master them. A note in his journal indicates how hard it was for Dilthey himself to re-experience certain emotions of past times:

Whoever is captivated by his topic, feels such close afffinity [wahlverwandt] to it that all movements, emotions, and desires associated with past events occur in his soul for a second time. How fortunate is he! . . . But I struggle in vain to wrestle life from this alien material [of the Reformation period]; I do not know whether I will ever be able to re-create the spirit of that time in me. This distrust of human nature . . ., [a nature] which to me has always been an object of high admiration; this haste for the hereafter and for extrasensory (übersinnliche) knowledge, which I hate; this life of sects, which is totally incomprehensible to me.[11]

In studying an event such as Luther's reformation, the historian deals with "a religious event of such an eruptive force — of such an energy in which life and death are at stake — that it lies beyond the range of experience of contemporary man" (GS, vol. VII, 215). Yet, it is possible for him to understand what moved these people. By studying the evidence, the historian "sees" that in the monasteries a technique of communication with the unseen world took place, which gave the souls of the monks a steady direction toward the beyond; he "sees" how the doctrine of the invisible Church led to the liberation of the individual; he "sees" Christianity as an enormous power that shapes life in the family, in the professions, in political matters, everywhere. In following Luther's career, we experience (erleben) the development of the Reformation (GS, vol. VII, 216).

It is significant that Dilthey used the word "seeing" in his description of an act of historical understanding. It indicates that for Dilthey the historian in spite of his act of re-experiencing remains an observer, visiting the past as a traveler. The identification with any past actor is only temporary, and results in a partial transformation of himself. The historian does not "go native." His knowledge of the past does not result in a substitution of one limited horizon for another equally limited.

In his 1868 review of Adolf Bastian's *The Peoples of East Asia*. Dilthey described the process by which a traveler comes to understand cultures alien to him. In studying an Oriental religious culture such as Christian or Buddhist, he said, it is not sufficient to analyze the Holy Book and the writings of a few Fathers, in the hope of squeezing out of these writings a system of doctrines: such a traditional scholarly study affords no insight into the actual nature of the lived religious convictions.

It is more fruitful to investigate the manifold forms of religious conviction — the living motives, the still existing circle of representations — if one wants to experience [*erfahren*] what this . . . culture means. Thus only the traveler, who now talks with the monks in their own language at the shores of the Irawadi River, now with the prince, now with the scholar of Mandalay, and then with the inhabitants of the monasteries at the shores of the Menam River — [the traveler] who does not meet all [these people] with the prejudices and the existing onesidedness of the missionary, but who as a student of divine and human matters approaches co-students and who attempts to understand them — only such [a traveler] will really grasp the faith and ideas of these nations of East Asia in their psychological roots and in their emotional motives [as they exist] in their free variety (GS, vol. XI, 208).

In summary: by seeing the human world as a text, and by turning to Schleiermacher's hermeneutics for assistance in interpreting this world, Dilthey acquired an unusual perspective on history. Any "text" — written or other — approached from Dilthey's hermeneutic point of view is seen as a message or, to put this point differently, any text which is thus approached is expected to communicate a message that will affect the interpreter and his readers. As the text always originated in another person in his otherness, a stranger, interpretation is a process of communication with another; this other has anticipated, or at least hoped, to be understood by the interpreter and his reader — for otherwise he would not have taken the trouble of sending out a message. The text as approached in Dilthey's hermeneutics is seen as inviting interpretation, as actively holding itself ready to start the process of communication.[12] Also, his hermeneutic perspective made him consider the past as something alien requiring interpretation and appropriation. Thus, he saw the past as a world from which he could learn. The world of the past was a world of others in their otherness — that is, a world in which autonomous others have expressed themselves in various products, and have disclosed their intentions, feelings, moods, insights, and desires by means of symbols. He expected that knowledge of this alien world would benefit him by expanding his horizon. But it could only be so if this knowledge were correct.

We have seen in chapter II that Dilthey wanted the "philosophical" study of history to provide modern man with insights into the true nature of human life. This would positively affect their self-consciousness. Yet in order to be fruitful for the praxis of life, these insights had to match reality, they had to be objectively true. The problems of objective historical knowledge and of valid interpretation of historical evidence loomed large in Dilthey's mind.

In clarifying how the expressions of human life — the life-expressions or *Lebensäusserungen* — could be interpreted like written texts, Dilthey distinguished three classes of "life-expressions," or three kinds of "objectification" of experiences (GS, vol. VII, 205-207): rational statements, overt actions, and experiential expressions.

To the first class belong concepts, judgements of philosophy, and the abstract systems of logical thought (GS, vol. VII, 205). These, Dilthey felt, belong to pure reason because they have no direct relationship to experience. They do not refer to the concrete life-context from which they originate. Their content is consequently basically the same everywhere and at every moment. Being abstract and transparent, the expressions of pure reason can be understood completely and unambiguously.

The second class of life-expressions are overt actions. Actions are oriented toward a goal but they do not always specifically communicate an intention to others. Nevertheless, they are meaningful, for they are prompted by an intention. An action expresses, however, only part of a person's being: it is a one-sided expression — or a symbol — of the fullness of the actor's life. In order to understand an action, the observer therefore has to know more than the action itself, namely, the circumstances, goals, means, and general context from which it originates. On the basis of its larger context, the observer will be able to "make sense" of the action he studies, as it enables him to understand better the lived depths from which the action originated.

The third class of life-expressions, experiential expressions, are the explicit expressions meant to communicate an experience — an intention, a feeling (*Erlebnisausdrücke*); to this class belong the objectifications of mind — the visible products of human behavior, such as religious and philosophical systems, works of art, monuments, and institutions. Such expressions can contain more than their creator realizes, for "he lifts [them] out of the depths [of life] which consciousness does not illuminate" (GS, vol. VII, 206). Emerging from the recesses of human life, these expressions are only partially accessible to reason. Their interpretation is neither logically correct nor false: life-expressions have to be judged with regard to their untruthfulness or truthfulness to life. For indeed, life-expressions can be intentionally or unintentionally deceptive: "distortion, lie, deception [often] disconnect in this [class of expressions] the expression and expressed" (GS, vol. VII, 206). Deceptiveness occurs often in the practice of life. Dilthey stated that only great works of art are, by contrast, undoubtedly truthful to life.

Actions and experiential expressions provide the historian with his "texts." Historical knowledge is like reading: understanding meaning by means of an interpretation of symbols. The historian has the same function vis-à-vis historical evidence as the literary critic vis-à-vis his text: he explains and communicates its meaning to the public.

But how can the reader know with certainty, or "objectivity" what the actors of the past have said and experienced? In the natural sciences, any object of investigation — whether it be an animal or a mineral — can, at least in principle, be completely known; every aspect of such an object can be perceived. The certainty, or objectivity, of scientific knowledge stems from the purely physical nature of the objects studied by the natural scientists. These objects obey natural, unchanging laws; they cannot express a hidden meaning. Physiologists and chemists determine the material of which the object consists; biologists and physicists discover its structure, and explain its behavior by the laws of inorganic and organic nature. Thus known, the object can no longer surprise us. Scientific knowledge subjects the objects it knows; it is trustworthy, indubitable, "objective" because it dominates what it knows. Can the interpretation of symbols — apart from the expression of pure reason — ever be complete to the extent that the phenomenon to which they refer is completely known, and unsurprising?

Dilthey did not think so. The objects investigated by the human scientist are more than purely physical objects bearing easily decipherable and conscious messages. They also have an invisible meaning, an unconscious message, which may contribute to a larger structured meaning, or may provide a clue to a hidden process. Interpretation is always tentative and leaves room for other views. The symbol cannot, as symbol, contain in itself what is symbolized. This gives the interpretation of any symbol an element of incompleteness and uncertainty. Historical *Verstehen* deals with material that "has more than one meaning" (*mehrseitig*) (GS, vol. VII, 227), and this invisible, or "spiritual," element of meaning has to be deciphered on the basis of visible material signs that can only refer to it indirectly. But this does not mean that interpretation is arbitrary, that everything can be legitimately read into a text. It was precisely the goal of hermeneutics to "provide a theoretical foundation for establishing the general validity of interpretation on which all certainty of history rests, and would ward off the thrust (*Einbruch*) of romantic arbitrariness and sceptical subjectivity" (GS, vol. V, 331).

Dilthey found in the material embodiment of an expression of human experience a barrier against subjectivism. He wrote that after authentic works of art, philosophy, religion or literature have been created, these objects exist independently from the observer — having become fixed in enduring material. The interpreter can consequently always return to them and thus counteract the momentary subjective, and arbitrary elements in his interpretations (GS, vol. V, 319).

The permanent object, moreover, loses its ties to the passing world of the time of its origin. With the passing of time, the lasting truth concerning life it embodies becomes more readily visible. From the existence of historical evidence in the form of lasting objects, letters, books, buildings, and so on, Dilthey concluded that, given the appropriate training in hermeneutic skills, it is in principle possible to know and understand the past more or less objectively.

Thus, the material to be interpreted is fixed. But the interpreter remains part of the life of his own time. Thus, a further problem remains to be solved; namely, what the implications are for the objectivity of the historian's knowledge of the past — implications stemming from the fact that he is himself a participant in the historical process and has a mind shaped by his personal and cultural experience; that he is not a detached observer with a blank mind which can mirror truthfully whatever is presented to it. If, as Dilthey affirmed, interpretations are inevitably colored by the specific life experience of the historian's own time,[13] how can it be claimed that this knowledge really discloses past life? Dilthey felt that this indeed was the central difficulty in the art of interpretation — a difficulty he could not solve.

To acknowledge the interdependency between knowledge and experience, he introduced the conception of the "hermeneutic circle," a term which he believed to be first used by Schleiermacher in his reflections on text interpretation.[14] In his historical survey of the development of hermeneutics in *The Project for the Continuation of the Structure of the Historical World in the Human Sciences*, Dilthey states that in the study of literature the hermeneutic circle contains three relationships of mutual dependency: between single words and the totality of the work, between the work itself and the mentality of its author, and between the work and the literacy genre to which it belongs. In each case, the problem is how to relate the known or experienced part (the discrete words or the text by itself) to the larger — and at first unknown and never totally knowable — context that gives the parts their meaning:

Given is the succession of the words. Each word is determined — undetermined [*bestimmt-unbestimmt*]. It contains in itself a variability of meaning. The means of syntactically relating those words to each other allows, within certain limits, several meanings [*sind mehrdeutig*]. The meaning originates when the undetermined becomes determined by the [syntactical] construction. In the same way the value of the composition of the whole — consisting of the parts formed by the sentences — has within certain limits several meanings. It [too] becomes determined by the whole (GS, vol. VII, 220).

The literary interpreter can understand only what his experience has prepared him to see. The interpreter uses his experience as a tool to diclose the possible being of the unknown. Interpretation is always "to a certain degree," remaining tied to the experience of the interpreter (GS, vol. V, 330). This circularity, inherent in all interpretative activity, puts a limit to how far any interpreter can go with his interpretation.

A further obstacle to objective knowledge of a literary text is its individuality. The literary work as it stands there in its contingency, concreteness and individuality can neither be grasped in its details nor in its total being. Quoting Leibnitz, Dilthey stated that *individuum est ineffabile* (the individual cannot be expressed) (GS, vol. V, 330).

Diithey pointed out that the same circular relationship between understanding and experience exists in philosophical and historical knowledge. In philosophy, the dependency of knowledge on the knower's experience limits the validity of the classification and interpretation of world-views. Systems are classified by comparing separate systems and by emphasizing what they have in common. But in so doing, the interpreter has already an initial idea of what the basic systems are. "Here one is trapped by the circle," for an anticipatory notion of what the system is "itself the result of judgments and induction, which [in turn] presupposes a conceptual system" (GS, vol. VIII, 161). Moreover, "in various periods the differentiations are related to totally different parts of these systems taken as important. So we are trapped here, too, by the circle . . ." (GS, vol. VIII, 161).

As far as the knowledge of the past is concerned, the circle occurs on two levels: first, on that of the mutual dependency between the historical reconstruction of the actual course of events and the larger meaning these events have; second, on that of the mutual dependency between the historian's life-experience and his interpretation of the past (GS, vol. VII, 162).

Dilthey illustrated both points with a reference to Barthold Niebuhr's reconstruction of Roman history:[15]

Everywhere his criticism is inseparable from his reconstruction of the real course of events. He had to state how the existing tradition of the older [periods of] Roman history emerged, and which conclusions could be drawn from this origin in order to determine its historical value. At the same time, he had (on the basis of a factual argumentation) to deduce the fundamental features of the real history. Doubtless this method moves in a circle — and when Niebuhr uses simultaneously the conclusions drawn analogously, the knowledge of these developments was subjected to the same circle . . . (GS, vol. VII, 162).

But Dilthey interpreted the dependency of the historian's interpretation of the past on his previous experience in a positive way. He argued that "life and the experience of life are the ever freshly flowing sources for understanding the social-historical world. Departing from life, the understanding penetrates into ever new depths" (GS, vol. VII, 138). These words indicate that he hardly saw the hermeneutic circle as a vicious one which corrupts knowledge. Here Dilthey seems ready to abandon the ideal of objective historical knowledge in favor of a dynamic conception of the study of history as a forever incomplete continuing exploration of unknown areas of human experience. But his thought took another direction instead: he modeled his conception of the understanding of history after the interpretation of works of art. In order to understand the exemplary function of the interpretation of works of art in Dilthey's approach to history, we must once again briefly turn to theological hermeneutics, now with a focus on its conception of truth and objective knowledge.

In theological hermeneutics, the interpreter could safely assume that the Author of the texts he studied spoke truth: God is good and has infinite knowledge. Thus in correctly understanding what the author said, the reader knew the objective truth about his inner reality — himself — and outer reality, God and His creation. But a human author, being not as good and having only limited knowledge, could not speak truth about reality: he could at most speak truthfully about inner and outer reality as he experienced it. This means that by re-experiencing the author's experience the reader learns only subjectively experienced truths, truths which are not very reliable. In the nineteenth century it did not worry very many people that past or present authors had not much to say about the nature of reality. Reality was no longer perceived as a creation having a deeper nature or meaning. All that people wanted to know was what the demystified reality of concrete daily experience was like.

Dilthey, allergic as he was to metaphysical speculation, wholeheartedly agreed that past and present authors had no truth to offer about the nature of reality. But he maintained that humans can nevertheless speak truth about the one area of which they have personal experience: human life. In fact, all the products they produce express human life and speak about life. According to Dilthey, works of art disclose life most truthfully, providing the observer with real or objective truth about human life. As Dilthey considered historians in many ways similar to artists, the histories they compose as similar to works of art, and history itself as a work of art created by the master artist, life, his conception of art will make us better understand his hermeneutic approach to history.

Seeing histories as creations of conscious life, Dilthey saw temporal coherences or "histories" — such as the history of Rome — as objects that are comparable to works of art. By object I mean in this context a free-standing entity having a shape of its own. Generally speaking, objects can be known objectively because a distance separates them from the observer. Dilthey's conception of history as an object can be best illustrated by the way he treated a person's life history as an object that can be known objectively.

An individual's history forms, according to Dilthey, a structured temporal whole that can be known as it is in itself — objectively.[16] The subject himself has in the course of his life interpreted his personal history in various ways according to his changing moods and interests. Such interpretations are passing, arbitrary and subjective. Dilthey maintained that an objective view of a life history is nevertheless possible when the various interpretations have finally become synthesized into one point of view, at the last moment of a person's life (GS, vol. VII, 233). If the object of investigation is another individual's life, it is possible to know it even better, because that life can be seen as a whole at the temporal distance from the investigator.

Dilthey applied the same reasoning to the history of mankind.

An objective view of history is only possible when — among the many points of view which afford opportunities of seeing the coherence of the whole and which makes it possible to select the parts that essentially constitute it — one is chosen which allows [the investigator] to discern this coherence itself, how it has happened (GS, vol. VII, 262).

This synthesizing point of view is only possible at the — hypothetical — last moment of history: "One has to wait for the end of history in order to possess the complete material for the determination of its meaning" (GS, vol. VII, 233). Dilthey's notion that the end has to arrive before the meaning of an individual life history and collective history — that is, its structure — can be seen, indicates that for Dilthey a history is a free-standing completed object.

Dilthey more than once referred to the past as an object.[17] His comparison of the past with a city at night might make this clear. Looking down from a hill upon a city in the evening, the observer notices hundreds of lights constantly go on and off in a confusing variety, comparable to the "emerging and falling off of emotions" and values experienced by the individuals of history. He then commented that these lights "belong to a world completely alien to us, a world that exists in and by itself, as it were, as an object (*gegenständliche Welt*) cut loose from us (*abgerückt*)" (GS, vol. VII, 256).[18] But if history can be seen as an object, it was to Dilthey not like an object pertaining to the world of nature. It had been created by man — that is by conscious life — and therefore expressed meaning.

To Dilthey, it is life that the human sciences strive to understand. Given the spontaneous, creative nature of life (including history), the symbols that express life most adequately are works of art, the most perfect expressions of the creative force. Life cannot be captured by logical — theological, philosophical, or scientific — formulas: it has to be intuitively grasped. Art is man's most truthful expression of life, and the artist — the great writer, painter, dramatist, musician, architect — has the most profound understanding of life.

A work of art is, according to Dilthey, a special kind of object because it exists self-sufficiently. It is more autononous, so to speak, than ordinary objects, because it is capable of leading an existence completely independent from its creator and from its observer. As Dilthey wrote, in great works of art "a spiritual element detaches itself from its creator" after its completion. Existing by itself, for its own sake, a work of art no longer carries any reference to its creator. It "stands there by itself authentically – fixated, permanent" (GS, vol. VII, 207). Existing as a material object independently from both creator and later observer allows the true and "certain" (*sichere*) knowledge of an artistic impression: the observer can always return to it attempting interpretation, fixed as it is in a tangible work (GS. vol. V, 319). By systematic effort, the interpreter can counteract the passing interests that keep him captive at any one moment.

Dilthey held that some life expressions deceive – but an authentic work of art never (GS, vol. V, 320). The true artist avoids the day to day struggle for life that consumes the existence of most people. The products he creates are not of direct practical use. Because the artist holds himself aloof from the struggle for existence, he does not have to lie and to deceive. His interest is not reality as it is lived from day to day. but the very roots from which ordinary existence originates. Dilthey conceived of art in hermeneutic terms as the most appropriate disclosure of life: art is "an organ for the understanding of life" (GS, vol. V, 274); it "attempts to express what life is" (GS, vol. V, 280). Works of art have truth-value: they exhibit truth in their very structure – a structure of words, of sounds, or of materials.[19] He called the artist "a seer who perceives the meaning of life" (*Sinn des Lebens*) (GS, vol. V, 394).[20] The experience at the basis of the artist's expression cannot have been arbitrarily made up; it is received, as it were, from life itself. The task of the artist is the same as that of the philosopher and the religious genius: to articulate life in a form understandable to others, a form adapted to the historical situation of the moment. A great work of art does not lie. It does not dangle before the eyes of the observer a world that is alien to its author (GS, vol. VII, 207). Inside and outside match. It is an authentic expression of the author's experience of life. Such a work is as a disclosure of reality, always truthful:

The work of a great poet or discoverer, a great religious genius, or a real philosopher can only be the true expression of the life of his soul; in this world of ours – filled as it is with lies – such a work is always true. In contrast to every other expression which is fixated in a sign, it can be interpreted exhaustively and objectively (GS, vol. V, 320).

Works of art acquire a Hermes function: they communicate reality's real nature to man.[21] Works of art reveal, or "say," in their specific artistic way something of importance about reality to man – not in audible words, like a living human being, but by exhibiting what they have to say in the way they are.

As entities having a "voice" of their own, and wanting to be understood, works of art figure like subjects instead of like objects: as autonomous sources of meaning, in their own way addressing man.[22] The past seen as an object discloses a meaning as well, expressing life, and the study of history has the same liberating effect on man as the contemplation of works of art (GS, vol. VII, 216). Both open up perspectives on life which a person limited by everyday circumstances can never reach by his own efforts. The past may be likened to a city of noble buildings which may now lie in ruins. Or it may be likened to a text which, however obscured by time, is in itself a work of art. For Dilthey, the most truthful text is not the written one which can be copied and altered but is the solid unique object — sculpture, painting or building — which through symbols communicates its truth to the observer-historian. But a written text might also have perfect coincidence between form and content, which, for Dilthey, constituted the highest form of art. An example would be a Bible from the early Middle Ages: written and illustrated with great care, on exquisite material, decorated with gems, so that the sacred message of God to man was given the most precious embodiment.

If the historical past is a work of art, life of the present has to be identified as the creator of history. Dilthey felt, indeed, that just as a work of art detaches itself from the artist, the past detaches itself from the moment of its origin in order to stand by itself, revealing its true and permanent form. The present has no real meaning because each present is in itself an isolated, short-lived and passing moment embodying ephemeral interest and emotions. Even after a present moment has passed and has become solidified as past, it will still be interpreted according to the ephemeral needs of the subsequent moments. The "real," or, in platonic terms, the "ideal" form of the past can only be distinguished long after the events have happened, when their accidental elements have vanished from sight. While the stretches of the intervening past grow larger and the field of memory increases, the true or real aspects of past events become less and less affected by emerging-and-disappearing emotions. Then passing, accidental interests, stemming from the moment of origin, are unmasked as mere "deception" (*Täuschung*). Then the "real" or ideal form of the past — its "true" or "objective" form discovered by the historian-artist — can be established.

For the understanding of the past a distance is needed similar to that required for the understanding of works of art. Thus, Dilthey saw the past as a work of art created by the master artist, life; and he saw the historian as an artist. He compared the historian to a painter, and historiography to painting. The past is an object for the historian, one with which he has a life relationship. In this relationship, some features strike him as significant, others as insignificant. The historian discloses the past in his own way by writing history. Just as the artist in painting a portrait brings out the features of his subject that seem to him to be characteristic and essential, so the historian stresses, in his rendering of the past, those events that seem significant to him.

All those aspects of an event that are not a necessary moment for the representation [*Darstellung*] of its significance, sink away. . . . The visual arts are distinguished from photography or wax reproduction in the same way in that they bring to bear the significant feature. In the variety of momentary experiences of images, whether they be of landscapes, of interiors or of faces, the perception [*Auffassung*] of the significant moments changes constantly. All the time we do not have before us an objective reproduction but a living relationship [*Lebensbezug*] (GS, vol. VII, 75).

Rather than copying everything that has happened — than merely reproducing the past object — the historian creates an abbreviated version, a "type."[23] Such a type expresses the hidden truth of past reality better than the visible "brute" past itself in all its complexity. The visible past — the facts as they happened — is a symbol that requires interpretation. Like the visible letters in a book, the facts of history refer to a dimension transcending mere visibility.

Dilthey realized, however, that an interpretation of a work of art can never be final, it can never be as objective as scientific knowledge of the mere things of nature: a symbol does not coincide with the hidden reality it hints at. But he insisted that interpretation can nevertheless be valid: the connection between symbol and hidden reality that is indicated in the interpretation can do justice to the reality behind the symbol. How can we evaluate the validity of an interpretation? Nobody can prove by logical or empirical means whether an interpretation of a work of art does justice to it; nor can it be logically or empirically proved whether an artist, philosopher, religious genius, or a historian for that matter, does justice to life. The criterion of an interpretation's validity is a sense of quality rather than a sense of logic. The closeness to life of the artist, the philosopher, and the religious genius is reflected in the quality of authenticity of their work. Thus, the authenticity of their works bears witness to the truth concerning life they disclose. Similarly, an interpretation's validity of historical evidence cannot be proved by logical means. Rather, the quality of the historian's work persuades us of the truthfulness of his rendering of past life.

Strongly resisting the element of arbitrariness in such "artistic" interpretations, Dilthey contended that it was possible to lay down the ground rules for interpretative processes. He did this for literature in *Poetic Imagination: Elements for a Poetics* (1887), and for history in later essays on the structure of the human-historical world. In the historical essays, he suggested a set of categories by which to approach the past – categories which he claimed to have deduced from "life itself."[24]

Thus, although Dilthey acknowledged the subjective element in the hermeneutic circle, he never succumbed to solipsistic constructivism, the position that meaning only exists in the eye of the beholder. He maintained in particular that the historian does not create the historical synthesis he describes, but finds it in history.[25]

He also contended that, although the historian himself selects his topic, and designates his "logical subjects of history," as Dilthey called them, such selections are justified by historical life itself. He wrote, for instance, that economic life "creates" for itself societies (*Genossenschaften*); that scientific life produces centers "to realise its [science's] tasks"; that in all cultures religious life creates strong organizations (GS, vol. VII, 135). These logical subjects are thus not the fictitious creations of the historian as mistakenly believed; they are real entities formed by the life of history itself.[26]

But, in the final analysis Dilthey was unhappy to be forced to recognize the impossibility of obtaining complete objective historical knowledge. Like most thinkers of his age, he could not completely discard the emotional need for objective truth – which, for him, meant complete truth. A careful reading of Dilthey's works shows that it was his views concerning the nature of objects and of other persons that kept him from fully embracing and developing the hermeneutic approach he himself had intitiated.

In Dilthey's thought artifacts and histories are mind-created free-standing objects, to which he ascribed intrinsic meaning. Artifacts and histories therefore confront the historian like works of art: as autonomous entities that communicate meaning. But on closer inspection it turns out that this meaning is not actively communicated by the object's "speaking" to the interpreter – that is, by a communicative act of self-disclosure on its part. The meaning of cultural objects, as Dilthey saw it, was their fixed inner structure. The object's meaning is at all times the same, although we may interpret it differently on the basis of our varying personal experiences. This fixity is in the nature of objects in general when we contrast them with genuine subjects, which are human beings. Acting spontaneously, subjects continuously transcend their existence of any moment. They are, in Sartre's words, continuously ahead of themselves. In order to be known, they need therefore to communicate their inner states to the observer, who thus becomes an interlocutor. Genuine subjects cannot passively be studied, they have to make themselves known by expressing themselves, by "speaking." And, of course, such subjects also receive communication through hearing. For Dilthey, cultural objects could not participate in dialogue, for they could neither speak nor hear. He could not conceptualize the communicative element in understanding.

It is true that Dilthey attempted to see life as actively disclosing itself and the meaning of the past as an active disclosure of life. But the meaning with which he felt most comfortable was the meaning that accrues to an object as the result of its place in a fixed system. Similarly, he attempted to see life itself as *mehrseitig* (GS, vol. VIII, 143). But he did not make completely clear whether cultural objects and life are *mehrseitig for us,* because of the limitations of our understanding, or because of their specific nature. If their meaning is merely inexhaustible *for us* because of our limited reason, their *Mehrseitigheit* is a regrettable condition; if, on the other hand, cultural objects and life themselves are *mehrdeutig,* this condition testifies to the depth and richness of life. Dilthey seemed inclined to opt for the first of these two interpretations; this made the hermeneutic interpretation of man's products in the end seem inferior to scientific knowledge. In this regard, he was led astray by the philosophical tradition, which following classical Greek thought, conceived of being as an eternal object to be contemplated. This classical conception of knowledge[27] was mediated by the modern rationalism which relied on intuition in order to know essences, and by empiricism and positivism which relied on visual observation to know the phenomenal world. In this tradition, the eye functions as the primary organ of knowledge; be it the inner eye of the mind in contemplating being and essences, or the outer eye in observing the phenomenal world. The physical eye is the instrument par excellence of modern natural science but natural science's object is no longer being which is truth itself, but nature, a powerful obstacle to man's desires that has to be subdued by the knowledge of its laws.

Because modern scientists approach their objects of investigation as entities to be subdued — to be silenced and made manageable — they have experienced difficulties in understanding human beings and their products. The nineteenth-century positivists attempted to solve these difficulties by reducing human beings and their products to the status of objects — of entities that do not act spontaneously. This was, however, precisely the approach against which Dilthey protested. But Dilthey, steeped in the Western naturalist tradition, and seeing cultural objects primarily as objects, that is, as entities having a fixed meaning, could nevertheless not complete the trail he so imaginatively started to its logical end.

In the final analysis Dilthey felt that works of art, histories, and life as a whole are enigmatic to us, merely because we cannot see them in their totality. If we could, the riddle would be solved. But the origin of the riddle is in us — in our finiteness — not in the meaningful objects or in life. Neither these objects nor life as such are riddles, they do not present themselves as mystery, actively inviting our responses. They do not do anything — they just are what they are. It is only we who are baffled when faced with their complexity.

As a result of Dilthey's conception of artifacts and histories as objects — and the corresponding ideal of objective scientific knowledge — the past sinks back from the reality-disclosing status of art to that of a common "object" of scientific investigation. Indeed, the spell of the Greek conception of being as reality as it silently and immutably exists by itself, has not quite been broken.[28] It is amazing how far Dilthey with his hermeneutic approach to historical knowledge went beyond the traditional conception of objectivity and scientific truth. But his hermeneutic solution to the problem of historical knowledge represents a conclusion reached after long and arduous mental labor. He could not bring himself to wholeheartedly embrace it.

Dilthey was as ambivalent concerning the ontological nature of the past's others as he was concerning the nature of cultural objects, and very much for the same reason. On the one hand, Dilthey was fully aware of the radical otherness of the past's actors. On the other hand, he saw them as part of the self — either the latent generalized self, or the developing self of mankind. The past's others figure in Dilthey's thought to a certain extent as others in their otherness because they are experienced by the interpreter as radically different from him. But this is only so because he is not yet aware that the same features exist in himself. Their otherness is only apparent. In reality, the past's others are parts of the general human self. For this reason, Dilthey felt that he could explain understanding (*Verstehen*) as a monologue of the general human self and not in terms of communicating with the past's others.

Thus we see that Dilthey's ambivalence concerning the ontological nature of works of art, artifacts and histories on the one hand,

and that concerning the status of others on the other, are intimately connected. With regard to both areas he failed to conceptualize the element of communication between subjects who are exterior to each other.

This may have been caused primarily by his rejection, as a modern philosopher, of a transcendental reality; reality is this world, and all humans participate in this reality. Thus, in knowing ourselves we know others, and vice versa. The recognition of the existence of other human beings as radically others was still suspect in Dilthey's eyes, because it reminded him of that traditional radical other par excellence, God. Dilthey had never been moved by his theological studies, he had never been personally touched by the God of his Lutheran church who reveals himself to man in the Scriptures. Thus, the Judeo-Christian model of the Other disclosing himself in the Word was not the personal experience for him as it had been, for instance, for Kierkegaard.[29] Thus, he did not see the effect of a literary work on the interpreter as the result of a successful communication, that is, of a genuine interaction between the interpreted object's active desire to be understood, and of the interpreter's active desire to understand.

But although Dilthey could not for these reasons wholeheartedly accept the hermeneutic approach he initiated, he was nevertheless on his way to seeing historical evidence and histories, and reality as a whole as disclosures of meaning, or texts to be read. The hermeneutic conception of reality as an act of self-disclosure with its important consequences for the study of history and culture, will be the topic of the next chapter on Dilthey's hermeneutic philosophy of world-views.

CHAPTER FIVE

DILTHEY'S PHILOSOPHY OF WORLD-VIEWS
(*WELTANSCHAUUNGSLEHRE*)

Dilthey had maintained in the *Introduction to the Human Sciences* that because history had shown pronouncements of truth to be historically conditioned, a critique of historical reason was necessary. He felt that it was imperative first to solve the antimony between man's historical consciousness and his need for certainty — between history and reason. This could hardly be done be devising any new metaphysical system, for such a system would again be historically conditioned; it would be of relative validity only, and would not, as a result, command much respect.

Dilthey maintained therefore that only a new philosophy could resolve this problem. Instead of focusing on unchanging reality "out there," as had been done in traditional metaphysics, he proposed a philosophy that was to study itself. This new philosophy — the philosophy of world-views — was thereby to be a "philosophy of philosophy" (GS, vol. VIII, 206) — a "meta-philosophy."[1]

This philosophy of philosophy would have to acknowledge the achievements of traditional philosophy; while at the same time it would have to express the modern historical consciousness (GS, vol. VIII, 7). Historical consciousness, after having performed its destruction of metaphysical systems, would be called upon to "assist in solving the marked contradiction between the claim to validity of every philosophical system and the historical anarchy among these systems" (GS, vol. VIII, 78).

In order to resolve the antimony between philosophy and history, Dilthey felt that first the origin of the conflict had to be understood. His point of departure in investigating the seeming weakness of reason was that philosophies clearly do not originate in pure reason, but in human, culture-bound consciousness and its historical life.[2] The study of past philosophical systems had taught him that they reflect the state of consciousness in their past epochs: "The way in which a period's knowledge is synthesized [into a unified system] is conditioned by the state of consciousness [prevalent at the time]." It is always "a subjective and passing expression" of that state, for in contrast to pure reason, consciousness is a shifting awareness of reality colored by changing emotions. Consequently, "a mood [*Gemütsverfassung*] always underlies any ideal of life and world-view and they are valid only in the historical ambience [*Umkreis*] in which it predominates" (GS, vol. VIII, 7).[3]

Thus Dilthey had reached the conclusion that the products of concrete human reason are never exempt from entanglement with concrete existence. They are rooted in the historical life of their time. Here, Dilthey's conception of mind is important. Dilthey conceived of mind as a mediating activity between the human organism's living will and the external world — as the continuously shifting or "living" relationship between the human organism and the context of its life-activities. He stressed repeatedly that no "object" exists without a human "subject" — as objects become objects only for a subject; and that no experiencing subject exists without an experienced external world: "A mere inner life or a mere external world is never given to us; both are not only always together, but [exist] together in a most lively relationship [*Bezüg*] to each other" (GS, vol. VIII, 16). "The world as an independent entity is an abstract notion" (GS, vol. VIII, 17). We perceive of the world what our living experience of it allows us to see.[4] This meant to Dilthey that lived experience, far from obstructing our view of a supposed reality, discloses it to us, and provides partial but real insights.

Knowledge is the experienced relationship between man and his external world raised to conscious awareness or "mind"; so mind is the experienced awareness of the world. Because we never see reality apart from experience, we can never see reality "as it is in itself."

The conception of mind as a mediating activity between inner and outer worlds had important consequences for Dilthey's view of knowledge, the product of mind's activities. Knowledge is not a reflection of reality, but is a reflection of our experience of it. We now must consider this point in more detail. Dilthey saw "knowledge" as a "symbol" of reality. Statements containing factual information about reality do not present us with reality as it is — they do not provide us with real, objective, or scientific knowledge about reality — they merely refer to, or hint at, relationships that are themselves not given to our perception and consciousness. The following important passage summarizes Dilthey's position on the relationship between perceiving subject and external world:

Everything man perceives about the world is always the relationship of his consciousness [*Lebendigkeit*] to its [the world's] properties which he cannot

change. By the unchangeable fundamental law of his situation he is tied to
these relationships. What he sees, dreams or thinks of as this world, is always
this relationship, nothing else. His world is as little a product of his consciousness as it is an objective fact. . . . From [this consciousness] the differentiation and connection of the functions which perceive the world, and
from [the world's] objective character which thus becomes perceptible,
follows every interpretation of the phenomena that surround us. Such a
relationship of functions makes it possible for us to perceive something of
the world that would otherwise be invisible to us. What is so perceived is an
expression of this relationship — only a symbol of the enigmatic coherence
of [total reality]. The objective coherence itself never enters our consciousness (GS, vol. VIII, 27-28).

Statements of knowledge — including philosophical systems — then,
are symbols pointing to a reality of which we are a part, but which
nevertheless remains mysteriously hidden from us, and of which
we keep discovering new and unexpected aspects as our experiences
change. Man's inability to ever see reality as a whole — the total
coherence of things, and his dependency in the process of knowing
on experience explain why in the course of ages man's philosophical
systems have changed so much: man's new experiences of reality
caused him constantly to revise his understanding of it, his world-
view.

The Dilthey called world-views the intellectual and intuitive interpretations of reality. A world-view is a philosophical system in
the broadest sense of the word — an understanding, or an interpretation, of reality. A world-view never contains a copy of reality
as it is. A world-view is only a symbol of, or reference to, reality. It
is a hypothetical construction, in images or rational formulas, on
the basis of our experiences which are scanty in view of the total
coherence of things of what reality is like, in short, an interpretation
of reality. And, as we have seen in the previous chapter, the difference between interpretation and knowledge is that the former
is only tentative, hypothetical, apt to be revised on the basis of
new evidence, new experience. Dilthey believed that truly scientific
knowledge — the products of pure reason, the objective knowledge
concerning nature — does not change; it increases during the course
of history. Philosophical interpretations, in contrast — being the
products of experience, and expressed in images and rational
formulas —vary.[5]

The relationship between man and reality, or inner and outer
worlds, as seen by Dilthey is decidedly different than that between
finite man and unchanging being in the philosophies of post-
Socratic classical antiquity or in Christian doctrines. Generally
speaking, the traditional philosopher had to detach his mind from

the changing visible reality of concrete experience; he had to free his reason for the perception of eternal truth; his bodily existence was experienced as an obstacle in the quest for truth. According to Dilthey, man does not have to efface himself in the face of being in order to really see and understand it. He does not have to divest himself from his individual characteristics that are bound to person-alize – not "distort" – his view. On the contrary: the more experi-ences with reality a person or culture has had – the more he or it is an individualized and specific person or culture – the more aspects of reality will disclose themselves.

What man "knows" about the human world is thus a product of the lived interaction between inner and outer worlds.[6] Dilthey distinguished two types of products, and two types of knowledge, emerging from the interaction between the human organism and its environment: the individual personality which he called the acquired soul-structure, and the collective world-view.

The first and most basic product of the interaction between man's inner will and his external world is the image an individual has of the world. This image is mediated by the individual's personality structure, or self, which has emerged in the course of his intercourse with the external world. The personality structure is, as it were, the glasses through which the individual sees the world.[7]

The second product is that of world-view formation – the creation of religious, philosophical systems and works of art. Although a world-view can be and is held by individuals, Dilthey uses the term mostly for those shared collective interpretations of reality prevalent during major historical epochs.[8]

Dilthey explained the genesis of world-views in the following way: the personal experience of life causes man to reflect upon life (*Lebenserfahrung*). This awareness of life is colored by a "mood," or emotion (*Lebensstimmung*), created by the specific nature of the experiences (GS, vol. VIII, 81). When emotions are shared by the community, they become the basis for the development of world-views. The world-views present in religion, poetry, and metaphysics articulate the significance and meaning of reality experienced at a certain time and place; they represent a solution to "the riddle of life" (GS, vol. VIII, 82).

As far as the means used in the world-view's interpretation of reality are concerned, Dilthey maintained that the interpretations presented in world-views explain something complicated by means of something simple. Such a process, he said, is not uncommon: it occurs in ordinary language, when a speaker uses metaphor, personi-fication and analogy. Religion, myth, literature and philosophies interpret reality by using visual and literary symbols (GS, vol. VIII, 82). Dilthey called world-views and philosophies "symbols of the various aspects of consciousness in their relation [to the world]" (GS, vol. VIII, 8).

A world-view contains, therefore, both a practical "ideal of life" that provides guidance for human conduct — as well as a theoretical "image" of what the world is like and what man's place is in it.[9] "The great historical states of consciousness in various times and [in various] peoples express themselves in the total mental coherence [*seelische Gesamtverfassung*]; this [coherence] expresses itself in the [people's] view of life, it conditions the [people's] intellectual world image [and] the goal it strives for, expressed in its ideal of life" (GS, vol. VIII, 27).

The problem that had stimulated Dilthey's reflections on the nature of world-views was the antimony between history and philosophy. He concluded at this point that this problem cannot be solved by means of reason and logical arguments because world-views are not products of pure reason, but of lived experience. This view of the origin of world-views in lived experience gave Dilthey a new perspective on the conflict between world-views and the existing anarchy of philosophical systems. He stated that conflicts between world-views occur when one of the many possible relationships between inner and outer worlds is fixated in a theoretical world image, and is subsequently mistaken for scientific, pure knowledge — and hence for the only valid image — presumably expressing the only valid way of experiencing reality and the only true world-view. Clashes between world-views occur in "the process by which the objective world images are made autonomous in the scientific consciousness" (GS, vol. VIII, 8).

By anchoring philosophy — or, as he would say, world-views — in personal and cultural experience, Dilthey did not reduce traditional philosophy (or his own thought, for that matter) to a purely subjective enterprise. He denied, indeed, that philosophies are arbitrary creations of imaginative thinkers. They are articulations of man's encounters with reality. This point leads to the heart of Dilthey's conception of world-views: his affirmation that world-views are valid because they are based upon man's experiences of reality.

Dilthey accepted the validity of world-views — interpretations of reality — because they are grounded in the collective lived experience of the really existing perceptible world. They express an experienced aspect of a real reality — a reality which is not thought up by man, but which exists independently from any human observer.

The reality of the external world, which he defined in his 1890 essay "Contribution to the Solution of the Problem of the Origin of our Belief in the Reality of the External World and its Validity, is, indeed, of crucial importance in Dilthey's conception of world-views; it validates experience as reality's disclosure. Actual experiences of reality cannot be refuted. This is an important point which deserves some closer scrutiny.

A personal experience, such as the pain of childbirth, or a culturally conditioned experience, such as the experience of nature and society as a struggle for life, cannot be contested: these experiences are facts. If a person states he is in pain, one can only accept it, and try at most to understand what he experiences and why: it makes no sense to deny that the other is in pain. The same reasoning applies to collective culturally conditioned experiences. One can from one's own point of view object to any specific *interpretation* of the feelings caused by childbirth as pain, or to the *interpretation* of nature as a scene of violence, but the experiences themselves are present for the experiencing person and culture.

At this point we understand how Dilthey's conception of world views led him to the novel conception of the philosopher as reality's interpreter, and to that of reality as a text to be interpreted. As a literary text is "actualized" in the interpreter's readings, so is reality "actualized" in man's interpretations. Interpretations of literary texts say something about the text's meaning; however personal and one-sided the interpretations may be, the text is always present in it. According to the philosophy of world-views, human experiences — being conscious experiences — are lived interpretations of reality; they are as such valid because reality — the "text" — is present in them. Similarly, the articulations of experiences in personal statements or collective world-views are accepted as valid in this philosophy. The manifold ways in which human existence has been — and is — lived, are seen as so many lived interpretations of reality. Dilthey's hermeneutic perspective makes us see the meaning of human existence as its being a lived interpretation of reality; man's specific value — his nobility — is his ever-present relationship to reality — ever present because human life cannot be lived without such a reltionship: man exists in the interpretative relationship to reality — every present because human life cannot be lived with such a relationship: man exists in the interpretative relationship to his environment, he *is* this living relationship.

Dilthey's conception of philosophy includes expressions of the relationship between human organism and external world that are beyond philosophy proper, in religion and literature. Dilthey wanted to conceive of "philosophy" in a much wider sense than was usually the case in academic circles. For Dilthey philosophy is present wherever a person attempts to lift himself consciously above mere activity: "Reflection [*Besonnenheit*], which aims at elevating everything to consciousness; the resulting spirit of criticism, the testing of preconceptions – philosophy . . . is this function, everywhere present in human history" (GS, vol. VIII, 219). In this sense, philosophy is not something marginal or unnatural; it does not conflict with life. On the contrary: it originates from the thoughtful experience of life itself. "Interpretations of reality," in the form of worldviews, emerge wherever we find man.

Underlying the understanding of life by poets, artists, religious thinkers, and philosophers is what Dilthey calls a "religious" feeling – that is, an awareness of "the invisible," which itself originates in a heightened experience of reality: ". . . life itself . . . points to something that penetrates it from the outside, that comes from its own depths – as an alien force, as if it came from invisibilities" (GS, vol. VII, 266). One of Dilthey's examples was Calvin's heightened awareness of death, which prompted the reformer to elaborate his stern puritan world-view.

Religious thinkers, artists, and philosophers articulate in myths and images their experienced relationships to reality; the philosopher does so by lifting "to consciousness the world image, the ideals, and goals that animate his time. He tries to hit the common root of life. Upon these roots of life and reality he throws the light of logical thinking" (GS, vol. VIII, 32). Dilthey urged philosophers to study the experiences of reality contained in religious thought and artistic expression, for "the artist and the religious thinker can see some aspect of the world, – a symbol [referring to] the world [as a whole]" (GS, vol. VIII, 28). In a sense, the artist and religious thinker may have a better access to reality than the philosopher, because their intuitive approach to it is more suited to reality's nonrational nature. He considered it very unfortunate that their rich material is commonly neglected, if not despised, by the philosopher.

Thus, in Dilthey's thought, the philosophers fulfill very much the same function vis-à-vis reality as a reader vis-à-vis a text. One can see interesting convergences in the work of literary critics such as Austin Warren, René Wellek, and William Empson. Warren and Wellek describe a poem as a "structure of norms" of which only a few are realized in the reader's actual experience of the poem.[10] Together, these norms "make up the genuine work of art as a whole." Similarly, according to Dilthey's philosophy, reality's "norms" cannot be experienced all at once; while all the experiences together would give an insight into reality as a whole. Moreover, as Warren and Wellek state, a work of art has a dynamic structure: "it changes throughout the process of history while passing through the minds of its readers, critics, and fellow artists."[11] The work is "historical": it has a development in the form of "the series of concretizations . . . in the course of history."[12]

Similarly, reality, like a work of art, has what today we call with Gadamer, an "effective history (*Wirkungsgeschichte*).[13] The work's history can be reconstructed from the reports of its critics and readers about their experiences and judgments, and from its effects on other works of art, so the history of reality can be reconstructed by studying the history of its interpretations in philosophy.

More recently, William Empson has discussed a problem in literature analogous to that seen by Dilthey in philosophy. With regard to literature, Empson wrote, the notion of a generally accepted poetics by which to judge poetry is unpopular these days. People feel that because a poetics is always inadequate, "it must always be unfair."[14] The result is a "general lack of positive satisfaction in the reading of any poetry"; the reader doubts whether his interpretation is right, and whether he ought to allow himself to like it.[15] The lack of standards by which to evaluate poetry has thus led to a "sterility of emotions such as makes it hardly worth-while to read poetry at all."[16] In philosophy, Dilthey saw exactly the same problem: the collapse of moral standards by which to evaluate conduct — be it in past or present — had caused moral scepticism and a malaise in philosophy.

However, Empson developed a solution to this difficulty. He said that it is the literary critic's business "to extract for his public what it wants; to organise what he may, indeed, create, the taste of his period."[17] Likewise, Dilthey's philosopher articulates for his age what his contemporaries experience to be the meaning of life. Both critic and philosopher need therefore not so much to know, in Empson's words, "what is over there," but to realize "what is necessary to carry a particular situation 'off'"[18]

The extent to which Dilthey actually used the interpretation of art as the model in devising his human sciences and his later philosophy of world-views, can be seen in his 1883 book *The Imagination of the Poet: Elements for a Poetics*. Here, Dilthey wrote that the problem in literature and the human sciences is exactly the same:

Can we know how processes operating everywhere [*überall wirkende Vorgänge*] produce these various groups of literature, differentiated as they are according to peoples and times? Here we touch the most profound fact of the human sciences: the historicity of the life of the soul, which is evident in every cultural system which mankind produces. How is the sameness of our human nature which expresses itself in uniformities connected with its variablity, its historical nature? (GS, vol. VI, 108).

The problem for the poet, and for the readers of the poet's products is, indeed, the same as that of the historian, the economist, and lawyer, and those who are dependent upon their productions: can the student of literature, and the student of man and his history

discover universally valid laws which can be used as rules in the process of [literary and other] creation, and as norms for critical judgment? And how are the [specific] technical approaches of a given period and nation related to these universal rules? How in the world do we overcome the difficulty with which the human sciences are saddled: to deduce universal rules from inner experiences which are to such a significant extent personal, complex, and yet indivisible? (GS, vol. VI, 107).

The comparison of reality with a work of art indicates that the diverging interpretations of reality in world-views do not result only from the limitations of the human mind, but also from reality's richness in possible meanings, its poteniality for alternative readings. Dilthey ascribed to religious thinkers, artists and philosophers an important function is social life. These gifted individuals remember the important moments of their personal life more vividly than ordinary people, and lift the content of their experiences to consciousness; then they transform these private experiences into universally valid symbols. Generally speaking, philosophy as Dilthey saw it clarifies for the society in which it functions, what at a given time life is all about. The specific ways in which philosophy fulfills this function depend on the general cultural situation in which it finds itself – such as the time, the place of origin, living conditions – and also on the personality of the philosopher.

Dilthey stated that in the present age, characterized as it is by the collapse of the universal science of metaphysics, philosophy has the task of interpreting life on the basis of contemporary experience of human existence. He felt that in this experience the element of life's historicity stands out most clearly. Thus, it is the task of the contemporary philosopher to open himself up fully to this historicity of human existence, and then to articulate what this experience tells us about reality and to formulate what it means. This is what Dilthey himself attempted.

A philosophy's appeal depends on its closeness to life as experienced at the moment. The more that a religious thinker, poet, or philosopher is in touch with life, the more authentic (*echt*) is his world-view: "every true world-view is an intuition which emerges from the standing-in-the-middle-of-life [*Darinnenstehen im Leben*]. . . . This standing-in-life occurs in the positions [one takes] towards [life], in the relationships to [it]" (GS, vol. VIII, 99). It is not content that decides the fate of philosophy, but philosophy's closeness to life, the mood it expresses and its degree of authenticity. Because human experience is valid in itself, its truthful presentation in works of religion, art, or philosophy are valid too.

Dilthey contended that it is the quality of authenticity, not the logical arguments, that convinces us of a philosophy's truth. All philosophical and religious systems are full of logical contradictions and false reasonings; they "have selected one aspect of things and eliminated others, they distort what lives by means of a strong will." Such systems "live" and expand nevertheless, and they do so "in spite of their logical failures, because of the vigor of their basic thought and because of the mood [*Gemütsverfassung*] expressed in them" (GS, vol. VIII, 33-34). As we have previously seen, Dilthey ascribed a will to power – a will to expand and to attain permanence and fixity to them. Authors may gain a large audience in their time, and convert many people to their point of view, because their readers – their contemporaries – share the same basic mood with their authors. Successful philosophical systems are not the isolated creations of geniuses or scholars, fantasizing in their ivory towers; they are vitally connected with the religion, social life, art, and literature – in short, the cultural life of the time, which make up "the emotional structure of history, from which it receives its imprint" (GS, vol. VIII, 35).

Dilthey considered his philosophy of world-views as the appropriate philosophy for his age. Realizing that both the relationship between the experience and knowledge of finite beings, on the one hand, and, on the other hand, the total coherence of things will always be partial, he did not claim universal validity for his philosophy.

Dilthey felt that his historical philosophy made possible a higher level of understanding reality (GS, vol. VIII, 161). His philosophy of world-views "lifts the human mind above the confidence, caused by [mind's] limited essence, that it has found in any of these world-views the [complete] truth" (GS, vol. V, 380). The historical consciousness at this stage philosophically "elevates itself above the attempts to build systems"; however incomplete the relationship between finite consciousness and total reality, "the historical consciousness is nonetheless the high potency of the systematic building of systems which [results] in the one-sidedness of a world-view" (GS, vol. VIII, 161).

In his meta-philosophy, claimed Dilthey, philosophy had finally understood itself for what it is. From the point of view of the individual philosopher, philosophy is a self-reflection on the nature of consciousness — reflection on what man does in thinking, in creating images, and in acting. From the point of view of history, philosophy is "the developing consciousness of what man does" — a consciousness which culminates in modern historical awareness.

While the system-builders of the past and their followers, all committed to the truths they articulated, were submerged in the stream of history without realizing it, Dilthey's meta-philosopher is part of the same stream, but knows it. Instead of a search for "the truth," his philosophizing is the critical empirical review of the life of the past and his own time. He does not want to learn any specific truth and to serve it. He is committed to study with detachment the many truths formulated throughout history the better to become aware of life's historicity, and to experience one new truth about it — the truth that fits the age — that life has no single truth.

The human sciences as presented in the *Introduction* were still oriented toward the search for objective knowledge of the human world; in their later form of the philosophy of world-views, they are oriented toward collecting the many truths man has found — truths that are symbols of a hidden reality. With his meta-philosophy, Dilthey had thus absorbed historicism: the historicity of human life was acknowledged in it. The realization of life's historicity had opened contemporary man's eyes for a new truth: that truth has many faces. But instead of undermining the vigor of present life, Dilthey's philosophy used it to stimulate life by making man aware of his sovereignty over the past — and thus, over the present and future as well. Dilthey claimed that the philosophy of world-views made possible a new systematic and empirical study of human life — be it a more modest study than the previous metaphysical systems. Philosophy's goal remained the establishment of the values, goals, and rules of conduct for human life; but its method differed from previous metaphysics: it had to take into account the limitations of reason, and to find its point of departure in the conditioned life of mind.

He indicated that the first step toward the new study of human life had been the discovery of the many questions posed by reality, and an insight into their interrelationships. The next step — the one proposed by Dilthey — is the realization of the conditions under which reason functions.

Thought will always be conditioned by its situation: "There

are always walls enclosing us. [We will always remain] attempting wildly to free ourselves from them: [we must realize] the impossibility [of such attempts], for the historicity of human consciousness is its fundamental characteristic" (GS, vol. VIII, 38). But realizing the extent to which thought is conditioned, the student of world-views can study the conditionedness of all thought.

Dilthey gave explicit directions for such a systematic study of thought, that is, world-views. He felt that the study should focus on structural features, those features which all world-views share, regardless of content. As products of different experiences of reality, world-views are all different. But because they are interpretations created by the same psycho-physical structure – man – and about the same reality – the external world – the philosophical systems that articulate world-views share certain basic features. First, they provide answers to the questions posed by the riddle of life – birth, procreation, death, misfortune, and so on – and they provide them in a coherent manner. Thus, the task of the student of world-views is to discover the logical and emotional coherence among these answers. Second, in each world-view a constant relationship exists between intellectual world-image, ideas concerning good and bad, and goals pursued by individuals and the community (GS, vol. VIII, 85). This relationship must be analyzed by the philosophy's student. Third, world-views have a developmental pattern and a common structure.

Dilthey defined the structure of a world-view as the coherence governing a society's vision of reality. Such a vision answers basic questions posed by reality, and thus inspires an ideal of life and a conception of the highest good; furthermore, it provides basic rules of conduct. Dilthey proposed a comparative study of world-views in order to find their structural regularities.

World-views and their crystallizations in philosophical systems are formed in the course of man's experience of life. They raise the predominant life-experience, including all purely physical experience, to the level of consciousness. Because a philosophical system develops organically with the life of the time. Dilthey considered a philosophy a living thing, comparable to a natural organism:

. . . a living entity displaying a structure similar to that of an organism; like [an organism], it is an individual belonging to a class; it must be sustained by the blood of a human heart if it is to survive; and according to its ability to live, it has a limited life span, a definite potency [*Macht*] to acquire power and establish itself [*sich geltend zu machen*] (GS, vol. VIII, 33).

The interpretations of reality contained in any world-views vary in history at least as much as those made by an individual during his lifetime. As a result, these

views of life, artistic interpretations of the world, religious dogmas, and philosophical formulas cover the earth like a vegetation of countless forms. Among them, a struggle for life and space seems to exist, like the struggle raging between plants in the soil. Some of them, supported by the powerful greatness of their author, acquire power over man (GS, vol. V, 379).

Like a scientist examining the specimens of nature. Dilthey approached the study of world-views:

As a botanist orders the plants in classes and investigates the law of their growth, so must the analyst of philosophy discover the types of world-view and the lawfulness of their development. Such a comparative approach raises the human mind above its confidence resulting from his conditioned situation, that it has grasped truth itself in one of these world-views (GS, vol. V, 380).[19]

Dilthey distinguished three main types of world-views. First is naturalism; it subordinates the will to the animal instincts that pervade the body and disciplines it in relationship to the outside world. Within this type of world-view Dilthey includes both sensualism and materialism. Second, in subjective "idealism of freedom"; it advocates the primacy of life, and more recently, of the individual. Finally, is "objective idealism"; it aims at compromise between the first two world-views.

Literary works, religions and philosophies embody, each in its own style, one of these three types. Although no world-view ever embodies one type perfectly, one is usually dominant.

In summary, Dilthey's proposed meta-philosophy would investigate in a systematic and in a historical way the relationship of the inner world of man to external reality and would study the relationship between philosophical system building and human nature in order to achieve a better grip on life.

Dilthey claimed to have overcome the moral scepticism caused by historical relativism by having restored reason to a new form of sovereignty over life. In accepting the philosophy of world-views, reason is no longer fooled by life, so to speak, it no longer basks in the illusion of its own freedom and purity, and it no longer lets itself down by the realization of its limitations and impurity. Reason's present realization and acceptance of its conditionedness frees it to play with past philosophies and to use them for its own advantage.

Dilthey did not want the meta-philosopher to copy the past in his behavior — actually to live past ideals. He wanted him to acquaint himself with these ideals, and to feel free to try each of them out in appropriate situations. In this way, the philosophical study of history would not cripple the human scientist, preventing him from leading an active, fruitful life. On the contrary: history would help him to master life, to become sovereign over it.

The freedom to choose between the solutions offered by the past in order to solve contemporary problems represents in Dilthey's eyes his victory over historicism. In his meta-philosophy, he felt, reason had again defeated history.

As the objectivity of the great historian does not urge him to master the ideals of individual epochs, so has the philosopher to investigate by means of a historical and comparative study the reflecting consciousness itself which conquers these objects, and to take a point of view [*Standpunkt*] above them. In this way, the historicity of consciousness completes itself in him (GS, vol. V, 380).

The notion that reason is at this point in history free to play with past philosophical systems — representing reason's sovereignty over the past — is an important element in Dilthey's thought. It is based on his assumption that the number of solutions to the problem of life was limited, and that at this point all major answers had been given.

According to Dilthey, it has always been reason's fundamental task (*Grundproblem*) to solve "the riddle of the world," and of life itself in a universally valid way. The riddle of life is like a knot that has to be untied. In practice, however, the riddle of life has been solved in many ways — ways that were far from being universally recognized. The history of philosophy expresses in rational formulas the ways in which life has been experienced at the various epochs of history; it articulates how the human organism and the external world — both "givens" as far as their fundamental structure is concerned — have been related to each other.

He maintained that there exist only a "limited number of possibilities" for untying the "knot" of life successfully (GS, vol. VIII, 138). The view that the number of solutions to the riddle of life is limited leads to a conception of history in which nothing new can really happen:

. . . all possibilities in which man can relate to the riddle of the world and life are tried out. In its historical context the achievement of each philosophical position is the realization of one possibility under given conditions; each one expressed an essential feature of philosophy, and through its limitation indicated the teleological coherence which conditions it. For it is part of a totality in which the complete truth is found. (GS, vol. V, 365).

When philosophical thought would have explored all the ways man could possibly relate to reality (GS, vol. VIII, 139) — when man would have tried all aspects of reality — the human mind would have at its disposal the total knowledge of reality. With complete knowledge of reality available, man would finally have reached a position of sovereignty vis-à-vis the world.[20] At this point, philosophical thought would have reached its consummation; man's restless search for truth would come to an end. In a way, the history of philosophy — and history in general — would come to a standstill, because no more genuinely new solutions could be developed. Here, we recognize an echo of Hegel's posthistorical stage in reality's history.

According to Dilthey, a turning point in the history of philosophy — and in history altogether — will be reached when the human mind will have tried all the possible solutions to the riddle of life.

Dilthey was not the only thinker at his time to toy with the conception of a posthistorical future: Augustin Thierry thought likewise that he witnessed "the providential termination of the labor of all centuries since the twelfth."[21] Vilfredo Pareto felt that the alternatives for action had by and large crystallized.[22] Gottfried Benn maintained that in the future man had to take into account only what had been achieved so far.[23] And, last but not least, Karl Marx expected a posthistorical age after Communism would become established. In the preface to *A Contribution to the Critique of Political Economy* (1859), Marx spoke of the bourgeois relations of production as the last of the antagonistic forms of the social process of production — the form that "brings the prehistory of human society to a close."[24] In the 1844 *Economic and Philosophic Manuscripts* he called Communism "the riddle of history solved," knowing itself to be this solution.[25] The posthistorical age inaugurated by Communism does not mean a restoration of an earthly paradise. But it will bring a qualitative higher level of human existence, as under Communism man will understand the true nature of his situations and therefore will be able to find real solutions for his problems.[26]

Dilthey's ideal of a posthistorical age — an age in which the labor of history would have ceased, and man would finally relax and enjoy the world; an age in which man would dominate history and nature, and would freely shape the future as he saw fit — expresses his desire for sovereignty and autonomy, his desire to be free from the power of time, and to domesticate it. The posthistorical ideal betrays his confidence that such a conquest of time was possible and, indeed, achieved, because all solutions to the riddle of life are available. In this sense, he remained true to the

Enlightenment conception of man as the creator of his own destiny. Dilthey's goal ultimately remained to master life by means of objective knowledge. In one of his preliminary studies on world-views, Dilthey reiterated that the relativities must be connected with universal validity. The empathizing with everything past must become a force to shape the future (GS, vol. VIII, 204).

After having absorbed all manifestations of human life from primitive times till the present, man will be able to distill from this knowledge, goals for his progression into the future: yes, in the historical consciousness itself, rules and energy will be contained which enable [him] to turn to the uniform goals of human culture – free from all pasts and sovereign over them (GS, vol. VIII, 204).

That is, the complete knowledge of human life gathered in the course of history which would then be practically useful. "The coherence of the human race is in universally valid thinking and the clear goals found upon it, the commonality of tasks, the healthy sense for what can be achieved, the deepened ideal of life: all these things receive a foundation in historical consciousness, which is no longer abstract, no longer merely conceptual, and thus no longer evaporates in unlimited idealism" (GS, vol. VIII, 204-205).

Dilthey's conclusion is that by gaining this knowledge, the historical consciousness would in principle overcome its own shadow, historical relativism:

It is not the relativity of each world-view that is the last word of the human mind which has reviewed them all, but the sovereignty of mind in regard to each of them – and at the same time the positive awareness of how, in the diverse ways in which the mind operates, the one reality of the world exists for us. In contrast to [a philosophy of] relativism, it is the task of the philosophy of world-views to... describe [zu Darstellung zu bringen] the relationship of the human mind to the riddle of the world and of life (GS, vol. V, 406).

It is interesting at this point to compare Dilthey's hermeneutic philosophy with Husserl's phenomenology, because Husserl in 1911 objected against Dilthey's "historicism" – a term Husserl used synonymously with historical relativism. In the years following Husserl's publication of the *Logical Investigations* (1900-1901), Dilthey and Husserl had been very close to each other.[27] Dilthey hoped, indeed, that Husserl's phenomenology could aid him in his attempt to develop a foundation for the human sciences. One can readily understand Dilthey's delight in finding what he thought to be a kindred spirit, for Husserl combatted positivism and historicism.[28] Both men attempted to re-establish the power of reason. Husserl contended that the positivists naively accept the things they study at face value, while being unaware of the ways in which their perception itself distorts the objectivity of their knowledge. To correct this serious fallacy, Husserl suggested the phenomenological method of "bracketing" — the pure description of phenomena in such a way that the observer frees himself from his personal and cultural prejudgments about things, and opens himself up for the things he studies. In regard to psychologism, Husserl advocated turning away from the analysis of the thinker or observer, and toward "the things themselves."[29]

Although both thinkers pitted themselves against the same attitudes, their solutions nevertheless diverged in important respects, because of their different evaluations of time and concrete experience. A close reading of the *Logical Investigations* shows the extent to which the thrust of Dilthey's hermeneutic philosophy differed from Husserl's phenomenology; for instance, in connection with Husserl's ideal of "pure description."[30] For Dilthey man is a temporal, historical being — part of the stream of time and history. As a result, the individualized concrete experience of man is his primary datum, the beginning and the end of his philosophical reflection. Husserl, by contrast, with his famous call "back to the things themselves," went beyond subjective experience. Dilthey rejected the possibility of knowledge of things as they are in themselves; things are always part of the larger context of life. Instead of "bracketing" himself, the philosopher had to immerse himself in the life of his time; in actual experience, reality was disclosed.

Equally illuminating for the difference between hermeneutics and phenomenology are Dilthey's and Husserl's respective treatments of the term "meaning." Dilthey maintained that the changing ways in which man has expressed himself about life represent precisely his changing experiences of life. He stressed the temporal, historical nature of life and of the experiences man has of life. He explained this by stating that the same images and the same experiences can never return: if different individuals repeat the same sentence, each person will nevertheless understand that sentence each time somewhat differently than the others; even if the same person repeats the same sentence, he will each time understand it somewhat differently, because in the meantime life as a whole has changed (GS, vol. VI, 172). In the *Logical Investigations*, Husserl denied, however, that changes in the understanding of meaning of phenomena can be explained by any reference to some change in life, or to reality itself. Changes in meaning occur as a result of the more or less accidental subjective acts on the part of the knower. These acts vary, while the things themselves — that is, their intended content — remain the same.[31]

Husserl distinguished between logical judgment, which does not change, and the knower's changing experience of such judgment which is somehow not important in itself. He defined a logical judgment as "the identical asserted meaning which is one over against manifold, descriptively quite different judgment experiences [*Urteilserlebnissen*]."[32] His goal was to clarify epistemologically the logical ideas, concepts, and laws by means of an examination of the concrete subjective experiences of these judgments. To Dilthey, the meaning of the phenomena pertaining to the human world is located in the phenomena themselves. A facial expression, or an artifact, disclose something of themselves to the interpreter. During the process by which reality's meaning is interpreted, new meanings are continuously formulated; this process has no logical terminus because on the basis of new experiences the interpreter will continue to discover new meanings. The "naive" experience of the world can never be transcended in one final interpretation: it can only be enlarged and deepened. Instead of bracketing himself, the interpreter has on the contrary to get into ever closer contact with the "roots of life."

In contrast, Husserl contends that change in meaning has to do not with the nature of the phenomena, but only with our experience of them. Central to his approach is the notion that "all thinking and knowing pertains to objects or situations [*Sachverhälte*] in such a way that in their being-in-themselves [*Ansichsein*] real or possible acts of thought or meanings, [they] make themselves known as an identifiable unity in variety [*Mannigfaltigkeiten*]."[33] In Husserl's perspective, the objects to be known are in themselves clear and visible. The philosopher aims at the "pure descriptions"[34] of them. Husserl defends for philosophy the principle of scientific objective knowledge, "the principle of being without prejudice."[35]

Their approach to the concept of expression represents another telling difference between hermeneutics and phenomenology. To Dilthey, all phenomena of the human world are meaningful; they reveal an "inside" because they have — more or less consciously — been created; their outside hides an inside (GS, vol. VII, 205). All phenomena of the world of man are, therefore, *eo ipso* expressions.

By contrast, Husserl accepted as expressions only phenomena which had been created with explicitly communicative intentions. In his view, phenomena have meanings only when they are intended as communicating a message, when they result from a conscious intentional act. Meaningful phenomena do not refer to themselves, as Dilthey felt, but to their author. For instance, a gesture of which the person himself is not aware, Husserl does not consider an expression in the proper sense of the word – it has in itself no meaning; meaning accrues to such an unintended expression only because of the interpretation by others in perceiving it.[36]

According to Dilthey, even an unconscious or logically absurd expression means something or makes sense somehow because it is an expression of an inner state, however vaguely articulated and confused it may be. To Husserl, an expression had to make sense in regard to an expressed content. He explained the understanding of an expression in terms of finding "the appropriate images" in fantasy, on the part of the knower – images that correspond to the expressed content; if no images occur, the expression is senseless.[37]

To Dilthey, the way in which man has expressed himself is as significant as the content he has actually attempted to express; the concrete historical expression is as essential as the inner state to which it refers. He did not separate form and content. To Husserl, the concrete expression represents a contingent element, while the thought, the "ideal-identical meaning" represents the essential one.[38] "The meaning of the sentence is not multiplied with the number of persons and acts, the judgment in an ideal logical sense is one."[39] Husserl finds this a matter of clear-cut evidence.[40] According to him, the "real" meaning exists by itself "over there," in the things which we experience, the meaning originates in us. While Husserl advocates that "general objects"[41] should be approached disinterestedly and without prejudice, suggesting that man is able to transcend time, Dilthey realized that finite man cannot have unprejudiced knowledge: man is a creature of his personal and his culture's experience, that is, of time.

We may sum up the preceding comparison between hermeneutics and phenomenology by stating that with his philosophy of worldviews, Dilthey believed that he finally had found a possibility for objective knowledge of the human world. Husserl, however, believed that he had secured a better foundation for objective knowledge. Husserl failed to appreciate Dilthey's way of overcoming psychologism, historicism, and positivism because he remained religiously inside of the traditional metaphysical framework which stresses the selfsame nature of things and of being – their having an "essence." Husserl approached phenomena from the perspective of their nonmundane ideality, their state of being that has no connections with the observer. He consciously ruled out the possibility that phenomena themselves might change their essence, their *"eidos,"* by positing that phenomena do not generate new meanings of themselves on their own account or in conjunction with their observers. Meaning as Husserl sees it is either in the invisible spirituality of the speaker behind the concrete visible phenomena, or it is in the mind of the observer interpreting these meanings.[42]

Because of his susceptibility for the powerful "saying" nature of works of art, Dilthey based his philosophy upon the insight that phenomena — at least, the phenomena of the human world — themselves express life, that they themselves "say" something, that phenomena are not exterior to the meaning they express, that they are themselves, in fact, the organs of meaning and saying. Dilthey's point of departure thus precludes notions of a self-same ideality of things; it inaugurates, in contrast, a conception of phenomena as having an active "speaking" nature, as being autonomous sources of meaning, as confronting us as others.

But, as pointed out above, Dilthey himself believed to have founded a new science by which to know human reality objectively in the form of the systematic study of man's collective experiences of life. In a letter to Husserl dated June 29, 1911, Dilthey indignantly refuted the former's charge of "historicism." Having severely suffered from moral scepticism, Dilthey had recovered from his "historical malady." Ultimately, the knowledge of life provided by it would conquer man's uncertainty concerning history.

However, in one way Dilthey almost succumbed to the other manifestation of the malady: the idolatry of history. He acknowledged that it is (at least currently in history) impossible for man to know the goal of history and the task of man in history. He suggested that during the intervening time, whenever a person had to decide to which ideal or course of action he had to commit himself, he should entrust himself to "history" — to the prevalent ideas of his time. After all, history is, according to the German historicist outlook, the manifestation of creative, conscious life; it seemed contrary to reason to assume that life might be consciously and knowingly evil; life — including the life of one's own time — simply had to be a beneficent force. In a preliminary study for the address for his seventieth birthday, Dilthey wrote:

The historical consciousness shatters the last chains which philosophy and science were unable to break. Now man stands completely free. But at the same time it saves the unity of the human soul, [saves] the overview of the mysterious coherence of things which is nevertheless apparent to our living nature. We may confidently revere in each of these world-views a part of the truth. And when the course of our life brings some aspects of the mysterious totality closer to us, when the truth of the world-view which expresses this aspect captivates us, we may then safely surrender ourselves to it: truth is present in each [aspect] (GS, vol. VIII, 225).

Similarly in "The Essence of Philosophy," Dilthey wrote that the philosopher whose self-confidence is undermined by the historical consciousness — once he realizes that he can produce only a historically conditioned work — should "surrender himself quietly to the power of the historical consciousness, and see his daily task from the point of view of historical coherence, in which the essence of philosophy comes to realize itself in the variety of phenomena" (GS, vol. V, 364). In passages like these, Dilthey came dangerously close to the idolatry of history, allowing life, which "knows best" to take the place of a higher power such as Nature or God, and to invite faith in the world as it is.

Dilthey, however, never deified life as it is, or *de facto* history. He was too much puzzled by life's contradictions, its cruelty and injustice, and, most of all, by the phenomenon of death — the incomprehensible reverse of — life to have any blind faith in what life brings. Cruelty and death, though part of life, contradict what one would like to see as life's real nature.

From life's changing experiences . . . emerges its face [*Antlitz*] full of contradictions, lively and at the same time ordered, rational and arbitrary, disclosing ever new aspects, and thus perhaps clear in details, but totally enigmatic in its totality (GS, vol. VIII, 80).

The awareness of having to die himself, and of the presence of death in nature, undermines man's trust in the goodness of life.

The center of all incomprehensibilities are procreation, birth, development, and death. Each living person knows about death, but cannot understand it. From the first look at someone who has passed away, death is incomprehensible for life; on this, our relationship to the world as to something other, alien, and frightening is founded. . . . The strangeness of life increases as man experiences permanent struggle in society and nature — constant destruction of one creature by the other, the cruelty reigning in nature (GS, vol. VIII, 80-81).

In another passage Dilthey mentioned "the most terrible and terrifying riddle" of ever so many mysteries of life (GS, vol. VIII, 143-144): death, procreation, family relationships, the cruelty of nature, the corruptibility of all that lives, and the contrast between free will and external necessities.

Such problems — contradictions contained in the many-sidedness of life — increase with the progression of thought. Actuality and thought, living and law, mental and physical, moral rule and hedonistic urge for happiness, [and] the profound mystery of time's corruptibility and the identity of our own existence, which requires the resolution [*die Aufhebung*] of becoming into being — who could enumerate all these riddles? (GS, vol. VIII, 144).

In evaluating Dilthey's thought, his reservations toward life should be kept in mind; these distinguish him both from the earlier Hegelian idealists and from the nationalistic historicist historians of the contemporary period. These reservations point to the existentialism of later thinkers to come.

Dilthey seems also ambivalent in another way. The traditional urge to find "the" truth — and the intimation that he himself had found it — conflicts curiously with Dilthey's remarkable willingness to grant validity to human experience as such, and its translation into divergent world-views. He continued to see that each successive world-view was the response to one particular aspect of life's riddle:

> The elaboration of world-views is determined by the will to fixity on the part of the world-image, of the estimation of life, of the conduct of the will. . . . Religion as well as philosophy search for fixity, effectiveness, dominance, absolute validity. But mankind has not progressed one step on this road. At no major point has the struggle between world-views led to a decision. While history selects among them, their main types stand side by side — sovereign, indestructible entities, which cannot be logically justified (GS, vol. VIII, 86-87).

The tone of this passage suggests that Dilthey still feels that the absence of progress in developing "the" total world-view invalidates the existing historical ones, and that the partial truths contained in world-views are all on the same "low" level, and therefore somehow basically untrue and invalid. In spite of himself Dilthey degrades the intrinsic validity of human experience. He still experienced the traditional, emotional need for the certainty of some "eternal" knowledge too intensively truly to appreciate the truth value of diverging personal experience.

Dilthey experienced his inability to solve the riddle of life, and to establish objective, scientific and universally valid knowledge concerning life and man's task in it as a painful defeat. In the 1903 address Dilthey depicts himself as a person who sees the all-important goal of overcoming the anarchy of opinions, but who "will soon succumb on the road leading to it without being able to reach it" (GS, vol. V, 9). In spite of his despair, Dilthey held fast to the belief in the one truth, based as it is on the one life, however contradictory it may seem to us.

Acknowledging that Dilthey did not completely embrace his own philosophy, we can step aside and take a look at the promises his thought holds for the study of history and culture. The novel conception of the historian as a Hermes-figure who transmits the life experiences of the past's radical others to those who, figuratively speaking, have stayed at home in the present is interesting. An example will clarify the impact of this conception. The past as text, written in different scripts — documents, artifacts, behavioral patterns — and in a foreign language — requires translation.

It is hard for us, for example, to make sense of Medieval animal trials. Animal trials in which animals would be brought to court after having hurt a human seem an absurdity, pure superstition, a misconception about how the world works on the part of ignorant people. We do not expect that to know about such trials will add to our understanding of reality. Such knowledge at most will be usefulness to historians who want to study the past for its own sake. But if, in contrast, we interpret Medieval animal trials as an expression of the close bond which then existed between man and nature, these events begin to mean something to us; they then make us realize, for instance, how much we ourselves are removed from feeling such a bond, and what may be lacking in our own lives. The seeming absurdity has become relevant. Further study may show us that such animal trials fitted in a sophisticated world-view, according to which man and nature were both part of a cosmic history. The seeming absurdity is at that point not only an emotional pointer to what we may have lost, it acts as an intellectual stimulus forcing us to think about the philosophical preconceptions underlying our own notions concerning the distance between man and nature we experience in our lives.

In approaching the past in this way, the hermeneutic historian learns not only about the past, but about himself, and about human life in general as well. He translates the cultural expressions of past experiences of reality — as is appropriate for this Hermes-process — in terms of experiences we understand, and discloses to his readers new layers of reality's meaning. Thus, he restores the communication between past and present — a communication which has been broken as a result of intervening changes in life.

At this point, comparison between the historicist and the hermeneutic approaches to history is indicated. Historicists such as Ranke had professed a profound respect for the alien past. But besides stating that every epoch is "equally close to God," they could not justify the respect toward the past on the part of the historians. Dilthey, in contrast, validates alien experiences and the behavioral patterns resulting from them: the past requires respect not only because it was lived by people — whom we should respect as fellow humans — but also because it teaches us about reality.

This latter remark — that past experiences teach about reality — leads to the question of their relevance. In the historicist perspective, past experiences had lost their relevance — their meaning — for us. Historicists simply explained the behavior of the people of the past by an appeal to the context of the period — its different moods and standards — and warned writers not to judge the past "unhistorically" in terms of present standards. In spite of its professed respect for the past, historicism could, however, very well be combined with a cleverly masked disdain for it: by seeing the past's strange features as exponents of the obsolete culture of the time. For instance, the Medieval superstitions were justified at that time: after all, the people did not know any better. But today, these beliefs have lost their relevance. With its concept of time's irreversible stream, historicism sterilized the past. The past of the historicists can no longer touch us existentially. The past of the hermeneuticists, in contrast, retains its validity and can touch our lives today.

Furthermore, historicists had no means to defend themselves against the richness of the past — sometimes even to the point of losing touch with their present, submerging themselves nostalgically in another period. They gave up their former cultural identity, and went native, so to speak, building and furnishing their homes according to historical styles, attempting to restore worlds of the past. The hermeneutic historian, in communicating with the past, remains himself.

Second, Dilthey's philosophy provided important source of inspiration for both Gadamer and Habermas, whose perspectives on history are so different. The ambiguities in Dilthey's thought were, indeed, such that he could serve as an inspirator to both.

Dilthey firmly rejected as "metaphysical fog" (GS, vol. I, 112) the assumption of an overall goal for history and historical laws. But having rejected these determinants of history's course, he remained highly ambivalent about what then might move history: the transpersonal creative force of "life," or man himself. On the one hand, he stated that life creates history and that man simply follows its course. On the other hand, he stressed that man increasingly has emancipated himself from history and is about to enter the posthistorical age of mastery over it. By identifying life with the actions of man, Dilthey avoided having to make a choice between these two interpretations. As a result, his philosophy of world-views has been developed in two directions: what we may call the "artistic" based upon the analogy between reality and a literary text, and what we may call the "Promethean" based on the view of man as the maker of his own history.

The artistic conception of history exemplified in the work of Gadamer is nonprogressive and nondevelopmental. It maintains that if history is, indeed, the series of embodied interpretations of reality, it cannot evidence progress. Every generation approaches reality in text in its own way. Because of the ensuing lack of continuity between interpretations, the successions of interpretations of reality are not logically connected with each other. Thus, notions and civilizations do not consistently develop toward the possession of an all-embracing knowledge of reality or ideal life.

Thus, the artistic concepts of reality lead to a view of the historical process as an unorganized amalgam of cultures, each in its own way disclosing reality. Past cultures, located, as it were, in timeless space, are studied for their own sake, outside of any developmental framework. They all speak truth, and all are of direct relevance to the present. The life-experiences of past cultures are not obsolete, only expressed in ways later ages find hard to understand. Gadamer maintains that texts say something to us, and continue to do so long after they have been written. Whoever withdraws from the reciprocity of such a relationship destroys its moral claim (*Verbindlichkeit*).[43]

Suspension of judgment is required for genuine understanding, which has, logically speaking, the structure of a question; it keeps possibilities open.[44] In interpreting a text, the interpreter should not make his own point of view unassailable. In hermeneutic understanding the alien is accepted into the own world.[45] Hermeneutic understanding is thus not knowledge to master the known, or to take possession of it (it is not *Herrschaftswissen*). It is putting oneself under the claim of the text, and keeping oneself open for its claim to truth.[46] "Whoever wants to understand a text is willing to have something said by it."[47]

The past is seen by Gadamer as a huge library rather than as a road to truth. On the other hand, the Promethean view espoused by Habermas continues to stress development and even progress. This view holds that history is consciously made by man, who is able to shape history as he sees fit because of his ability to anticipate a desired future on the basis of his memory of his past experiences. Because man does not simply remember what objectively has happened, but interprets his experiences in a personal way; he has a certain freedom in projecting the future. At this point in history, now man has understood that there is no objective goal or law, he realizes that it is up to him what the future becomes. Habermas works out Dilthey's philosophy of worldviews in this direction.

To Habermas, the promise of Dilthey's hermeneutic approach is the latter's grounding of the subjective elements in knowledge in the mind's capacitv to interpret reality in different and novel ways. On the basis of these interpretations, man is capable of creative actions which generate consciously projected novel futures. Habermas' model is, however, not the understanding of art or that of others, but the understanding of self, as effected, for instance, in psychoanalytic treatment. In *Knowledge and Human Interests*, he sees history as the species' "self-formative process."[48] The critical social scientists's role is to society what that of the analyst is to the individual: to discover the "real" truth about society's past as opposed to the distorted truth contained in ideologies. As a result of this "analysis," mankind will be able to consciously realize its true nature, and project its future in accordance with it.[49]

Third, the significance of Dilthey's philosophy of world-views for history lies in the possibility it creates for the historian to focus on non-Western cultures which, from the early nineteenth century, were not deemed suitable objects for historical research. In Dilthey's philosophy of world-views, no basic difference exists between, on the one hand, past alien world-views and the cultures they inform, and, on the other hand, present ones. All cultures embody interpretations of reality.

The hermeneutic approach which bridges the gap between the once and the now can therefore be fruitfully extended to build a similar bridge between the here and the there — between the familiar world of our own experience and the alien worlds of present and past other cultures. From the realization that reality genuinely has been known in other periods, it is only a short step to the realization that truth has been spoken in other parts of the world as well. In both cases the other culture expresses in its works of art, religion, philosophy, and in its political and economic system its interpretation of reality.

A period located elsewhere in time is moreover in the same way alien to us in our present as a culture located elsewhere in space is alien to us in our space. A present — or past for that matter — culture located elsewhere in space can be understood for that reason by the same methods of understanding as a culture belonging to the time-frame that we consider our past.

The convergence of the understanding of past and present alien cultures is illustrated by the example of Medieval studies in Europe and the United States. In Europe, people identify with the Medieval past which still surrounds them in many forms. Thus, the study of the Middle Ages is to a large extent a historical study of the historian's familiar world, a study of his historical "self." In the United States, in contrast, Medieval studies although practiced in the universities' Departments of History, figure as the study of a genuinely alien culture. But on both sides of the Atlantic the same methods of study are used.

The effect of classical works belonging to our own tradition, such as Plato's philosophical texts, the Greek tragedies, and the plays of Shakespeare is like the effect of the Middle Ages in Europe, still more or less direct, requiring an amount of specialized training in order to be understood. Chinese vases, Islamic mosques, African masks, and Indian relics or poems, in contrast, − like the study of the Middle Ages in the United States − require more strenuous efforts in order for their richness to be understood. But the same type of hermeneutic understanding is involved.

By being understood, a cultural product loses the character of being alien and miraculous. It begins to make sense. We develop a relationship to it. It becomes a Thou rather than an It. When kept at a distance, every cultural object is an alien It − a mere object. When we attempt to really understand an alien cultural product, the alien It − whether a Shakespearean play or an African mask − becomes a Thou. Potential Thou's do not occur only in our own tradition, they also occur in other civilizations and their pasts. They will be recognized as such when we attentively turn toward them, and allow ourselves to be addressed by them. The attitude underlying the artistic concepts of reality is one of positive expectation that the past will speak truth. The non-Western cultures of the present and their products can, however, be approached with the same positive expectation. Then they, too, will speak truth.[50]

The hermeneutic starting point to the study of history and culture as initiated by Dilthey is the positive expectation that the others have something to teach us, that their experiences can serve for us as windows on the reality that lies outside of our personal and cultural limited experience. Because the hermeneutic study of history stimulates a study of history as retrospective cultural anthropology, it is therefore very much compatible with contemporary structuralist approaches to history, such as that of the *Annales* School, which focuses on history's "deep" environmental, social and economic structures; that of Michael Foucault, which focuses on the ways in which the epistemic fields of past epochs were organised; and that of Lévi-Strauss, which focuses on the discovery of universal structures of the human mind. In this sense, Dilthey gave an important impulse to structuralist studies.[51]

Conversely, Dilthey has also contributions to make to the study of cultural anthropology. First, as we just have seen, Dilthey's philosophy offers a theoretical foundation for the validation of the world's divergent cultures. Second, it sees the cultural anthropologist, like the historian, as a Hermes-figure. The cultural anthropologist engaged in interpreting the meaning of the "texts" of non-Western cultures, and explaining the meaning to their readers at home. Cultural anthropologists learn to understand "the language of experience" of the culture under investigation – a language spoken in its world-view, morality; its behavioral patterns and social organization; and its artifacts – for these express, each in its own way, a society's language. The specific "grammar" of each language – the structural pattern of a culture – testifies, in its own way, to a specific experience of reality.

The approach to the study of culture hinted at in Dilthey's philosophy of world-views has much in common with that of the cultural anthropologist Clifford Geertz: Geertz states that "doing ethnography is like trying to read . . . a manuscript . . . written not in conventionalized graphs of sounds but in transient examples of shaped behavior."[52]

These promises offered by Dilthey's work, the possibility it offers for widely diverging interpretations, testify to the richness of his thought. Whether their diversity resulted from a conscious refusal on Dilthey's part to impose his will on the material that offered itself to his reflection, or from his inability to do so, is of little importance. An authentic philosophical oeuvre, like a great work of art, has many possible meanings, and generates many responses in its interaction with its students and observers in the form of new interpretations.

This analogy of a philosophical work with a work of art does not, however, free the student-observer from the obligation to respond, and thus to reflect critically on what is offered. On the contrary: any work is honored most appropriately by engaging in a dialogue with it – a dialogue which stimulates further reflection. Such a dialogue with Dilthey leads us to identify factors which inhibited the full development of his thought, and to identify steps that have been and other steps that will be necessary for the further development of the hermeneutic approach he initiated.

Dilthey, like others of his era, continued to experience history as progress. As long as time actually was experienced as a medium of growth, life as a process of progressive developments, and history as a progress in civilizational achievements, the nonprogressive, "artistic" understanding of human life Dilthey hinted at, could not be accepted. Only the cultural anthropologists of the next generation, persons who experienced the shock of World War I, and who realized, as a result, the illusion of progressive developmental history, were able to approach other cultures without pretensions of their own superiority. It took historians much longer − in fact, till the 1960s − to shed this attitude, and the corresponding belief in the progress of Western civilization.[53]

The promise of Dilthey's artistic view of history − the insight into the relevance of other cultures' past and present world-views, being disclosures of reality − can therefore only fully be understood in our own time − after the "betrayal" by history. Today, we realize that what seemed a betrayal from the point of view of a progressive conception of history, has turned out to be the very means by which our eyes are opened again for the relevance of other cultures' world-views − the means by which our cultural isolation has been broken, and our channels of communication with the world's other cultures have been opened up again. The next step in the further development of the hermeneutic approach is therefore its application to the study of non-Western cultures.

Similarly, the promise of the Promethean view of history is taken up today by those who, like Habermas, no longer believe in automatic historical progress, but who nevertheless are not willing to give up the hope that man might be able to consciously shape his future. Habermas' announced next step is therefore the further reflection on the communicative aspects of achieving progress.[54]

The second factor that kept Dilthey from fully developing his hermeneutic approach was his conception of objects. I have already touched upon this subject in chapter III. By exploring Dilthey's philosophy of culture we realize again that we are confronted in his writings with two conceptualizations of objects, as natural science objects − as fixed entities having a definite essence, and as works of art − acts of self-disclosure or processes of becoming being. If the human organism and the external world were, as Dilthey maintaned, fixed entities, and could relate to each other in but a limited number of ways, possessed a limited number of attributes, and thus, were restricted to a limited number of combinations, then history would, indeed, be finite. Then a posthistorical state of mankind could indeed be expected to occur at some time in the future. Objective knowledge − knowledge from all points of view, resulting in a complete picture of reality − would be a possibility.

If, on the other hand, the human organism and external reality were meaningful entities, autonomous sources of meaning, having, like works of art, a "living" structure as acts of self-disclosure − if they were entities which *are becoming*, as it were, as long as they exist as that particular structure − then history would never end, and man would forever continue to interpret reality, and would be invited to be attentive to its disclosures.

Because he took his cue for the understanding of objects from common objects, Dilthey opted for the former conception of things, and of a history followed by a posthistory.

The third next step in the development of the hermeneutic approach is therefore the development of a conception of objects — of cultural objects, and perhaps of natural objects as well — as existents which are not passively there, but, like works of art, actively *are*.

In dealing with Dilthey's philosophy of history, the next chapter will offer an explanation of why ulimately Dilthey could not free himself from a progressive view of history — a view so clearly in conflict with his hermeneutic philosophy of world-views.

CHAPTER SIX

THE MELODY OF LIFE: DILTHEY ON THE MEANING OF HISTORY

While during the nineteenth century the reassuring faith in a power steering from above the world's course was declining, the faith in history increased. History was seen as the force that gave the world's affairs direction and that eventually would purge the world from its evils.[1] The Christian hope for a "new heaven and a new earth" was thus transformed into the secular hope for a better earthly future. Although for many people God had died, most people could still see their lives as meaningful — as steps in the grand historical process in which the imperfect world was slowly recreated into a perfect world of prosperity and justice.[2]

Dilthey shared his age's belief in history. He could therefore be little satisfied with a conception of the past as a collection of cultures "chaotically" existing side by side in a timeless void. An aimless history, the coherence of which was merely a construct of the historian's mind, made human life seem pointless; therefore he could not help but think that together the past's cultures form a coherent temporal whole.

In his hermeneutic philosophy of world-views, Dilthey advocated the intrinsic meaningfulness of individual cultures. In his philosophy of history, he saw history as a coherent temporal whole. This chapter analyzes Dilthey's speculative philosophy of history, his reflections on history's meaning.

A review of six major ways in which history has been conceptualized in the Western tradition will provide an insight into the way the problem of history's meaning presented itself to Dilthey.

In Western historical thought two major discussions on the structure and meaning of the past stand out. The first discussion concerns the question whether the past is to be conceptualized as a timeless field of experiences or as a temporal linear succession of events. The second concerns the question whether past events have a symbolic meaning, for instance reflecting God's will, or simply a "literal" meaning, describing events. In the Western tradition, a continuous shifting has taken place between the conception of history as a field and as a line, and between the ascription to historical events of symbolic and of literal meaning.

Chronologically speaking, the oldest conception of history — primarily political history — in the Western tradition is a cyclical one. From classical antiquity until far into the eighteenth century the world of man's affairs was considered part of the realm of nature. Man's institutions followed the same pattern of birth, climax, decline and death as the other things of nature. According to this view, natural phenomena repeat themselves without ever producing something novel that could serve as the basis for further development. Nature and human life, including human history, evolves in cycles. This involves a conception of the past as a cosmopolitan field of timeless experiences — as the stage upon which the basically unchanging drama of man was performed time and time again.[3]

In this classical conception of the political history, the chronological order of history's events had the function of facilitating their memorization. It did not indicate a direction of the historical process, for political history was not seen as a linear process. Because of its lack of direction, cyclical history makes upon us — used as we are to a history that receives its meaning from its direction — the impression of being "meaningless."

This cyclical conception of political history of classical antiquity could easily be harmonized with later Christian conceptions of life based on biblical views of history. St. Augustine, for instance, pointed out in his *The City of God*, written during the years 413-426, that earthly life revolves in cycles, but that at one point God will decide that it is time for the Last Judgment and the end of the world.[4] While the visible movement of the City of Man — political history — was cyclical, the invisible history of the City of God — the history of salvation — was linear. In the meantime, man lived the timeless drama of human life, choosing between a virtuous life leading to eternal life, or a depraved life leading to damnation. Life's meaning was the individual's relationship to transcendental reality. This second "mixed" conception of history remained important in Medieval thought.[5] During the Renaissance the cyclical nature of history was re-emphasized. Bodin's *Method for the Easy Comprehension of History* is a good example of this conception of history.

The third conception of history is that of being a providential design. A discussion of this kind of historical meaning of history's course can only arise in a society which sees its past as a coherent succession of events in linear time[6] — that is, as a history in the proper sense of the word. In the Western world, Jewish and Christian thinkers were the first to see some events of the past as parts of a linear history.[7] While still conceiving the past was an enormous field of cyclical ups and downs, they believed, however, that a few sacred events, directly inspired by God, marked the outline of mankind's history of salvation.

The fourth conception of history is that of its being an expression of allegorical or mythical meaning – a symbol. According to the early Christian and the Medieval tradition, the historical events described in the Bible could be interpreted in three ways, or, to put it differently, these events had three meanings: first, they had a "historical" or literal meaning: they simply described what had happened at that time; second, they had an allegorical meaning they referred to the Christian doctrines. Third, they had a mystical meaning, pointing to the eschatological future when the promises of the revelation will have been fulfilled.[8] Biblical history thus was a "book" that could be "read" as the Bible itself; like the Bible, biblical history revealed history's author and his intentions to mankind. This way of seeing symbolic meanings in historical events described in the Bible was carried over to contemporary history. For instance, Medieval political figures were often identified by their opponents as the Anti-Christ prophesied in the Book of Revelation; the actions of these monstrous persons signified God's intention to end the world. Bad harvests signified the wrath of God. According to this perspective, historical events are symbols: they express God's nature and His intentions for mankind.

As a result of the Reformation, however, the "literal" meaning of the events described in the Bible and of contemporary history increasingly began to predominate. The eighteenth-century scientific approach to history, which focuses on the causal connections between events, completely discarded the spiritual meanings. Thus biblical history, and the contemporary historical process as well, lost their symbolic dimension. They no longer expressed God's nature and intentions. The became plain "literal" history.[9]

Something analogous happened to nature. During the Middle Ages, nature, too, had been considered a "book" – a revelation comparable to the Bible itself.[10] Under the influence of modern science, however, the universe was increasingly seen as a mechanically functioning object produced by mindless nature. Nature, too, was losing its spiritual symbolic dimension.

From classical antiquity until the eighteenth century, the three conceptions of history discussed so far – cyclical, providential and symbolic – coexisted. During the eighteenth century, they lost importance, becoming supplanted by linear secular conceptions. The most important of these is that of history being a developmental structure.

During the Enlightenment, many people had become sceptical about Christian conceptions of universal history. Voltaire, in his 1756 *Essay on the Manners and Mind of Nations, and on the Principal Facts of History from Charlemagne to Louis XIII*, ridiculed Bossuet's theology of history. He pointed out that a universal history which excluded the civilizations of China and India was a farce.[11] But Voltaire did not yet offer a theory by which to link the succession of historical periods into one chronological system; each generation or period stood on its own, being given a new opportunity, as it were, to attain a state of rationality. But his contemporary, Turgot, ordered the events of history into a linear diachronic system of continuous chronology.[12] In this sketch of universal history, the providential Christian interpretation of the past as history is transformed from sacred into secular history. Turgot thereby saw secular history as civilization's steady progress.

Thus, the past became conceptualized as a sequence of events having occurred in linear time instead of as an amalgam of events having occurred in the timeless field of the world — as an accumulative and developmental process of civilizational growth instead of as a supernaturally guided succession of sacred events. The organizational principle connecting history's events no longer came from without — from God — it came from within — from the created world's own nature. Till Darwin's *Origin of Species*, the natural world was still seen as static. But the human world had become, in the eighteenth century, a historically developing totality.

The Enlightenment philosophers rebelled against the Christian supernatural conception of providential and symbolic history — they contended that history had no transcendental dimension — that it was a purely natural and rational process. The realization, during the Enlightenment, that human history and its discrete entities — such as institutions or civilizations — follow their own "natural" courses, intensified the tendency toward "literal" history already noticeable in the Reformation interpretations of biblical and contemporary history. History's entities and events had no symbolic meanings; they were not creations of God, but of nature. As mindless nature did not express anything, history's historically grown entities did not require interpretation. They had to be approached just as all other things of nature; they were objects for scientific investigation.

This nonexpressive, nonsymbolic history still had, however, a "meaning" — the "literal" meaning of being *this* or *that* structure. From the eighteenth century onward, history's meaning is thus identical with its "literal," or observable, diachronic structure, most commonly identified as civilization's progress.

But during the next century it turned out that it was extremely difficult to determine what exactly was history's structure – and thus its meaning. The determination of history's structure became the topic of both overt speculations of philosophers interested in history – such as Kant, Hegel, Comte and Marx – and of covert speculations of historians – such as, for instance, Michelet, Burchardt, or de Toqueville. The historians refused to philosophize about history. They advocated empirical research. But by the way they told history's story, they nevertheless smuggled into their empirically researched account a speculative philosphy of history.[13]

History's sixth conceptualization is that of being discontinuous – that is, of being no history at all. This conception is the idealist position. The idealist historians of the Historical School claimed that although nonmiraculous or natural, human history is nevertheless not part of the mechanically functioning world of blind nature. Opposing their positivist colleagues, they maintained that human behavior is not determined by laws comparable to the laws of nature, and that consequently, a human behavioral product like history is more or less unpredictable. As a result of their statement that human behavior does not conform to general rules, the links connecting human history's events were weakened. The history of idealist historians became less rational, its structure less intelligible than that of the positivist historians believing in historical laws. Now that history's meaning had become "literal," that is identical with its structure, history for the idealist historians lost its meaning along with its structure. The refusal of professional historians of the Historical School to identify any direction in the historical process, and the disillusion of many late nineteenth-century and early twentieth-century middle-class intellectuals with regard to the progressiveness of Western civilization reinforced this trend toward the belief that history is formless and meaningless.

In Max Weber's writings this sixth major conception of history – the conception of a discontinuous history that is therefore meaningless – is articulated with particular clarity.[14]

We can now summarize the ways in which history's meaning had been determined so far. The meaning of history depended, in the first instance, on the historian's overall conceptualization of the past as either a field of experiences, or as a coherent series of events. If the past was conceptualized as a coherent series of events, the meaning of this history depended, in the second instance, on whether past events were seen as mind-created products, or as the products of blind natural forces. In the first case, the past had a spiritual or symbolic meaning. In the second case, the past had a literal or structural meaning. The past could also be conceptualized as an incoherent series of events; in that case, it has neither a symbolic, nor a literal meaning. These traditional ways of solving the problem of history's meaning are interpretations which — like the trodden paths through a rough terrain — interpret the area and prescribe for many succeeding generations how they will reach similar goals in the area.

Dilthey's originality in approaching the topic of history's meaning lies in his rediscovery of the symbolic interpretation of history — a path that had not been used since the beginning of the modern period and was completely overgrown to the point of becoming invisible. For the traditional Christian interpretations of history as having a providential or symbolic meaning did not seem to square with the experience of the perceptible world as the only and ultimate reality. The modern conception that history means what it is and the correlative conception that history means nothing because it has no structure are expressions of the modern age's non-Christian orientation. But during the nineteenth century, very few people, however alienated from the Christian faith, were ready to contemplate the possibility of history's meaninglessness, and of having to live in an absurd world,[15] to use Sartre's expression. Most people continued to believe in history as the force that could overcome the world's evils. Their non-Christianity had not yet become nihilism. Thinkers such as Dilthey, even though rejecting the theological and philosophical doctrines of the past, continued therefore in the nineteenth century to speculate about history's structure and meaning.

When Dilthey started his career as a scholar, he was confronted by two conflicting approaches to history's meaning: on the one hand the unified systems of a structured or meaningful progressive history exemplified by the German Hegelian and the French philosophical approaches; and, on the other hand, the Rankean empirical approach in which no attempt is made to order the events and the periods of history into any unified meaningful system.[16] Although Ranke was interested in universal history, he declined to express any opinion concerning its meaning; he felt that the totality of history' structure — and thus its meaning — could be known only by God. Many historians less committed to the Christian faith similarly declined to express opinions concerning history as a whole; they refused speculations about history, and advocated strictly empirical research. Dilthey saw his task as the search for some synthesis between the philosophical and the empirical approaches —

a synthesis in which abstract metaphysical speculations about history are avoided, but in which a sense of history's meaningfulness is nevertheless preserved.

Dilthey's first move in the interpretation of history's meaning was to accept the view that history's events form a unified temporal structure, and to simultaneously reject the view that this structure has the form of a progressive historical development.

In the *Introduction to the Human Sciences*, Dilthey investigated the nature of the structures found in social and cultural life — of, as he called them, "cultural systems," such as educational, economic, political and religious systems, art, philosophy, science, nations and epochs. Raising the question of how the existence of such cultural structures could be explained, Dilthey stated that sociology, in his time connected with the name of Auguste Comte, claims that it can explain the "interconnections" or relationships structuring the present world of men, while the philosophy of history, at the time mostly associated with the name of Hegel, claims that it can explain those of history (GS, vol. I, 90).

As far as the past is concerned philosophers of history claimed to have found overall historical structures. These structures make the temporal totality of history intelligible, either by means of a plan of history, an idea regulating history, or a formula explaining the law of historical development. In this way a meaning is ascribed to history. The common characteristic of these philosophies of history is that they are constructed on the basis of a priori clues — like God, Reason, and Progress — singled out by philosophers on the basis of abstract thinking as the most fundamental datum of reality.

Dilthey termed explanations of history by means of such a priori logical statements, mere "superstitions" (GS, vol. I, 91). He wrote scornfully that the speculative philosophers of history tried to "force history to betray her ultimate secret" and added that neither in history, nor in nature for that matter, is there "such a last and simple word . . . expressing its true meaning" (GS, vol. I, 92). Dilthey stressed the extreme complexity of the historical world. The structure of history, he wrote, is too "immensely complicated" to be caught in any single formula. Such a formula might not be wrong, but it would always by "a poor and insufficient expression of the powerful reality" (GS, vol. I, 96). According to Dilthey, abstract thought can never grasp the concrete historical process:

The philosopher who investigates the historical world has to get directly in touch with the raw material of history, and has to master all its methods. He has to subject himself to the same law of hard work on the raw material as the historian (GS, vol. I, 92).

Although Dilthey rejected the means by which the philosophers of history attempted to explain the past he was fully in agreement with their *goal* — which was to understand "the structure of the whole [*Gesamtzusammenhang*] of which the historical-social reality consists" (GS, vol. I, 92). Dilthey thus accepted the view that history is from beginning to end a temporal unity with an imminent structure, nature, or "meaning." Only detailed historical research can tell what history's structure had been:

If there is a kernel of truth hidden behind the hopes of a philosophy of history, it is this: historical research, based on a mastery as complete as possible of the various human sciences. As physics and chemistry are the tools of the study of organic life, so are anthropology, the study of law, and political sciences, the tools for the study of the course of history (GS, vol. I, 94).

Philosophers of history do not realize, however, that the meanings they attribute to history are merely reflections of their own value systems (GS, vol. I, 97). Dilthey pointed out that the meaning attributed to universal history does not make sense outside of that particular observer's social system. As an example he mentioned "the powerful idea of progress." Assertions of progress in history reflect more the personal experience of the observer with his "happy feeling of having a task in life and being able to fulfill it" than a genuine theoretical effort to find history's goal and structure. The idea of progress would have been invented — projected into the past — even if history had exhibited no progress at all (GS, vol. I, 97).

He believed that it would eventually be possible to reconstruct the complete course of history on the basis of solid historical research. It seemed only logical to assume that the knowledge to be gathered by the human sciences would result in the factual reconstruction of a universal history (GS, vol. I, 95). But he doubted whether it would be possible to reach trustworthy knowledge in the area in which the philosophy of history claims competence — namely that of the meaning, the goal and the value of history. Although he did not clarify what he understood to be history's meaning, he apparently felt that it was not identical with any "literal," observable structure.

After having published the *Introduction*, Dilthey developed his hermeneutic approach to historical evidence and to reality as a whole. He considered the phenomena of the human world to be mind-created expressions of meaning that require interpretation. As we will see now, Dilthey did not only ascribe symbolic meaning to artifacts and cultural structures, but also to history's diachronic structures — the temporal coherences we call histories. A comparison between the life history of a natural organism and an individual will clarify the reasons why Dilthey in his later phase ascribed symbolic meaning to human history.

Plants and animals do not project their life histories; they live totally in the present. Having no center of awareness — no mind — they are at the mercy of outside influences. As a result, their lives occur haphazardly. If their lives display patterns of organic growth and decline, these are natural and impersonal patterns — not personal patterns created from the inside. Dilthey felt that such natural life histories are meaningless because they do not express an inner force.

A person, by contrast, creates his own history; he is aware of the diachronic structure of his life. A person increasingly dominates his inner forces and his outer environment. His life realizes a plan that he has projected on the basis of his previous experiences. Thus, a person's life history displays a personal pattern which expresses his inner self or personality. Dilthey felt that because they are the outward expression of an inner force, human life histories are meaningful in a way natural ones are not. They have a symbolic meaning that is absent from natural history. Thus, Dilthey re-introduced into historical thought a category that had been banished from it in the modern period. But his reflections on history's meaning still express a profound ambivalence toward history's symbolic nature.

Dilthey distinguished two types of meaning in a person's life history, subjective and objective. The subjective meaning of a person's life history is its structure as it is interpreted by the subject at each of its consecutive moments. Thus subjective meaning changes constantly in the course of life, varying with the subject's moods. To the subject, his past life appears as a symbol to be interpreted. A personal history's objective meaning is its structure as it will be fully visible at life's end. Then it will no longer be a symbol but a finished object that can be known objectively.

Thus it turns out that a life history's subjective meaning is the result of the subject's self-interpretation while he finds himself in the middle of his life. A life history's objective meaning is the result of a subject's self-observation when he has reached the end of his life. We may express this differently by stating that as long as a person stands in the middle of life, his past is incomplete, its contours cannot be clearly seen, that consequently it appears to him as a symbol requiring interpretation, as a text that leaves room for diverging interpretations. Having reached the end of his life, in contrast, the outline of his life is clearly visible, his past has become

complete, its univocal form or meaning consequently can be objectively observed. His past has become an object of observation.

This would mean that a life history has only provisionally a symbolic meaning, namely, as long as it is incomplete. But obviously
this cannot mean that a completed life history simply by being
completed loses its character of being an expression of an inside
force. Even the completed life history is still a symbol in that
sense. But Dilthey could not figure out what to make of a completed
life history. On the one hand, he stressed that a person cannot
remove himself from life in order to observe it objectively from the
outside. Nor can any human observer be objective about the life
of another, since in some sense, being human he shares this life.
Thus, life was always a symbol to be interpreted instead of an
object to be observed. On the other hand, Dilthey looked upon
past life as something from which a person can indeed remove
himself over the course of years, achieving a distance from which
it could be objectively observed. But he could not conceive of
understanding another, or the symbol the other has created, as
a genuine self-disclosure on the other's part. If he could have seen
understanding of others and their products as a process of communication, in which the other figures as an autonomous source
of meanings revealing its inner world in concrete exteriorized
symbols, he might have understood that even a life history still
remains a symbol, even if it is completed and fixed in material
signs, remaining partly hidden and forever disclosing new aspects
of itself. The reason for Dilthey's inability to do so is that he
could not live with the thought that everything in the world is
not destined to be known and mastered by reason. The emotional
barrier posed by the desire to dominate makes Dilthey's analyses of
the symbolic nature of a history that will never come to an end and
will never completely be dominated by man all the more remarkable.

As Dilthey used the meaning of individual life as the model for
that of history, it is necessary for the understanding of Dilthey's
conception of history's meaning to first analyze the process by
which individual life's subjective meaning is gradually transformed
into its objective meaning.

In the act of living, the discrete moments of an individual's life
receive a preliminary meaning by being positively or negatively
experienced by the living subject. As each moment is experienced differently, according to the subject's changing moods, his
life is therefore experienced as a "chaotic" succession of negatively
and positively experienced moments:

The individual values of the experienced present stand separated from each
other, standing side by side. One can only compare them [not order them in a

hierarchy]. Life seems from the point of view of [experienced] values as an endless manifold of existential values, negative ones, positive ones, of individual values. It is a chaos full of harmonies and disharmonies — but the disharmonies are not dissolved into harmonies. No sound-complex filling a present has a musical relationship to previous or following complexes (GS, vol. VII, 236).

In hindsight, however, reflective mind comes to discern the structure of the course of its life as a whole. Mind, as Dilthey put it, with its ability to discern meaning, can overcome the passing of time, or the mere series of discrete moments, by seeing the coherent form of its past.

We may clarify this process in the following way. Human life is lived in time, which is a succession of moments, so that life happens piecemeal. But the discontinuity of human life is only apparent. Beneath the appearances is a real lived unity. A reflective mind can discern the real but hidden coherence of seemingly discrete experiences which make up the structure, or the meaning of a life. In Dilthey's words: ". . . the categorical relationships of value and goal as separate aspects of the understanding of [an individual's] life are absorbed in the totality of this understanding [of meaning]" (GS, vol. VII, 236). Thus, in reflection, the preliminary pleasant or unpleasant meanings of each momentary experience gives way to their final and enduring meaning.

Dilthey felt that at the end of a person's life, the objective and subjective meaning of his life history coincide — almost. For at this last moment, a person has subjectively — that is, in experience — the objectifying distance toward his previous life required for the objective knowledge of his life's structure. At the person's death this meaning is fixed forever. The person can no longer speak his changing mind. He is no longer an autonomous source of meanings. The symbols he created share his death. The meanings of life's moments as they were experienced by the living person are subordinated to its dead totality.

Dilthey attributed the same type of symbolic meaning to history at large, and discerned in it the same two meanings, subjective and objective.

Like individual life, history is meaningful as an outward expression of conscious life. Its pattern is created from life's inside. According to Dilthey, history thus also has a symbolic meaning. This means that for Dilthey history's meaning is not merely history's concrete structure — a structure that has to be seen — but that it also is a symbol to be interpreted, a text to be read. Thus, history's subjective meaning was its structure as interpreted by historians at different moments of time. Its objective meaning was its structure as observed by a historian standing at history's last moment.

In contrast to a person's life, however, the life of mankind will never reach a final moment. It will never come to an end. It would seem therefore that the objective meaning of history's events — their place in history's structure — can never be established. In theory, history might be an object that is in the process of completing itself. In practice, it remains a symbol requiring interpretation.

As in personal life the subjectively experienced moments are subordinated to the totality of the life history, so in collective historical life the subjectively experienced "moments" — history's periods, or cultures — are subordinated to the totality of history. Representing the supreme achievement of the conscious mind, history's diachronic whole is more important to Dilthey than the parts of which it is composed. Time is to him still the medium for a truly human life. In his philosophy of history, Dilthey thus remained more clearly committed to the Enlightenment conception of history than in his philosophy of world-views.

In order to clarify the relationship between subjective and objective meaning — that is, between the shifting momentary experiences of history's meaning and its lasting final meaning — in individual and historical life, Dilthey used several structural analogies from two other areas of symbolic expressions, literature and music. He referred, for instance, to the meaning of words in a sentence. A word means something in itself, but only in a vague, undetermined way. For example, all speakers of the English language know, more or less, what is meant by the word "table"; but what it means in a particular sentence or text can only be clarified when the word's larger context is taken into account. The context determines, or solidifies, one of the many possible meanings. Similarly, a discrete event in personal life — such as a wedding — is experienced right away as meaningful; but this meaning is at first an undetermined one, becoming fixed in the further course of life; of the many possible meanings of the event, eventually one meaning is actualized.

Dilthey also used analogies between discrete letters in a word

As words have a meaning [*Bedeutung*] by which they designate [*bezeichnen*] something, or [as] sentences constructed by us [have a meaning], so, on the basis of the determined-undetermined [*bestimmt-unbestimmten*] meaning of the parts of life, its structure [*Zusammenhang*] can be figured out. Meaning is the special kind of relationship which the parts of life have to life as a whole. This meaning we understand as we understand words in a sentence: on the basis of memories and future possibilities (GS, vol. VII, 233-234).

and discrete grammatical structures on the one hand, and the totality of personal life and history on the other, to clarify the objective meaning of human history's events.

> The doctrine of an objective value of life [is] metaphysics — it transcends what can be experienced. But we experience a unity of life and history in which every part has a meaning. Life and history have a meaning as letters in a word. There are in life and history syntactical moments as there are particles and conjunctions [in language], and they have a meaning (GS, vol. VII, 291).

It is illustrative of Dilthey's bewilderment concerning historical meaning that he illustrated the diachronic coherence of history by referring to the relationship of letters in a word and of words in a sentence. While a word means something in itself for those who know the language — even though its meanings vary contextually, an individual letter means nothing by itself. A word is a symbol in a way that a letter usually is not.

Dilthey used yet another analogy: the relationship between the moments of time and their coherence within diachronic human life and the sounds of a musical composition and their coherence in the composition's melody. In listening to a musical composition, one sound-complex at a time is heard, but its musical beauty lies in its melody in which the successively perceived sound-complexes are harmonized to form a whole. Echoing St. Augustine's remark about a psalm,[17] Dilthey asserted similarly with regard to a melody that in order for its meaning to be truly appreciated, it must be perceived in its totality. Human life — and thus history — is like a melody, a unified meaningful structure which is not the sum of discrete experiences but the consciously experienced "melodic" structure of its totality. In Dilthey's words: "Life is like a melody, in which [discrete] sounds are not expressions of the real realities that are intrinsic to life. Life itself is the melody" (GS, vol. VII, 234).

Life is, as it were, the composer of its own structure. Because it is a conscious force, life cannot but create forms or structures. Thus, the symbolic meaning of life's manifestations — history — originates in life's inner tendency to produce meaningful wholes.

By comparing human life with music, Dilthey indicated that the discrete moments of human life are devoid of their true meaning when experienced without a context — "in themselves," or one by one — just as the discrete notes of a musical composition are meaningless when heard separately. But human life is neither produced nor experienced that way; the discrete experiences are at the very moment of experience already part of life's larger structure —

pregnant with their true or objective meaning, the meaning that will become clear in the future. Life's melody thus emerges from its own depths. In contrast, the forms and structures of history, those have-been's that are now fixed, are silent. In order to become heard they must be consciously attended to by the historian and the reading public. The melodious forms of history have to be "heard." In order for history to say or "mean" something, the texts in which its meaning is embodied need to be read, the melodies need to be sung.

Dilthey not only indicated that history had a melodious form, he also described what that form was like. On the basis of his interpretation of the past's symbols he composed his own interpretation, his own reading or performance, writing, as it were, his own text to historical life's melody.

Dilthey saw that history's periods were not at all linked smoothly in an overall developing system. He was struck by history's discontinuities.[18] But this insight into the specific character of periods never undermined his belief in history's ultimate coherence – its melodious structure.

In order to solve the problem of how the various periods "fit" into this "total structure of the times," Dilthey suggested the Darwinian model of evolutionary biology.

The concept and knowledge of the evolution of the world and of successive stages of different forms of life was already grasped by Buffon, Kant, and Lamarck. Other writers produced epoch-making studies on higher civilization; and, beginning with Winckelmann, Lessing, and Herder, such studies applied the concept of evolution everywhere. Finally the study of primitive societies yielded the missing link between the evolutionary theory of the natural sciences and the newly won historical knowledge pertaining to, and based upon, the development of political history, religion, law, morals, language and literature in all nations. Only then could the evolutionary theory be consistently applied to the study of the entire natural and historical development of man. . . . (GS, vol. VIII, 77).

The biological theory of evolution reconciles unitary history with the intrinsic validity of each of its periods or structures; for each period is a necessary precondition for the next. It also illustrates the relative value of historical forms. "The theory of evolution . . . is necessarily linked with the recognition of the relativity of every historical form of life" (GS, vol. VIII, 77). Concerned in particular with the confusing variety of philosophical systems, Dilthey wrote that the theory of evolution explains that no such system can claim absolute validity because each is equally a creation of life. The variety of philosophies, and of human life in general are "connected with ongoing life; it is one of its [life's] most important and instructive creations" (GS, vol. VIII, 78).

Although Dilthey — not believing in a teleogical orientation of history, or in historical laws — had professed, in the *Introduction*, not to know the actual direction of the historical process, he attempted to sketch the general outline of this process. He rationalized his attempt by suggesting that at this point in history, its subjective meaning — its meaning as he interpreted it — and history's objective meaning — its meaning as a hypothetical outsider would observe it at history's end — almost coincided. He adopted the Hegelian thought that at this late point in time, artistic interpretation was almost scientific — that is to Dilthey empirical — observation. Thus, Dilthey complemented the Darwinian model of history's course with a Hegelian model of historiography — a model according to which mind — that is mankind — gradually succeeds in knowing its own history. Thus, by means of his Darwinian conception of history, and his Hegelian conception of historiography, Dilthey solved the conflict between the individual values of history's periods of cultures in favor of history's totality. In so doing, he sacrificed the symbolic conception of history to the scientific one.

In looking back upon mankind's past, Dilthey identified history's structure, and thus, its meaning, as mankind's development toward autonomy. He looked upon mankind's history in the same terms as a person's development. The outcome of a person's successful life history was a strong personality structure able to enforce its will on its environment;[19] that of mankind was the strong culture of the Western world able to dominate the rest of the world. With the progression of time, he "observed" that the human mind in the West had progressively liberated itself from the fetters of dogmatic thought. "Describing" Western history, he wrote that with humanism and the Reformation modern man had become "adult" (mündig) (GS, vol. VII, 89). He interspersed his account of the subsequent intellectual history of the Western world with "not yets," "stills," and "at that points," thus indicating mankind's continuous progressive development. Decisive steps in historical progress were the American and the French revolutions, which showed the world that it was possible to bring great ideas into practice: these two events represented "an enormous progress over everything past. Humanity became conscious of its inner force. . . . It was from then on clear that the movement from higher ideas to greater [concrete] forms of life had no limits" (GS, vol. VII, 274). Finally, the "last step in the liberation of man" is brought about by the historicist insight into "the finitude of all historical phenomena, of every human or social structure, of the relativity of every kind of belief" (GS, vol. VII, 290). The identification of Western man with mankind as such is illuminating for his Enlightenment perspective on history: Western civilization represents Civilization as such.

This insight into the finitude of historical phenomena makes man sovereign over life, for it teaches him that there exists "no philosophical or religious system which can bind man. Life is liberated from knowledge based on abstract concepts; spirit becomes sovereign over all the cobwebs of dogmatic thought" (GS, vol. VII, 291). No longer restricted in his freedom by traditional philosophical systems or religious creeds, modern man can make of life what he chooses.

Modern civilization, with its mastery over nature and freedom from tradition, is grounded in the occurrence, in Western civilization, of strong personalities, or "soul-structures." Hence, mankind's progress has a psychological foundation in the historical development of the individual human mind. The increasingly powerful soul-structures of Western individuals enables Western civilization to achieve in the course of history its remarkable mastery over the earth, a development which — at least, Dilthey added, as far as the "historical" peoples are concerned (GS, vol. I, 20; see also vol. V, 212) — is accompanied by a decreasing dependency upon nature.

In this general progress of the human mind, Dilthey attributed great importance to the human sciences. The progress made in the latter is, indeed, an indication of the general historical progress. The development of the study of history is, in particular, indicative of man's progress because of all the human sciences it is the one most apt "to set man free."

Dilthey described the work of the historian in progressive terms, namely, as a cleaning and correcting of the traditional representations of the past, till the past finally can be seen as it had really been. "The darkness of experience is explained; the mistakes resulting from a narrow interpretation by the individual are corrected; the experience [of life] is itself enlarged and perfected in the understanding of others on the basis of our own experiences" (GS, vol. VII, 145). The ever-enlarging scope of historical knowledge supports the progress of the discipline "by the more intensive usage of the sources, by pushing back the boundaries of the unknown past."

Historiography progresses not only because of better methods, but also because of the progression of history, in which process ever more events are produced, thus enlarging the object to be understood. The progressive tendency of the human sciences is similar to the progress found in the natural sciences:

In the totality of the human sciences real progress is evident. The understanding of historical structures has been conquered for the historical consciousness.

history penetrates into the relationships between these structures as they constitute a nation, a period, a historical line of development. . . . How could one compare the contemporary historian's understanding of artists, poets, and writers with any previous understanding! (GS, vol. VII, 144-145).

The progress of the human sciences — disciplines with an intimate relationship to experience — is, indeed, a movement of "gradual enlightenment" (GS, vol. VII, 145). The development of the human sciences forms an "ascending spiral," resulting from "the circulating movement between experience [and] understanding, and representing the mind's world in general concepts" (GS, vol. VII, 145). Thus, Dilthey's text for history's melody was the familiar song of mankind's progress.

Dilthey realized, however, that the "melody" of human life and history can never become totally transparent to human beings. He was aware of life's irreducible irrationality. Some events, he realized, can never be integrated and made sense of. They remain dissonants — in life's melody — contingent and disruptive elements, causing suffering. In this respect, Dilthey seems on the verge of the later existentialist conception of a meaningless, or absurd, life and history. But in spite of his perplexity when confronted with life's riddle, he never gave up his faith that life is meaningful and that human history is ultimately a melody. He considered life's dissonants expressions of a mystery still too profound for man to understand.

In the next generation, Martin Heidegger and Jean-Paul Sartre responded each in his own way to Dilthey's faith in life's meaningfulness expressed in the latter's poetic conception of a melodious history. Heidegger further developed Dilthey's idea of meaningful symbolic history; Sartre elaborated on history's dissonants, interpreting them as an indication of its nonsymbolic nature, its meaninglessness, its "absurdity." A brief comparison of their philosophies and Dilthey's thought will be helpful for a better understanding of the direction of Dilthey's philosophy of history.

In Heidegger's philosophy, the concept of being takes in many ways the place of that of Dilthey's life.[20] Heidegger's being is — like Dilthey's life — an act of self-disclosure. But there exist two differences that are important in this context. Whereas Dilthey's life discloses itself to itself, Heidegger's being discloses itself to what it is not self: man. Moreover, whereas Dilthey sees the self-disclosing nature of being as a provisional element, ideally to be substituted by self-evident being, Heidegger maintained that self-disclosure is being's very nature; being is a movement that will never stop.

As far as Heidegger's conception of history is concerned, he contended that it is grotesque to conceive of man as the creator of history. The great epochs of the past reflect not ideas produced by men, but disclosures of being. The disclosures of being determine man's perceptions of reality, his experiences and, as a result, the way things are in a given period. In the introduction to his 1929 Inaugural Address, he suggested that a nonemergence (*Ausbleiben*) of being might be responsible for the disconcerting present state of affairs in the world.[21] The meaning of life as experienced at a certain period is not some opinion arrived at in a special effort by philosophers; each person, that is, man qua man experiences a disclosed meaning of life simply by being-in-the-world. Heidegger urged man not to ignore being as it discloses itself to him, but attentively listen to it, and protect it; thus, he called man at one point being's "shepherd."[22] In his thought we notice with particular clarity the dangerous aspect of such an emphatic affirmation of being's intrinsic meaning: the historicist idolatory of history.

With the notion of a "history of being" that was somehow to be followed or obeyed by man, Heidegger transformed his earlier existentialist philosophy of responsible, or "resolved" existence presented in *Being and Time*, into a philosophy of being that could be understood as an admonition not so much to interpret being, but to support uncritically whatever its manifestation, history, would bring. Thus, he encouraged an attitude that fitted only too well in the historicist tradition of German thought.[23] Heidegger's philosophy is a reaction against the Promethean view of man — that is of man who does not believe in a God and who therefore fancies that he can be the creator of his own world. Heidegger did not believe in the existence of a transcendental power, but he nevertheless refused to inflate man to divine proportions.

In Heidegger's philosophy being "happens" at the cost of man's ability to respond: being's happening deprives man from the possibility to initiate meaningful action; meaningful action originates exclusively in being. The limited but nevertheless creative freedom ascribed to man by Dilthey — seeing man as the interpreter of history — is denied by Heidegger. Man has to passively receive history as being's disclosure.

Now let us take a look at Sartre's philosophy of existence. Following the French tradition, Sartre protested against the depreciation of the human individual implied in German historiography and philosophy. The dangerous aspect of Sartre's vindication of the individual's responsibility for his own life was, however, an extreme depreciation of reality, leading to nihilism.

In his novel *Nausea* Sartre explicitly rejected the notion of the meaningful "melodious" structure of human life. Although he does not mention Dilthey by name, Sartre's analysis of human life's meaninglessness seems to aim directly at the latter. In listening to a jazz-song, the hero of the novel, the historian Roquentin, reflects upon the difference between the succession of discrete notes or sounds in time and the melody that is seemingly not part of this world. Roquentin's experience of music indicates that for him (and for Sartre) the realm of being and that of contingent human life are separated.[24] In the course of the novel Roquentin gradually realizes that he had wanted his life to have the quality of a transcendant melody. However, in a painful process of awakening, he realizes that this is impossible: man lives in time; his life is contingent.

First, Roquentin became aware that he could not retain his past as part of himself: "I can search the past in vain, I can only find there scraps of images and I am not sure what they represent, whether they are memories or justification."[25] He found himself confined to the moment of the present: "I am cast out, forsaken in the present: I vainly try to rejoin the past: I cannot escape."[26] As long as he had a past, Roquentin was able to imagine himself as the hero of the melody or story of his own life. Now he realizes that his memories are cut off from his present, that they sink away in the past never to be recalled as the lived experiences they once had been. A present experience can furthermore not be part of a melody or story, for nobody knows at the moment of experience what the future that would have to elevate the present experience to the status of being part of the story, might bring. In Roquentin's words: "Something is beginning in order to end: an adventure does not let itself be drawn out; it only makes sense when dead."[27]

The individuals — or, for that matter, mankind — can never live as heroes in their respective stories because the stories are still in the process of being written, and their endings are totally uncertain; human life and history, therefore, cannot have an inherent structure; thus, it cannot have intrinsic meaning. If a person's life is seen as having structure and meaning, it is so because this structure and meaning are given to it in hindsight. In itself, life is formless, absurd and meaningless.

In *Being and Nothingness* Sartre formulated this conception of the formlessness and meaninglessness of life in philosophical terms. His terminology is reminiscent of Hegel. Nonhuman reality, "being" (*être*), is the in-itself; it is totally absorbed in its own existence, opaque, without an interior, massive; it is totally isolated in its being, for it has no relationship to what it is not. Uncapitalized *être* indicates the deflation of Heidegger's *Sein*. Being (*être*) is pure positivity. Man, on the other hand, is pure nonbeing (*néant*), nonpositivity or "nothingness"; because of his dynamic consciousness, man is never identical with what he is at a certain moment. Conscious man is always ahead of himself — he never "is" what he "is."

Following the Cartesian tradition of a distinction between mind (*res cogitans*) and matter (*res extensa*), Sartre posited an absolute rift between the two regions of reality — consciousness, the origin of meaning, and being (*être*), the passive receiver of meanings ascribed to it by man.[28]

In Sartre's conception of history, man, in writing history, creates history's form and meaning. In his existentialist philosophy, reality outside of living man — the worlds of nature and of culture, the latter as far as it is embodied in concrete material forms such as books, paintings, buildings, landscapes — has no meaning whatsoever. These are realms of profound silence, the silence of the dead who — by having lost their ability to raise their voice and to directly address us — have lost forever, it seems, the ability to express themselves, to generate meaning.

To sum up: Heidegger continued to affirm the meaningfulness of man's life in time on the basis of man's actual experience of life's meaning — an experience that is "natural" to man, and that precedes reflection because it is grounded in being itself. As a result, Heidegger came to advocate submission to a presumed "history of Being," which is, in fact, an admonition to submit to destiny. In his philosophy and being Heidegger underevaluated man's active role in interpreting and shaping the world, and hence, man's responsibility for what he makes of it.

In Sartre's existenialism, in contrast, the relationship between conscious man and his mindless natural and cultural environment is totally ruptured. In the existentialist period of his philosophical career, Sartre formulated a philosophy of man's total alienation from reality; he insisted that the authentic person has to create his own subjective interpretation of life while realizing its intrinsic absurdity and meaningless. He maintained that man had to create the future without any sense of obligation to the past. Sartre thus underestimated in his early philosophy the value of reality.

In comparing Dilthey's thought to that of Heidegger and Sartre, we may comment that Dilthey is doubtless closer to Heidegger's historicist idolatry of history than to Sartre's existentialist despair. He differs, however, from Heidegger in that he does not consider concrete history as the *direct* expression of life or, in Heidegger's terminology, of being; he considers history as life's symbol.

Dilthey's hermeneutic philosophies of world-views and of history belong to what Paul Ricoeur has called the "exegetic" type of hermeneutics.[29] Exegetic hermeneutics considers a symbol as an entity that "wants to say." It sees a symbol — be it a work of art, a gesture, a history or reality itself — as an expression of a truth and beauty that the symbol in its material existence both reveals and hides. Ricoeur contrasts this type of hermeneutics with a more modern type, the "demystifying" hermeneutics of Nietzsche, Marx and Freud. These authors are deeply suspicious of the symbols they interpret. They consider symbols not as wanting to speak — as organs of truth, but, on the contrary, as phenomena hiding painful truths and ugly realities. Indeed, they treat symbols as symptoms. In contrast to symbols, symptoms do not "want" to reveal the reality that gives them birth. Whatever they say to the interpreter, they disclose involuntarily, against their "intentions." Only by careful study can the interpreter discover their meaning.

As an exegetic hermeneuticist, Dilthey approaches cultures and histories almost as sacred texts. With his interpretations, he attempts to articulate their truth and beauty. The philosopher of the demystifying type, by contrast, sees these same cultures and histories as distortions of reality. With his interpretations, he therefore intends to prepare the ground for a recreation of the reality underlying the symptoms. When successful, symptom formation no longer has to occur. This "recreation" of reality — by the Promethean man of the Enlightenment — is not envisioned as a restoration of its original beauty, for its original existence is seen as an ugly chaos. It is an original re-creation of the existing material.

From the demystifying point of view, the interpretations of symbols offered by the exegetic hermeneutic philosophers seem products of naive or complacent minds, closed to a critical questioning of the world as it exists. Exegetic hermeneutic philosophers are often branded as conservatives.[30] As far as Dilthey is concerned, we have had ample opportunity to point out that this view is not beside the mark. But nevertheless it is one-sided.

The promise of Dilthey's thought is, indeed, a conception of reality which — simply because it never is in itself — is in itself neither good and truthful nor bad and deceptive. Dilthey points toward a conception of reality as a symbol — as a work of art. According to this conception reality becomes what it might be in the interpretations of its readers. Then man is neither the passive contemplator of a supposedly true and beautiful reality, nor the active Promethean recreator of a supposedly deceptive and ugly reality. As the interpreter of reality, he shares responsibility for what it may become in his encounters with it.

Before this insight can be fully developed, however, it is necessary to take seriously the conception of reality as an autonomous source of meanings — an "other" confronting man. A first step into this direction was taken by Heidegger who conceived of being as an act of self-disclosure. A next step has been taken by Gadamer and Habermas. They conceptualized interpretative processes as communicative interactions between interpreter and interpreted as two partners in a dialogue. But even Gadamer and Habermas still conceive of the understanding of reality more in terms of a contemplation of a silent reality that needs to be seen than in terms of a communication with another who speaks and needs to be heard. A further step is therefore necessary: a reflection on reality's speaking "otherness" disclosing itself to us.

As far as Dilthey is concerned, however, we must state that he was still too much on guard against the "saying other" of metaphysics: the God of traditional philosophy and theology. He therefore could not envision a reality that in some respects would be comparable to a living — speaking — subject to a partner in a dialogue. But he came remarkably close.

PERSONALITY STRUCTURE AND DEVELOPMENT: THE KEY TO DILTHEY'S CONCEPTION OF HISTORY AND CULTURE

Although the central concern of this study is an examination of Dilthey's contribution to the study of history and culture, we have not yet taken the opportunity to investigate Dilthey's views about history's concrete course. Before turning to Dilthey's conception of concrete history, however, we must in this chapter review his psychology — his ideas on personality structure and personality development. For, as we have seen repeatedly, Dilthey used the experiential material of personal life for the understanding of collective historical life. Thus, an analysis of Dilthey's conception of personal history provides a key to understand his conception of human history at large. It will prepare us also to understand his explanation of human life's historicity and his views, respectively, of discrete historical developments and of overall historical development.

During the nineteenth century, psychology became a natural science. Positivism denied the existence of immaterial substances: thus, it discarded the substantive soul, and reduced man to his material body. Human behavior followed the laws of nature that everywhere in the universe regulate the movements of matter. Natural science psychology was therefore decidedly deterministic. This determinism was precisely what upset Dilthey, who defended man's moral nature.

When Dilthey started his career, the unsolved task confronting all scholars who were committed to a belief in human freedom was precisely the elaboration of a new psychology which could make human behavior intelligible without involving positivism's mechanistic natural laws, or theology's traditional soul. In the following historical survey I will describe the disappearance of the soul, the subsequent transformation of the science of the soul — psychology — into a natural science, and the reintroduction of a mentalistic conception of man. I will restrict myself to the developments within Germany.

During the eighteenth century, man's immortal soul — postulated by religion and metaphysics — had for the first time become an object of empirical, or scientific, investigation. With the publication by Christian Wolff, professor of philosophy at Halle, Germany, of *Psychologia Empirica*, a new natural science was proposed to provide empirical material for a new discipline, the *psychologia rationalis* (the title of Wolff's next book). Empirical psychology studied the manifestations of the soul in the material world. Thus, there existed from this point on two psychologies: empirical — or scientific — psychology, and nonempirical rational — or "philosophical" — psychology. Both disciplines, empirical and rational, had the same object of study: the human soul, but they approached it by different methods. This duality was rooted in the dualism of *res extensa* and *res cogitans* established by René Descartes. During the latter half of the Enlightenment, a "philosophy of human nature" founded upon observation and experiment became very popular.[1] For our purpose it is important to note that the substantive immortal soul, and the personal finite ego, or consciousness, were at this point undifferentiated.

Kant first distinguished between the substantive soul and the psychological ego: in the *Critique of Pure Reason*, he denied that the substantive soul, studied by rational psychology, could be studied empirically or scientifically. Given in experience is only the empirical or psychological ego — empirical psychology's topic of investigation. Kant contrasted the ego with transcendental consciousness, which could never become the object of an act of knowledge. A truly scientific or empirical study of the soul could therefore only focus on the "inner sense," or ego. Scientific psychology had, in other words, to restrict itself to the empirical study of human consciousness. The soul was beyond its scope.[2] From now on, philosophers speculating about the soul, and psychologists empirically studying its bodily manifestations, began to travel separate directions.

This separation between philosophy and psychology was not yet clear, however, in Romantic speculative nature-philosophy and German Idealism. Hegel, for instance, freely speculated about such entities as "Spirit," "Mind," and "Absolute Consciousness," which were basically transformations of Kant's transcendental consciousness. Also many thinkers combined nature-philosophical speculations with empirical research.[3] For a while, the philosophically minded students of the phenomena of consciousness could remain thinking that they were studying the soul; and the empirical psychologists could continue to see themselves as philosophers. Gradually, however, the substantive soul, in which many still believed, began to drop out of scientific psychological discourse.[4] Most nineteenth-century students of empirical psychology were trained as natural scientists.

Nineteenth-century psychology had also close ties to another natural science, brain anatomy. The former "soul" became physically localized, and identified as part of the body.[5]

The empirical researches of brain anatomy could be easily combined with Comte's popular philosophy of positivism. Comte considered only the objects of the physical world accessible to observation and scientific investigation. Psychology as an independent science of the soul could therefore, not exist. Comte assigned mental phenomena to the domain of sociology.[6]

Materialistic philosophers contributed their share to the disappearance of the soul. Philosophy, in the form of metaphysics, had traditionally been more congenial to spiritual concerns, such as Dilthey's, than natural science. But nineteenth-century philosophers such as Feuerbach, Marx and Nietzsche pinned themselves against traditional philosophical convictions, declaring that only the body has reality. As Nietzsche wrote, "soul is only a word for something about the body."[7]

The implied support of these philosophers for scientific psychology indicates one of the moving forces behind this psychology: the drive for man's emancipation from religious beliefs in favor of naturalism and humanism.

Thus, in the nineteenth century, philosophical psychology was no longer considered scientific, and scientific psychology had, by and large, become a natural science. For physicists, physiologists and anatomists, it was a "psychology without a soul." Even the existence of the mind, of consciousness, or of the psyche, was no longer recognized. In this scientific psychology, one of the points of departure for understanding mental life was the assumption that mental events are composed of elementary occurrences — discrete perceptions, associations and reactions: in order to understand these events, the scientist had to reduce them to their elementary parts. Scientific psychology's second point of departure was the doctrine of psychophysical parallelism, stating that mental phenomena could only be studied by means of their material-physical correlatives; the movements of matter, bodies and organisms. These material movements did not stem from mysterious invisible "forces," they were lawful movements of matter, hence, the movements of the mind could be scientifically studied.

At the end of the century, there were several new departures in the development of psychology: Wundt's version of scientific psychology, Bretano's psychology of consciousness, and Freud's psychoanalysis. Dilthey's descriptive psychology represents one of the first of such new departures now to be reviewed.

In 1875, a new dimension was given to scientific psychology by Wilhelm Wundt, who founded in Leipzig the world's first *Institute for Experimental Psychology*. Although Wundt accepted the idea that mental phenomena are accessible only through physical occurrences, he nevertheless distinguished between physical and mental phenomena. When a stimulus touches a nerve, it is a physical event. When the stimulus and the excitations of a nerve are experienced by a subject, it is mental phenomenon. Wundt thus separated psychology from physiology. In Wundt's physiological psychology the "soul" had become personalised and internalized. What used to be called the soul is "the total content of our inner experiences, our thinking, feeling and willing, as it is unified in consciousness."[8] Not only the material manifestations of the soul, but also its mental manifestation — a person's personality — is therefore studied experimentally and explained scientifically.

Between the traditionalist philosophers and theologians who continued to believe in the existence of a substantive soul on the one hand, and the scientific psychologists, who considered psychology a natural science on the other, emerged another school of scientific psychology: the psychology of consciousness. Its representatives emphasized the special character of the mental as opposed to the physical. They focused on the inner aspects of man, on man's conscious life, his intentional activities and his self-awareness, and they stressed the inadequacy of the exact methods and quantitative concepts of physical science used in empirical psychology. In doing so, they retained the concept of the mental as a fundamental category of human life.

As a result of the activities of this school, the intellectual space between the two extremes, the natural science view of man and its metaphysical counterpart, became populated by a confusing variety of divergent concepts: mind, consciousness, psyche, ego, person, self, intentionality — concepts which all aimed at capturing the active, free and spontaneous nature of the human mind.[9]

The first representative of the psychology of consciousness was Franz Brentano. In his 1874 *Psychologie vom empirischen Stand-Punkt*, he distinguished between physical and mental phenomena. Mental phenomena are not things that can be observed in the same way as the things of the external world, they are "soul-acts" (*seelische Akten*), and have to be studied by introspection. The soul-acts together form the "soul," the existence of which Brentano — a faithful, although unconventional Roman Catholic — still accepted. For him, psychology was still — or once again — a science of the soul. A later offshoot of this psychology of consciousness is the psychology of the person, represented, for instance, by Max Scheler. Scheler distinguished between ego, or consciousness, and the person: the ego is the support or seat of mental or psychic activity, the person is that of intentional acts.

In this context, the emergence of psychoanalysis takes on meaning. During the 1890s, this branch of psychology was developed by Sigmund Freud. Its central concept is the unconscious mind, which profoundly influences thought and behavior.

This brief historical survey has shown that at the end of the nineteenth century psychology had become a natural science, but that the natural science conception of psychology was being challenged from several quarters.

It is worth emphasizing that Dilthey was led to his interest in psychology by his interest in what he called "the life of the mind" – in what he saw as the mind's activity in religion, philosophy, the arts, and history in general. "Psychology" — which Dilthey understood to mean the general science of the human mind and its operations — thus, became a fundamental discipline for the other human sciences.

Instead of studying human behavior in a laboratory situation or in real life, Dilthey drew his material from his investigations of the mind's products — the great works of philosophy, theology, literature and the arts produced in the past, and the study of history in general. He also used the insights he had gained from his physiological studies performed while teaching at the University of Basel. But after his stay at the University of Basel, he never worked in a laboratory again; nor did he study living persons in any systematic fashion. Thus, Dilthey cannot be designated as a psychologist in our sense of the term; from the point of view of method, he remained a philosopher — a philosopher of finite mind – reflecting on the — finite — mind's concrete workings.

Because Dilthey considered the mind's cultural life as the hallmark of human existence, the study of mind was for him almost identical with the study of man as such. Dilthey, in the *Introduction to the Human Sciences*, accordingly called both "anthropology and psychology the foundation of all knowledge of historical life and all rules concerning the governance and continuation of society" (GS, vol. I, 32).[10] The psychology envisioned by Dilthey was a general study of the human embodied or finite mind. It acknowledged the human mind's active and creative nature, manifested in the sovereignty of man's will, the sense of responsibility for his actions, the capacity to subject everything to the power of his thought (GS, vol. I, 6); it thereby acknowledged man's spiritual, conscious, inner, or mental life (*geistiges Leben*).[11]

In the *Introduction to the Human Sciences*, Dilthey gave only tentative indications of his conception of psychology; eleven years later, in his 1894 article, "Ideas for a Descriptive and Analytic Psychology," he presented a full-fledged program for a contemporary psychology, while further interesting remarks on his conception of psychology are scattered in other essays, such as "Poetic Imagination and Madness" (1886), "Experiencing and Thinking" (1892), and "Contributions to the Solution of the Question Concerning the Origin of Our Belief in the Reality of the External World" (1890).

Convinced of the importance of the creative mind, Dilthey nevertheless categorically rejected the metaphysical notion of a substantive soul. He pointed out in the *Introduction to the Human Sciences* that the philosophers of the metaphysical period had attempted in vain to devise formulas for the interconnection between facts pertaining to mental life — to the soul as they saw it — and those concerning nature. The connection between a pure spirit and a material body postulated by the metaphysicians could not be explained. Dilthey accepted the modern science of nature, at least those discoveries that concerned external nature, but he realized that it could not be combined with the traditional philosophy of spiritual substances.

Instead of a contrast between body and soul, Dilthey noted a contrast between external and inner worlds. In his conception of man, the traditional soul is replaced by an "inner life," the "life of the mind," or "the life of consciousness" (*das Leben des Geistes*). Man's "spiritual" life (*geistiges Leben*) is his inner life, or the movements of consciousness. Because the relationship between the external and the inner world could be empirically studied, the old problem of the relationship between soul and body was reduced to manageable proportions. In this way, Dilthey could uphold the "spiritual" or moral nature of man to which he was committed, without however, suggesting the existence of any nonempirical substances, such as a soul.

The psychology eventually to be developed by Dilthey — in his 1894 essay treating descriptive psychology — was aimed at the understanding of the interaction between man's inner life — the origin of man's outwardly visible behavior — and the external world. Stated differently, he was concerned with the relationship between the mind's creativity and the constraints imposed upon the mind by the external world and his own internal world — between freedom and necessity.

Dilthey distinguished two perspectives in the study of man: those of inner and outer experiences. Seen exclusively from the point of view of man's inner experiences, the external world is considered as given in consciousness, and its laws are seen as determined by consciousness. Seen from the point of view of outer experience, the external world appears to man as existing independently "out there," impinging upon, and determining, his inner world. Dilthey saw these generally as the perspectives, respectively, of the human scientist and the natural scientist.

The human scientist considers man a source of action, the center of a will intent on achieving goals (GS, vol. I, 17). Using the perspective of inner experience, he studies the "creative power of the spirit" (GS, vol. I, 18) from the perspective of mind's freedom. As a living human being himself, the human scientist personally experiences this power. The human scientist's point of departure is therefor experience — especially his own self-experience.

The natural scientist, on the other hand, focuses on the assumed elementary occurrences which compose mental events. He approaches man from the outside, seeing him primarily as a passive entity without will subjected to influences from the external world. In this perspective, there is no place for the mind's freedom.

Dilthey called this external, natural-science psychology "explanatory" psychology (erklärende Psychologie) because of its aim of giving causal explanations for all human behavior. He characterized his own version of psychology, with its focus on man's inner life, as a "descriptive science."

Although he did not forthrightly reject explanatory psychology in his Introduction, he clearly did not think highly of it. The external approach of the natural scientist conflicts with the self-experience of man as an active and willing entity. Not derived from experience, explanatory psychology attempts "to deduce the total coherence of mental life from certain assumptions" (GS, vol. I, 32), for instance, the assumption that a person's mental life is composed of discrete basic elements. Because of scientific psychology's hypothetical assumption, its results too have a merely "hypothetical" character. By contrast, the human sciences in general, and Dilthey's psychology in particular, have as their starting point the unity of mental life as given in inner experience (GS, vol. I, 29). Their results are, therefore, more truthful and also more useful.

An emphasis on the mind's creativity and freedom did not block Dilthey's vision from recognizing the dependency of inner life on "outer" experience. This awareness of the limitations, or the finiteness, of the mind's freedom, its dependency on the outer world of nature and culture is, indeed, the central element of Dilthey's psychology. We must therefore examine in more details how Dilthey saw the dependency of the inner on the outer world.

The most elementary dependency of mind is that on the body and the further external world of nature. The human organism develops its individuality on the basis of the functions of the body, and its relationships to surrounding nature; the "mood of life (*Lebensgefühl*) for a person is, at least partly, founded on these organic functions; and the organism's impressions are, moreover, conditioned by its bodily senses, as determined by the external world. The organism's acts of will are, furthermore, often conditioned by the nerves. These insights into the mind's dependency on nature had crystallized during Dilthey's research at the University of Basel.

Dilthey concluded from this that mental life as such does not exist: man is not a "soul" accidentally connected with a body, but a living unity of "spirit" and "matter." A person's "mental (*geistig*) life is only a part of the psycho-physical living unity (*Lebenseinheit*) separated from it only by means of abstraction" (GS, vol. I, 15).

The second dependency of mind is upon the social world. A person lives not by himself; he is always part of a social structure. The object of psychology is the individual, but this individual is an abstraction taken out of the living coherence of the historical-social world in which he functions. Man as a totality is "an entity receiving impressions from the outside world and, conversely, affecting changes in it" (GS, vol. I, 30).

Psychology as a descriptive science is therefore the analysis of the general properties of social man: its goal is "to work out by means of abstraction the general properties which psychical individuals develop in this condition" (GS, vol. I, 31). It is thus not a psychology of the individual ego or of consciousness, but of the individual as part of, and as interacting with, his natural and cultural environment. In Dilthey's words:

The individual as an entity in itself, preceding history and society, is a fiction of genetic explanation; the individual studied by a healthy analytical science is the individual as being a part of society. Psychology's most difficult problem is [to acquire] analytical knowledge of the universal properties of this human being (GS, vol. I, 31-32).

Psychology as a descriptive science, then, focuses on the way individuals experience themselves, as parts of a natural and social context. Specifically, it focuses on their inner, subjective states as parts of nature and as members of society.

This latter social dimension of human existence caused Dilthey to envision what he called a psychology of "a second order" (GS, vol. I, 66): a study of the mental facts, or inner states, that accompany externally visible social relationships. He recommended, for instance, the study of the psychic bond connecting individuals, and the collectivities to which they belong. Some topics of study in this area he mentioned were the psychic relationships uniting rulers and ruled; the nature and limits of political authority, including the extent of freedom an individual has for accepting or rejecting the authority of his rulers; and the factors which make it possible for people to live together in social organizations.

When we now turn from the *Introduction to the Human Sciences* to Dilthey's 1894 essay, we notice his tone becoming more aggressive. Dilthey declared without ado that the current psychology, modeled as it was after the natural sciences, totally failed to understand the phenomena of mental life, that is, of life as it is actually experienced by human beings. The basic assumption of the natural sciences — that nature is causally organized — does not apply to man, and consequently a natural science approach to man simply does not work. Not only does it not work, but from the dominant position of scientific psychology, "extremely negative consequences follow for the development of the human sciences" (GS, vol. V, 145). Indeed, he now claimed that natural-science psychology has "enormously contributed to the heightening of the sceptical attitude [of modern man] and to a superficial, infertile empiricism — and also to a divorce of life from knowledge" (GS, vol. V, 145). Because it fails to appreciate human creativity, its influence on the study of history and on criminal law was particularly disturbing (GS, vol. V, 191-192). Scientific psychology could, indeed, never do justice to the richness of man's inner life, and to the phenomenon of the will "which so powerfully manifests itself in our life" (GS, vol. V, 142-143).

With the 1894 essay, "psychology as a descriptive science" became a detailed project for "descriptive psychology." Its task was to study two aspects of human mental life: a formal, and a substantive aspect — form and content.

As far as its formal aspect is concerned, Dilthey defined descriptive psychology's task as "the description of the parts and coherences that appear uniformly in every developed human mental life, as they are connected in one coherent system — one not thought but experienced" (GS, vol. V, 152). The object of descriptive psychology are the regularities and uniformities of developed mental life as they appear in a "typical" adult person (GS, vol. V, 152). This conception of the adult person will emerge later in this chapter.

As far as descriptive psychology's content is concerned, it had to discover what human life is all about. To that end, it had to study the articulations of life's nature and meaning, as expressed by great authors, such as Seneca, Marcus Aurelius, St. Augustine, Machiavelli, Montaigne and Pascal. The study had to systematize and make available these great men's intuitive understanding of human life (GS, vol. V, 153).

Other methods in descriptive psychology advocated by Dilthey are comparative psychology, developmental history, and experimental psychology (GS, vol. V, 157). Only these last three methods would qualify as psychological as we conceive of the term today.

Dilthey expected that as a result of the utilization of these various methods psychology would leave the laboratory and become an important tool for practising historians, economists, political scientists and theologians. He expected also that it would prove useful to persons engaged in everyday practical life (GS, vol. V, 157-158; see also vol. I, 32).

I will now examine some of Dilthey's suggestions concerning mental life of particular relevance to this study. First, I will analyze his suggestions concerning the mind's creativity in shaping order out of the chaos of incoming stimuli.

Dilthey was struck by the basic stability of man's mind both in perceiving inner and external events and in remembering them. Man's inner life forms a coherent unity, but this coherence is never given to conscious perception in its totality: "the light of awareness (*Gewahrwerden*) falls now on this point then on that one: mental power (*psychische Kraft*) can . . . evaluate only a limited number of links of the inner coherence to the level of consciousness" (GS, vol. V, 171). Conscious inner perception is therefore always partial and fragmentary. Its contents are changing constantly.

Although the contents of conscious perception are thus highly variable, the "same connections" that link these momentary contents of conscious perception nevertheless "return continually"; and consequently, these perceptions together form a unified pattern. The overall structure of an individual's way of perceiving inner events is, as a result, remarkably stable:

If one link calls forth a second link, or if a class of links calls forth another one; if, in some cases, this second link calls forth regularly a third or a second class of links a third link −; [and] if this [process] were continued in a fourth or fifth link, then a consciousness of the coherence of all these links − a consciousness of the coherence of whole classes of links − must emerge with general certainty (GS, vol. V, 171).

It is interesting to note at this point that Dilthey realized the existence of many contents of which the subject is not conscious. Yet he falls short of acknowledging the importance of the "unconscious" as the moving force of conscious life, a discovery left to Freud.

Dilthey observed the same stability in the mind's image of the external world. In the perception of external events, too, conscious perception constantly shifts from one particular to another, but because of the mind's habitual links between these particulars, a unified picture of the total situation emerges nevertheless.

Memory knowledge is characterized by the same stability; the mind retains because of these habitual links from its many past experiences also a more or less unified image of the past. In view of the chaotic number of stimuli reaching the mind at each succeeding moment, Dilthey felt that the mind's relatively stable image of reality was amazing. He explained it by the mind's capacity to "abstract" phenomena from their living context. In inner awareness, for example, a person concentrates his attention on one phenomenon out of the "chaos of events." He isolates this phenomenon out of the "fast stream of inner events," and focuses on it. He lifts it, or abstracts it in this way from its context: "only by means of abstraction do we lift a function, a link, out of the concrete coherence" (GS, vol. V, 171). This abstracting activity of the mind is the precondition of an individual's knowledge of the inner and the external world, and of his knowledge of the past as well. Knowledge is the personalized image of an aspect of reality, or of reality as a whole, which a subject constructs in habitually processsing his experiences in certain ways.

Fundamental to Dilthey's psychology is his conviction that the individual subject connects his inner and outer experiences and its memories into relatively stable images in a creative, personal way — that, in making these connections, the subject does not follow impersonal universal timeless rules, as Kant had believed. All knowledge is, to use Michael Polanyi's term, personal knowledge.[12] The images of the inner and the external world, and of the past are never completely fixed images, however. On the contrary, "the fate of an image . . . is dependent upon feelings and the way one's attention is divided"; images change "as parts drop out, or are removed"; new elements enter (GS, vol. VI, 99). The mind constantly rearranges images according to its changing moods: "there are no isolated elements [in the mind]. These are everywhere inseparable from their functions" (GS, vol. V, 196).

Dilthey insisted that to be aware of oneself, to perceive and to remember are, therefore, far from the passive acts of registering facts that the positivists assumed. Knowing processes are extremely complex operations in which various mental activities, such as the distinguishing of differences, or the seeing of similarities, as well as the acts of connecting, separating, abstracting, or unifying entities, and discerning uniformities of several are interrelated (GS, vol. V, 171-172). Far from being passive, the mind is therefore active — creating intelligible order out of chaos.

A related testimony to this active nature of the mind is its ability to spontaneously differentiate between what is significant and insignificant to it — a process which occurs in the very act of experiencing. Each experienced event has a certain value for the experiencing subject — it is experienced as positive or negative, important or unimportant. In experience, the mind automatically separates significant events from those it experiences as insignificant. These evaluations concerning the relative importance of events are due to the stable interconnections the mind sees among mental events.

The mind's capacity to directly realize what is significant gives the human scientist an important advantage over the natural scientist. As the world of nature is devoid of mind and does not display any conscious coherence, the natural scientist can have no immediate knowledge of what is of intrinisic importance in his objects of study. He has to establish himself — from the outside — the criteria by which to separate the important from the unimportant. The human scientist studying the world of man, by contrast, simply can become aware (in *Verstehen,* or empathy) which events the subjects themselves (the subjects whose products he studies) have experienced as significant. Thus, as Dilthey claimed repeatedly, the human scientist's insights are more certain than those of the natural scientist, who cannot go beyond framing hypotheses.[13]

From the above examination of Dilthey's conception of mind, we may infer that he saw the mind as a function of the total psychophysical human organism. Rejecting the metaphysical conception of a disembodied soul — presumably able to free itself from its material basis in order to contemplate eternal truths — Dilthey affirmed that "mind" and "body" — inner and outer life — form a living unity. In Dilthey's psychological perspective, "mind" is the human organism's center of awareness; this center processes the stimuli reaching the organism from inside and outside; it stores memory of previous experiences it has had with stimuli. Because the human organism's conscious center — man's "mind" — retains in memory its past experiences, it can evaluate, that is, interpret, incoming stimuli and respond to them in personal, creative ways.

Having the capacity to respond in a personal fashion to reality, the human organism can shape its own environment, building a world of its own; in doing so, however, the organism is conditioned not only by its natural, but also by its cultural environment.

An individual is always part of a social group. At each moment, one's mind takes account of personal past experiences; but however individualized these are, they are always infused with the experiences of his social group. Any individual begins to experience reality according to the directives received from those who raise him. Consequently, the individual mind's creations always bear the personal and cultural stamp of their "creator" — whether this creation be a philosophical system, a religious creed, a work of art, or an action. Such a creation does not mirror an eternal truth; on the contrary, it is anchored in its creator's individual and cultural experiences with reality; it mirrors the historical situation from which it emerged, it is part of the stream of history; it is through and through "historical."

The mind's personal input in creatively organizing incoming stimuli into patterns to form images of reality — or knowledge — and in doing so its dependency on previous experiences, together form the foundation for the historicity of human life.

Human life's historicity is thus grounded in the way a human organism operates — in man's finite mind's special capacity to creatively organize experience on the basis of past experience — individual and collective — and in anticipation of future experience. The variety of man's collective creations, of both past and present cultures, is testimony of the human mind's finite creativity. Indeed, only the human organism has this capacity to creatively respond to stimuli, for only it has a center of awareness, a "mind" strong enough to organize experience — the welter of incoming stimuli — into orderly patterns. Organic forms with a lesser degree of awareness can only passively react to incoming stimuli.

In the *Introduction*, Dilthey claimed that "psychology" — which was actually a philosophy of finite mind — should be the fundamental discipline for the human sciences. In the essay on descriptive psychology, he made the same claim even more forcefully, maintaining that "psychology" should not only be the foundation for the specifically humanistic disciplines, but also for the discipline studying the acquisition of knowledge: epistemology.

Dilthey's claim, in the essay just mentioned, of psychology's fundamental nature for epistemology represents an important step in his growing understanding of human existence's historicity — and, by the same token, a step away from his former positivist hopes — expressed in the *Introduction* — for an objective science of human life. Positivist thinkers considered epistemology — investigating the supposedly timeless rules of reason and of the conditions under which knowledge is possible — to be immune to subjective individual or historical factors. In denying the universal validity — the objectivity — of epistemology, Dilthey touched, indeed, a central nerve of positivist thought.

Because of his conception of the mind's functioning, Dilthey could not accept the Kantian notion of a "pure reason." Finite reason depends on experience. In his 1892 essay "Experiencing and Thinking: A Study of the Epistemological Logic of the Nineteenth Century," he rejected Kant's dualism of what is given to the thinking mind (experience) and the activity of thinking itself (GS, vol. V, 84). Reason and experience cannot be separated in this way: "the total structure is contained in life and experience, and manifests itself in forms, principles, and categories of thought . . ." (GS, vol. V, 83). A truly transcendent, or "pure," epistemology is consequently impossible. Knowledge is part of a person's individualized experience of life. Every bit of knowledge, every philosophy — epistemology included — is part of personal experience, and as such is grounded in time and history.

The intimate connection between experience and thought, or theory, causes for instance the introduction of historically determined linguistic and conceptual patterns into seemingly pure, abstract thought. Dilthey cited Kant's own philosophy as an ironic example of the dependency of reason on experience.

Dilthey's conclusion was therefore that "an epistemology without prejudices," unaffected by actual experiences and inherited beliefs is illusory (GS, vol. V, 151). Dilthey called epistemology "psychology in motion" (GS, vol. V, 150). Man's knowledge of reality is never an "objective" image of reality — that is, one in which it is pictured as it is in itself. Being man's organization of the data of experience, the image of reality — knowledge — is his personal creation; it is his personal interpretation of it.

In view of his statement that epistemology is "psychology in motion," it is not surprising that Dilthey has been accused of "psychologism" — the explanation of human behavior on the basis of personal motives. In grounding thought in experience, however, and in showing how experience is processed, Dilthey did not trace thought back to the idosyncrasies of individual thinkers. He saw mental products — thought systems included — as expressions of a historical "mood," as creations of history rather than of individuals. The related charge of historicism makes therefore somewhat more sense than that of psychologism. But both charges are, however, largely unfounded. For with his descriptive psychology Dilthey wanted precisely to overcome psychologism, just as with his philosophy of world-views — based upon the objective life-relationships between human organism and external world — he wanted to overcome historicism's shadow, moral scepticism.

The reason why psychologism and historicism could exert a paralyzing influence is not that they drew the attention to the variety of philosophical systems, value systems and cultures confronting man, but that positivist thinkers conceived of reality as a thing-in-itself, and combined with this conception the ideal of objective — impersonal and universally valid — knowledge. This ideal of objective knowledge automatically degrades individualized views of reality — views based on, and tied to, private and collective individualized experiences — to being merely "subjective" — and thus, from the positivistic point of view, invalid — knowledge. Indeed, psychologism's and historicism's insight into the individualized nature of knowledge only exerts an undermining influence in the framework of a positivistic notion of a reality "that is what it is," and its concomitant ideal of "objective knowledge" — knowledge as an exact replica of reality as it is in itself. When, by contrast, reality is conceived of as an act of self-disclosure, revealing ever new aspects of itself, and knowledge as man's creative articulation of these novel aspects, the variety in interpretations of reality no longer reflects a regrettable finitude of the knowing mind, but becomes a testimony to reality's richness and the mind's perceptiveness.

Dilthey could escape the undermining influence of psychologism and historicism that had threatened psychology and philosophy since Kant's discovery of the conditionedness of knowledge upon consciousness because he no longer subscribed to the positivistic notion of reality and its ideal of objective knowledge. His conception of knowledge was not that of being a passive mirror of reality, but, indeed, a powerful man-created image — an image that presents reality in new aspects.

Scientific and philosophical knowledge, as the personal organization of experiential data, is always individualized, but that does not make it arbitrary. Dilthey emphasized that the creative organizations of experiential data are based upon actual experiences with reality. Therefore its results are anchored in reality, and can be judged.[14] The various organizations of experience — individual images of reality — differ in quality and power. Some images are more powerful, more revealing — and hence more "true" — than other images, just as works of art differ in quality and power. The power — or the truthfulness — of any conversion of experience into image can be rated on the basis of its fruitfulness for human life — by taking into account the power the image has to open up new aspects of reality.

The term subjective knowledge, represents positivism's judgment of knowledge as a failed description of reality as it in itself is; the term personal knowledge — introduced by Michael Polanyi — better represents Dilthey's judgment of knowledge as a creative interpretation of reality — creative because it opens up new vistas upon it.

In summary, knowledge's individualized nature represents for Dilthey thus not a drawback, but, on the contrary, an enormous advantage. Because he can have this kind of knowledge, man can transcend reality as it confronts him, and can venture further on his exploration of its still hidden aspects.

After having analyzed the finite mind's creativity and conditionedness — the elements of freedom and necessity in human life — we now proceed to a central concept of Dilthey's descriptive psychology: the personality structure or "soul-structure" — with a more modern term, the self — a term which Dilthey, however, seldom used. Perhaps his most original contribution to psychology proper was this concept of the "acquired soul-structure" (*erworbenen Zusammenhang des Seelenlebens*) (GS, vol. V, 271), which is an individual's personality as it has acquired structure through experience. This concept of the shaped personality or self enabled Dilthey to give a completely naturalistic account of the origin of a personality as the historically grown structure of an individual person; it also gave him a means for clarifying the extent to which the mind can free itself from internal and external conditions, and to account for the historicity of human existence. In touching upon Dilthey's concept of acquired soul-structure, we thus come close to the hidden source of his conception of mankind's history as a progress in freedom. We now will further probe this important concept, beginning with the notion of the origin of the personality structure, or soul-structure, in the human organism's confrontation with external reality.

In his 1890 essay on the reality of the external world, Dilthey described the human organism in naturalistic terms as a "system of instincts" (GS, vol. V, 103), a "bundle of instincts, from which the most diverse strivings and volitions radiate in all directions according to feelings of dissatisfaction and need" (GS, vol. V, 102). The individual human organism becomes aware of itself as an independent physical and psychical entity — a self — in its contacts with the external world. With the consciousness of the external world, self consciousness develops; is, moreover, teleologically organized, for its goal is the satisfaction of its needs (GS, vol. V, 125). The organism's activities stem from its volitions. Indeed, its kernel is the will to satisfy its instinctual desires (GS, vol. V, 133).

A person's self-awareness as an individual originates in the experienced contact of this living and willing organism with the resistant external world. Dilthey already suggested in the *Introduction to the Human Sciences* that the experienced contact with reality is crucial for the development of an individual's personality for "the structural relationships here experienced become our guiding principles in our understanding of reality. In 1890 he asserted that the process of personality formation begins even before birth — for even an embryo has personal experiences — that is to say, an awareness of "I" and "not—I."

Anticipating Freud's conception of the reality principle, Dilthey wrote that the more each human organism realizes the resistance of the world to his will, the more it becomes aware of itself as an entity separated from it — that is to say, as an individual existing independently in his own right.

Dilthey summarized the development of the personality structure, or self, in its confrontation with reality in the following words:

The self often finds itself in changing states, which are experienced as a unity by the person's consciousness; at the same time, it [the self] finds itself conditioned by the external world, and acting upon it. In its consciousness [the self] grasps [the external world], and it knows itself determined by the acts of its sensory perception. As in this way the organism's living unity finds itself conditioned by the milieu in which it lives and to which it reacts; an organization of its inner situations thereby emerges (GS, vol. V, 200).

On the basis of this brush with the world the organism builds the ego's "goal-oriented unity." This unity has a teleological structure because of the organism's striving for fullness of life, for the satisfaction of instincts, and for attainment of happiness (GS, vol. V, 207). This structure explains the components of its life. For instance, bodily sensations — serving as signals to indicate what are good, and what are harmful, contacts with the external world — are clearly teleological in character (GS, vol. V, 208), as are the mental sensations of pleasure and pain. Moreover, the organism's instincts to feed itself, to procreate and to protect itself — all these "powerful instincts which reign throughout the animal world — the human social and the human historical world" — are similarly goal-oriented, serving the preservation of the species. So do reflex mechanisms, and, as just mentioned, pain, which is a warning signal against detrimental activities. Dilthey saw "nature" as having used the strongest possible means for self-preservation, for both individuals, and the species.

This type of teleology has nothing in common with a metaphysical goal toward which man would develop. The teleology of mental developmental processes Dilthey saw as grounded in the human organism's natural and instinctive — partly unconscious, partly conscious — strivings to satisfy its needs.[15] Viewed subjectively — from the perspective of the experiencing subject — the human organism's instinctual goal is happiness; viewed objectively — from the perspective of the economy of nature — it is the preservation of the species. Dilthey optimistically believed that ultimately these two perspectives coincide.

As the network of the mind's habitual positive and negative potential responses to the stimuli reaching it — stimuli from reality inside and out, and stimuli embedded from the past — the soul-structure performs a regulating function for the human organism's manifold activities. The organism's experiences with reality cause it to avoid unpleasant situations and to seek pleasant ones. On the basis of the latter, the organism gradually articulates an overall goal for itself — a leading orientation. The emergence of such a goal occurs in various stages. The soul-structure's "kernel," or "center," is formed by the organism's instincts and feelings — which are the soul-structure's raw material, so to speak — which confer on incoming impressions a certain measure of interest. On the basis of this interest, additional instincts and feelings call forth images; thus they establish a direction for the person's will. Interest becomes attention; attention becomes perception; and perception combined with remembered images causes, in the course of time, the emergence of an idea or goal toward which the organism as a whole is oriented. This orientation of the soul-structure gives unity to a person's life.

Because it contains "the rules on which the course of discrete mental events depend" (GS, vol. V, 182), the soul-structure calls forth, and determines a person's activities. The soul-structure functions, as it were, as the rules of a game; in Dilthey's words, it becomes the "rule and power that reigns over the discrete occurrences [*Regel und Macht . . . welche die Einzelvorgänge regiert*]" (GS, vol. V, 182); or, to put it differently the soul-structure functions as a "grammar" for a person's "speech acts" — his activities.

The soul-structure limits a person's freedom of development. A young individual can change his opinion frequently, but as he becomes older he will increasingly stick to his opinions and value-judgments: they are part of the way in which his personality has become organized in the course of time. As an adult, his consolidated character traits express his outlook on life, the core of his personality. Dilthey illustrated his conception of the relationship between freedom and necessity in human life with the example of instrumental music. Such music has "a direction, and activity that reaches out toward its realization, a progression of psychic activity itself, a determination by what has already passed but still the self-containment of various possibilities, a process of explication which at the same time is a creation" (GS, vol. VII, 231).

Because of the initial period of undeterminedness of the soul-structure, man has the potential of developing into many different directions.[16] This openness of the soul-structure to the environment is the basis for the variability — and thus the historicity — of human life.

The soul-structure regulates the individual's relations to external reality, to his internal reality, and to his past. A well-functioning soul-structure is therefore the very basis of healthy mental life. It performs its function of promoting mental health by consistently focusing on phenomena significant to it from both objective and subjective points of view. Dilthey explained this mental health function by contrasting the malfunctioning mind of a sleeping or mentally ill person with the well-functioning mind of a poet.

In an address delivered in 1886, "Poetic Imagination and Madness," Dilthey saw sleep and mental illness as preventing the soul-structure from focusing on distinctive phenomena of the inner and outer world; it is inactive, and so cannot organize perception. No knowledge can therefore be acquired in such states: during mental illness "a sick person cannot use the acquired soul-structure to process the images, feelings or impulses of which he must be conscious at each moment. Thus, the regulation of images by the fixed standards shared by all healthy people come to a standstill" (GS, vol. VI, 94). The soul-structure, as a force regulating the individual's relationship within himself and with his environment, has become unable to connect inner and outer world. The poet, by contrast, can better organize the stimuli reaching him than the ordinary person, thus creating powerful works of art which articulate aspects of reality that impressed him.

In the essay on descriptive psychology, Dilthey came back to the problem of mental illness and mental health. He stated that mental illness — such as illnesses accompanied by hallucinations — is, in fact, caused by the disintegration of the patient's soul-structure. Mentally ill patients can still reason, their minds still work; but their reasonings are faulty. Not being the expressions of a soul-structure developed in interaction with reality, such reasonings lack present contact with reality.

Thus, Dilthey clearly envisioned the possibility that mental illness has mental causes; he complained, indeed, that the psychiatry of his time was so much oriented toward the physical side of mental illness that its literature said nothing in the direction of mental factors (GS, vol. V, 120-121). Dilthey thus anticipated Freud in perceiving the importance of psychic factors in mental illness.

Just as mental illness is caused by a weak or sick soul-structure, so is mental health the result of a strong soul-structure. Dilthey affirmed a direct relationship between mental health and ego strength: the more healthy a person, the more powerful his soul-structure — this "large regulating apparatus" (GS, vol. VI, 96). The creativity of poets and artists in general was for Dilthey the most telling expression of strong soul-structures — soul-structures that can transform the many stimuli reaching them into powerful and beautiful images.

Reacting against the romantic notion that the poet is a sick, alienated person who has lost contact with reality, Dilthey stated, on the contrary, that poets are super-healthy individuals. In poets the soul-structure is the strongest; these creative individuals display great power in conjuring up images. The poet is therefore more healthy than the ordinary person, who in fact is less free in shaping his awareness, his perceptions, and his memories; or — to state the same point differently — who is more reality-bound.

Dilthey's evolution of poets as super-healthy, and thus almost as super-human individuals and as true culture heroes who can function as models for ordinary less strong, less artistic, and more reality-bound individuals, further explains why he expected so much from the analysis of literary masterpieces in contributing to psychology and the other human sciences; for in these works the functioning of the human mind could presumably be studied under optimal conditions. Dilthey maintained that animal and human organisms are both goal-oriented; in seeking pleasurable experiences, animals and humans both follow, as it were, the directions given to it by the inner and outer environment by adapting their behavior to them. Dilthey had, indeed, carefully studied Darwin while at the University of Basel, and he was thus thoroughly familiar with the importance of the phenomenon of adaptation in contemporary biological thought (GS, vol. V, 212).

But in contrast to Darwin, Dilthey saw a marked difference between animal and human forms of adaptation. For man, in acquiring a soul-structure, gains a degree of mastery over external nature and his own instincts which animals cannot achieve. Indeed, animals must forever blindly and helplessly follow their instincts; they can only act on their impulses. A fully developed human individual, by contrast, is no longer the slave of either instincts or environment; he rules himself and his environment by means of his soul-structure which is organized toward the pursuance of the goal he wants to achieve and the realization of ideals he has set himself; he is an autonomous, sovereign person, free to do what he consciously chooses.

Because of the soul-structure's power to actively shape a person's life, the mechanical explanations proposed by scientific psychology are – Dilthey felt – totally insufficient (GS, vol. V, 179). No wonder, then, that the soul-structure represents the most important object of Dilthey's psychology.

Dilthey suggested several methods for descriptive psychology's study of the soul-structure. We have previously seen that he maintained that our own soul-structure is not given to consciousness in its totality. Scholars cannot therefore study its functioning by analyzing the workings of their own psychic structure, or, for that matter, by experimenting with the consciousness of others. They must, therefore, turn to the end products of mental activity; first to creations of persons of genius, especially works of literature; but also to other, less individualized products – such as myths, religious customs, judiciary systems, and social organizations (GS, vol. V, 180). According to Dilthey, "What man is cannot be discovered by introspection, nor by psychological experiments – only by the study of history" (GS, vol. V, 180). The products of the mind studied by the historian of consciousness are "mental life transfixed into things" (GS, vol. V, 199).

Dilthey suggested furthermore several topics for the study of the soul-structure, such as the relationship between feelings and instincts; the fusion of feelings with each other; the transference of feelings to other, originally unconnected areas; the impact of the past on present in each consciousness; the emotional impact of people on each other; and mental activities by which feelings are translated into symbols – as is the case, for instance, in art and religion (GS, vol. V, 187).

As a further topic, Dilthey listed the soul-structure's volitional activities. He pointed repeatedly to the dependency of discrete acts of will upon the strivings of the total soul-structure (GS, vol. V, 189). Although such a dependency of the will on the soul-structure is not conscious, the soul-structure is nevertheless very real (GS, vol. V, 190). Dilthey stated emphatically that the conception of the soul-structure – or self – is not an hypothesis, or an abstraction but a reality. Because of its active conscious will, the soul-structure has its own life and its own independent kernel.

He mentioned other topics: "the various forms of individual mental life, the difference between the sexes, national characters,

and the great types of goal-oriented human behavior and of indi-
vidualities" (GS, vol. V, 190), as well as character types — such as
the ambitious, the vain, the cowardly, the strong. He considered
character types the result of specific relationships between instincts
existing within a person's soul-structure (GS, vol. V, 234).

After the description of the soul-structure, of the investigation
of its function in mental life and of the methods by which to study
it, one more important aspect of it remains to be examined: its
development. Dilthey conceived of personal development as an
increasing articulation of an individual's ideal of life — his general
orientation toward life — and as an achieving of personal autonomy.

Dilthey saw a soul-structure as both a synchronic and as a diachronic structure. As a synchronic structure, the soul-structure is
considered from the point of view of its present — a present in
which conscious and unconscious elements interact. As a diachronic
structure, the soul-structure is considered from the point of view
of its temporal unity — a unity which stretches from birth to death.
While within the soul-structures's living totality, the synchronic and
diachronic structures condition each other (GS, vol. V, 213), both
structures must be distinguished in order to better understand their
living interaction.

Dilthey described human life in dynamic terms, as a "perpetual
movement" (GS, vol. V, 218), in which the instincts "function as
an agent pushing the organism forward." Life's forward movement
is a progressive development because each new stage is conditioned
by previous ones. Besides being progressive, the soul-structure's
development is also continuous because the instincts press constantly
for satisfaction; development is, moreover, as we just have seen,
goal-oriented.

The diachronic structuredness of the soul-structure is the direct
result of the teleological orientation of the human organism. For in
the individual's pursuit of happiness the source of his happiness
becomes increasingly clear to him, and this crystallizes as his
conception of ideal life. The organism seeks to develop and retain
values that enhance its life. It attempts to realize values that fulfill specific needs — needs that have arisen in its encounters with
reality. These goal-oriented strivings of the organism cause "an
increasing articulation of mental life" (GS, vol. V, 217) — a process
leading eventually to a clearly articulated "ideal of life" (*Lebensideal*), according to which the adult consciously organizes his life.
This ideal, in turn, is then expressed in practical life as the individual's preferred activities, and his chosen environment.

Dilthey divided an individual's development between birth and

death in the three conventional stages of youth, maturity, and old
age. The stage of youth is one of enthusiasm: the adolescent wants
to rebuild the world. The stage of adulthood is characterized by a
mixture of freedom of the will and of action, on the one hand, and
resignation to the world as it is, on the other. Thanks to his soul-
structure, the adult has acquired a certain distance from and therefore mastery over himself and his life; but he has had also to adapt
himself to reality:

In a hard struggle, the young person's ideal of life and dreams for the future are
adapted to reality [*die Macht der Sachen*, the power of things]. The authority
[*Herrschaft*] of maturity emerges. Finished as the person he came to be, and
conscious [of his identity], he rises above the one-sided subjectivity of the
young person to the recognition of the value-coherence of reality, [a value-
coherence] which he no longer wants to create, but only wants to support
where he happens to be (GS, vol. V, 217).

Because the adult "has discovered what is valuable in the world
as it is" (GS, vol. V, 217), he no longer feels frustrated about the
impossible ideals of his youth. Dilthey clearly could not appreciate
a lasting commitment to social change, and he must have considered
adults remaining inclined to revolution as maladapted. With his
belief that the middle-class world as it is has "its truth," Dilthey
shows himself to be its loyal representative.

As Dilthey saw it, an individual's instincts and feelings are fully
articulated at the height of his life; a mature individual is a person
who knows what he wants, and knows how to fulfill his desires.
He has, indeed, organized his life specifically to satisfy his emotional
needs; thus, his inner instincts and feelings have received a concrete
external form in the various spheres of life. Dilthey saw a similar
increase in articulation, and realization in concrete forms of life,
of the goals pursued by the will. Together, these conscious feelings
and volitions and their manifestations in concrete existence,
represent the acquired soul-structure of the mature person, and
"its mastery over the discrete conscious occurrences" (GS, vol. V,
217).

The process of increasing articulation can continue far into old
age. But with the passing of years, a person's ability to be receptive
and flexible declines; now the past begins to dominate the economy
of the acquired soul-structure. This can lead to rigidity and lack of
freedom in responding to new situations. But in a truly "great"
individual – a person with a powerful soul-structure, such as
Goethe – the process of aging leads to the paradox of a free mind
that retains its flexibility and strength existing in an increasingly
enfeebled body. In such an aged person,

the form of the soul reigns supreme, while at the same time his bodily organs weaken; a mixed and subdued [gedämpfe] mood [reigns] over life; [it] stems from the control of a soul over its discrete emotional conditions – a soul which has absorbed many things (GS, vol. V, 225).

Dilthey is ambiguous about the relationship between life's stages and its totality from birth to death. On the one hand, Dilthey maintained that each stage of man's development has a unique value, for each fulfills a specific need appropriate to it. The most perfect life would be one in which the specific value of each moment is consciously experienced and appreciated (GS, vol. V, 218): development consists of stages of life; these strive each to win and retain a value of their own. Sad is an infancy sacrificed to the more mature years; silly a life of pushing ahead – of making earlier phases a means to later ones (GS, vol. V, 219). It is, indeed, life's nature to "drench each moment" with the fullness of values (GS, vol. V, 219); man should embrace these moments as they come wholeheartedly.

But while each moment is perfect in its own way, there is on the other hand progress in life, namely, in the form of an "increasing adaptation by means of a differentiation, an intensification and [a formation of] higher connections." At this point, we notice the by now familiar tension in Dilthey's thought, between the intrinsic value of part – the discrete stages of moments – and whole – the total course of the individual's life.

As far as an individual's life is concerned, Dilthey discerned moreover a progressive tendency toward "higher" stages of development. If regularly satisfied, the "lower" or "elementary" instincts decrease in the course of time, and make room for "higher" instincts.

Personality development thus involves a progressive series of stages, each displaying an increasingly richer unfolding of ever "higher values. In this process, the self steadily becomes more articulate, and it acquires increasingly "higher" connections.

To Dilthey, the crowning achievement of human life is the formation of a fully articulated soul-structure with its full awareness of its needs and ideals, and its corresponding life style designed to gratify those needs and to attain those goals. It characterizes the autonomous individual who masters both himself and reality to the extent possible for a finite being.

Because the mental development of an individual toward freedom and autonomy can only be described – not causally explained – it escapes the grasp of the natural sciences. Indeed, the emergence and development of autonomous mental life – represented by the soul-structure with its mastery over itself and its environment –

in the midst of unfree nature is, in Dilthey's eyes, "the greatest
riddle that resists the insights of natural science" (GS, vol. V, 223).
It almost qualifies as a miracle.

The autonomous individual is the truly human person. Such a
person is master of himself and nature, his whole environment. In
Dilthey's words, when he finds his power limited by external
factors — he has the wisdom to adapt himself to the inevitable:

> he is no longer at the whim of the play of stimuli. He bridles and controls
> his reactions, he selects where an adaptation to reality can further the satis-
> faction of its needs. And, most important, where he cannot determine reality,
> he adapts his own life-processes, and controls his unbridled passions and the
> play of imaginations by the inner activity of his will (GS, vol. V, 212).

The autonomous person is indeed the supreme achievement of
human life:

> All human development can achieve nothing higher than to form such a [soul]
> structure: sovereign, closed in itself, and significant [in itself] — adapted to
> the conditions of existence. . . . In all earthly reality, such a form of a soul
> appears as supreme (GS, vol. V, 220).

Here we may conclude that the concept of the sovereign individual is at the heart of Dilthey's descriptive psychology, as well as
of his philosophy of the human sciences in general.[17]

The autonomous individual is a supreme work of art created by
the subject himself. Already in 1860, Dilthey had referred to
human life as a work of art, formed "by receiving in contemplation
and activity all forces of the world, by integrating all features of
one's own nature into a unified form"[18] — the form referred to as
"soul-structure" by Dilthey's later writings.[19]

Throughout his career Dilthey emphasized that it was the task
of philosophy to support man's emancipation from immediacy, and
to free him from inner and outer constraints so that he could live
a free and "spiritual" life by mastering himself and his environment.
By articulating the ideal of the autonomous person, Dilthey wanted
to help his contemporaries to realize the ideal more readily.

Dilthey shared with Nietzsche, Weber and Freud this enthusiasm
for the autonomous individual as the fruit of Western civilization —
of civilization *tout court*. A brief comparison with these other
authors will demonstrate the extent to which the autonomous
person was, indeed, the age's cultural ideal.

Nietzsche, like Dilthey, rejected the person who merely follows
his instincts and the person who obeys tradition; he saw the emergence of the autonomous person as the final consummation of mankind's history. In the *Genealogy of Morals* he wrote that it took a

long time, and much suffering, before the autonomous person —
that is, the animal with a strong will and long-range goals, had
emerged — but that this end justified the means:

> The tremendous labor of what I have called "morality of mores" . . . the
> labor performed by man upon himself during the greater part of the existence
> of the human race, his entire *prehistoric* labor, finds its meaning, its great
> justification, notwithstanding the severity, tyranny, stupidity, and idiocy
> involved in it [the emergence of the person with long-range goals]. . . .[20]

Only at this point in history does educated man realize that the
person free from morality and customs had been history's goal:

> If we place ourselves at the end of this tremendous process, where the tree
> at last brings forth fruit, where society and the morality of custom at last
> reveal *what* they have simply been a means to: then we discover that the
> ripest fruit is the sovereign individual, like only to himself, liberated again
> from morality of custom, autonomous and supramoral.[21]

As we saw in chapter III, the autonomous person as Nietzsche
conceived of him was the person who could fulfill his promises;
Nietzsche described this type of individual also as the person in
whom mankind had found its completion:

> the man who has his own independent, protracted will and the *right to* make
> promises — and in him the proud consciousness, quivering in every muscle,
> of *what* has at length been achieved and become flesh in him, a consciousness
> of his power and freedom, a sensation of mankind come to completion.

Weber's thought on this point is similar. Weber rejected tra-
ditionalism and dogmatism as strongly as Dilthey and Nietzsche
did. He advocated for man a "negative totality of freedom of
movement in all directions — the breaking away from all 'shelter,'
from every practical and theoretical organization, from order and
security."[22] The freedom to go his own way seemed to Weber
characteristic of the truly human individual. He laid great stress
upon one's responsibility to act in full consciousness of the possible
consequences of one's actions. He wanted his contemporaries to
use their freedom to achieve only ends they had consciously
approved. In his sociology, he intended to show what the social
world was like, and how social structures function. On the basis of
the objective knowledge provided by the professional sociologist,
the politician and ordinary citizen decide sovereignly which course
of action to take. For Weber — as for Dilthey and Nietzsche — the
world had become the object and the raw material for sovereign
man.[23]

However, Weber did not, as clearly as Dilthey, Nietzsche, and
Freud, situate the autonomous person at the end of mankind's

development, although the growing rationalization he observed in the Western world seemed to point in that direction.

Freud, like Dilthey and Nietzsche, felt that the curbing of instincts, in particular the aggressive and sexual instincts, represented the precondition for civilization's historical progress. At the same time, however, he identified the repression of instincts for the sake of civilized living as the very cause of neuroses. Freud's psychoanalytic effort was aimed at making the neurotic person conscious of such repressions, thus giving him more mastery over himself:

> By extending the unconscious into consciousness the repressions are raised, the conditions of sympton-formation are abolished, and the pathogenic conflict exchanged for a normal one which must be decided one way or the other.[24]

The therapist accustoms his patients

> to an unprejudiced consideration of sexual matters like all other matters; and if after they have become independent by the effect of treatment they choose some intermediate course between unrestrained sexual license and unconditioned ascetism, our [the profession's] conscience is not burdened whatever the outcome.[25]

As a result of psychoanalytic treatment, the individual has become an independent autonomous person able to make his own decisions.

Dilthey and Freud were in many respects remarkably close. Besides their agreement that civilization had emerged as a result of constraining the instincts, they also shared the views that a person is a coherent totality of meaning, and that mental illness can be caused by mental causes. Moreover, both authors pointed to the fact that the same symbols recur throughout history in religion, myth, dreams, and insanity.[26]

At this point, a critical remark is in order. Dilthey's contribution to the study of man is his incomparably clear insight into the mind's organization, an organization which allows man to respond creatively to reality within the framework of his culture.

By maintaining, however, that in the contemporary age mind had become sovereign over itself and its environment Dilthey overestimated the power of mind. This would mean, that at this "late" point in human history, the mind is no longer conditioned by its own experiences, but could choose freely from mankind's complete experience — collected by historians — which perspective on reality he would use. Such a situation, however, could only exist in the hypothetical case of men being born as adults, having strong soul-structures. But as long as human beings are born as helpless infants without soul-structures, they will remain forever conditioned by personal and cultural experiences. Indeed, no matter how much time is given to the human race, man's biological organization makes it impossible for human beings to emancipate themselves from culture.

With Dilthey's descriptive psychology outlined, we can turn to the reactions of contemporaries to it. Dilthey's intentions in descriptive psychology have been widely misunderstood as being psychologism. Many of such misinterpretations of Dilthey come from the oddity and vagueness of his terminology. For instance, in conceptualizing mental life, he used such old-fashioned, metaphysically sounding terms as "soul" (*Seele*), "life of the soul" (*Seelenleben*), "spirit" or "mind" (*Geist*) and "spiritual" (*geistig*), along with more modern, and scientifically acceptable, terms such as "consciousness" (*Bewusztsein*) and "self" (*Selbst*).

Although Dilthey at one point called the development of a fixed terminology (GS, vol. V, 176) a major task of descriptive psychology, he nowhere defined *Geist, Seele,* or *Bewusztsein*; nor did he adequately differentiate between the *Geist* of an individual, and that of a society. In his writings, meaning shifts. *Geist* means at different times mind, consciousness, ego, self, and psyche; and, consequently, *Psychologie* means the study of all kinds of manifestations of this multifaceted *Geist*. The fact that Dilthey was, with von Brentano, the first to consistently resist psychology's domination by the natural sciences, and the fact that, as a result, little terminological clarity then existed in the area vacated by the traditional term "soul," only partially excuses Dilthey's vagueness.

An early example of a misunderstanding resulting from Dilthey's terminology was its interpretation by the Neo-Kantian Heinrich Rickert, professor of philosophy at Marburg, Germany. In his 1896-1902 publication *Kurlturwissenschaft und Naturwissenschaft*, Rickert made a distinction between *Geist*, which expresses itself in acts of evaluation, and *das Psychische*, which refers to the phenomena of the former "soul," as well as to modern "consciousness."[27] Rickert suggested the term *Kulturwissenschaften* for the study of the social-historical world. By thus rejecting Dilthey's term *Geisteswissenschaften*, he wanted to make clear that the study of the human world has nothing to do with "psychology," which was in his eyes the study of individual consciousness. He completely overlooked the sociological and social psychological element in Dilthey's work, and – finding support in Dilthey's terminology – accused Dilthey of "psychologism."[28]

A different criticism came from the psychological profession, in the reaction of Hermann Ebbinghaus, one of the founders of the older school of experimental psychology. In 1898 Ebbinghaus published in the *Zeitschrift für Psychologie der Sinnersorgane* a devastating article entitled "On Explanatory and Descriptive Psychology,"[29] focusing on Dilthey's essay on descriptive psychology. Ebbinghaus was clearly irritated by the aggressive tone of Dilthey's 1894 essay. The gist of his retort was that if Dilthey had known contemporary development in the field, he would not have written his essay. Dilthey was indeed not well informed on Wundt's ideas; in this respect, Ebbinghaus' criticism was, indeed, justified.[30]

Although Ebbinghaus praised the literary-historical and philosophical-historical perspectives offered by Dilthey, he stated that the article said little about "the truly psychological" — except for a few trivialities about the development of the individual. In this respect also Ebbinghaus was, to a certain extent, right; for Dilthey remained, after all, primarily a historian and philosopher. Ebbinghaus furthermore justifiably attacked Dilthey's refusal to accept hypotheses in psychology: if the scientist were only allowed to stick to what is one hundred percent certain, he claimed, "the stream of life and progress" in the discipline would be obstructed: science has progressed by discarding useful hypotheses that had later proved to be unfruitful.

But Ebbinghaus failed to see the fundamental issues Dilthey had raised. He omitted, for instance, to point out that Dilthey advocated a conception of mind as an active rather than a passive faculty. He also failed to see the importance of Dilthey's conception of the acquired soul-structure: he was of the opinion that the soul-structure was merely another way of talking about traditional causal connections serving to explain human behavior.

Although Dilthey's psychology thus did not meet with sympathy on the part of his contemporaries, it was, however, discovered by the next generation of scholars. While still active as a psychiatrist, Karl Jaspers, for instance, acknowledged his debt to Dilthey in his 1912 article "Causal and Understandable Connections between Fate and Psychosis in Dementia Praecox,"[31] and in his 1923 book *Allgemeine Psychopathologie.*[32] The psychiatrists Heinz Hartmann and Ludwig Binswanger were also much influenced by Dilthey's concept of *Verstehen* and of a "descriptive" psychology.[33] His influence on Plessner and Buytendijk has been mentioned above.

Dilthey's suggestions for a "psychology of a second order" came to fruition in the sociological investigations of Eduard Spranger, George Simmel, and Max Weber — to name a few.[34] Dilthey's approach to psychology furthermore later influenced *Gestalt* psychology developed between Wars in Germany, and further eleborated in the United States after World War II.

Indeed, it would seem that in the United States Dilthey's view was rediscovered during the 1940s by Abraham Mazlow and others, although it remains uncertain whether Dilthey's writings exercised any direct influence on this development.

The significance of Dilthey's psychology for the study of history and culture can be summarized in the following two points. First, his psychology — based as it is on the mind's creativity, and conditionedness — interprets the variety of concrete manifestations of human life as the expression of man's creativity, a variety which should be positively welcomed. Second, his psychology indicates that in spite of man's creativity, human life is nevertheless "historical," that is, conditioned by natural and historical or cultural circumstances.

The writings of twentieth-century authors such as Abraham Mazlow, Ludwig von Bertalanffy, and Oliver Sachs bear witness that Dilthey's psychology is as relevant today as it was in his own time.

Mazlow rejected for psychology — in terms that are strongly reminiscent of Dilthey — the reduction of complex things into simple elements — "this . . . has succeeded well enough elsewhere in science, for a time at least. In psychology, it has not." The view of the world as constructed of small elements is "artificial, conventionalized, hypothetical," it is a "man-made system imposed upon an interconnected world in flux."[35] Mazlow therefore constructed his own humanistic psychology on the interpretation of elements of mental life in the context of a person's total life situation.

Even more striking is the affinity between Dilthey and von Bertalanffy. In a 1971 article, "System, Symbol and the Image of Man," he pleads for a humanistic psychiatry that is remarkably similar to Dilthey's ideas about man as an open psycho-physical system, which is the more "healthy"the more his mental life — his soul-structure — is integrated.

Von Bertalanffy states that a "third revolution" is taking place in psychiatry (after the psychoanalytic and behavioral ones) in which the human organism is conceptualized again as "a holistic and active system." This revolution uses a model of man as an internally active psycho-physical organism, and it conceives of cognition not as a passive reception of stimuli or a making of photographic copies of reality. Rather "the organism is seen as creating the world it perceives, conceives and lives in"; and behavior is "an expression of imminent activity . . . of living creativity."[36] Von Bertalanffy describes the normal person as "an open system with respect to information received from outside." Instead of one-way causality and statistical chance, it works with "multivariable interaction and organization."

Von Bertalanffy illustrates the usefulness of this (Dilthean) model of man with an analysis of schizophrenia, contending that in the schizophrenic person the "subjective elements run wild and are disintegrated"; "not isolable symptoms," but "integration makes for the difference [with a healthy person]."[37] The regression found in schizophrenia is a "disintegration of the personality system, de-differentiation and decentralization," a "loosening of the hierarchic mental organization."[38]

Again, one is strongly reminded of Dilthey when he declares that the natural sciences are unable to "know the reality behind the phenomena of subjective and objective experience," but that "we [might] have other access to this reality in direct experience and its sublimation in art, music, analytical knowledge,"[39] that science is only one approach to reality; and when he contends that a psychiatry which uses the modern systems approach "can give some answer to the question of meaning, which is nothing else than connection within a whole or system."[40]

Finally, I will point to Oliver Sacks' 1973 *Awakenings*, as it also underlines the importance of the Dilthean approach to human behavior. Sacks describes patients who, after having contracted *encephalitis lethargica* during the years 1916-1927, "woke up" from their lethargy as a result of a new pharmacological substance. What struck Sachs was the difference in the patients' behavioral patterns after they had regained consciousness. He concluded that it is not enough to describe diseases in purely mechanical or chemical terms; diseases have to described also in terms of organization and project. The discrepancies between his patients' brain damage and their behavioral disturbances demonstrated to him that the character features of the individual – Dilthey would say his soul-structure – his personal "strengths" and "weaknesses," play an important role in deciding the course of a disease; it demonstrated also that other factors, such as the previous effects of the external world on the patient, and the circumstances and occurrences of his past and present life are also important.[41]

The next chapter will show that Dilthey's conception of individual development provides the historian with a useful model for historical developments of discrete social and cultural entities. It will show also how, on the basis of his psychological insights, Dilthey arrived at an interpretation of mankind's total history as the progressive emancipation of the human mind from nature and from tradition.

CHAPTER EIGHT

STRUCTURE, DEVELOPMENT, AND PROGRESS:
DILTHEY'S VIEWS ON THE CONCRETE
COURSE OF HISTORY

This chapter returns to examine again Dilthey's approach to history and culture, drawing upon his concepts of personality structure and development just discussed.

As he considered the person from this point of view of his individual creative mind, so he considered history from that of man's collective creative mind. His philosophy of life is, accordingly, still in many respects a philosophy of mind. But it is not a philosophy of abstract mind – of mind à la Hegel, originally existing by itself, independent of matter – but a philosophy of concrete, or embodied, finite mind. Consequently Dilthey was, in spite of his one-sided, mind-oriented standpoint in history, led toward many interesting insights – as he had been in psychology. Because he considered the structuredness of the human mind's operations as its very essence, he correspondingly developed a keen eye for the structuredness of historical periods and cultural developments. Because he realized the possibilities and limitations – or finitude – of the human mind in responding creatively to its environment, he developed remarkable insight into the role of culture in human life. He formulated, moreover, an interesting conception of historical significance, and he suggested a highly useful model of historical development.

Dilthey approached the past simultaneously from two angles: first, he reflected upon history's total course, as if he were an outsider to the historical process, using the familar diachronic perspective – considering history as the forward movement of human life. Looking upon the past from this perspective, Dilthey interpreted history in terms of the human mind's progressive development from tradition-bound forms of past human existence to the sovereignty over nature and history in the modern mind. With this interpretation from an outsider's point of view Dilthey gave an answer to the ancient question concerning the meaning of history, his speculative philosophy of history.

Second, he examined from an insider's point of view man's lived experience of history, using a novel, synchronic – or structural –

perspective, considering history as a static, temporal structure. Looking upon the past from this perspective, Dilthey interpreted history in terms of a structure in which past, present and future synchronically cohere to form a unified totality. He considered human life as it has been lived at various points of time in its day-to-day encounters with reality. On the basis of this perspective, Dilthey developed his philosophy of world-views.

I have discussed Dilthey's speculative philosophy of history in chapter VI, his philosophy of world-views in chapter V. In this chapter, I will investigate how Dilthey combined these two perspectives in his view of history's concrete course. Although ultimately the diachronic perspective dominates his interpretations of history, the synchronic impulse of his thought powerfully counteracts this diachronic impulse. From this tension between the synchronic and diachronic perspectives, a highly original perspective of history emerged — one in which the period concept has become the modern culture concept, and historical development the developmental notion of change in cultural patterns.

This chapter begins with a sketch of Dilthey's conception of what he assumed to be history's creator: diachronic dynamic life.

Dynamic life is the creator of human history. As a philosopher of life, Dilthey celebrated in his philosophy life's dynamism and creativity manifested in the richness of human history's products. "Historical life creates. It is constantly engaged in the production of things and values" (GS, vol. VII, 153). As an individual's life-history is the realization of that individual's creative energy, so concrete history is the realization of this inner force, conscious life.

In considering Dilthey's conception of life, a reader is struck by life's dynamism. Life is a forward-moving thrust. It moves on from one moment to the next, from past to future — temporarily embodying itself in ever new concrete forms. Human history's movement is fueled by man's most basic instincts: hunger, love and aggression (GS, vol. V, 209). These instincts prompt man to act and to work for a better future.

In man, life has reached consciousness of itself. Life's awareness of the present's insufficiencies and the future's possibilities urge it to move on, objectifying itself in ever new forms. For life can never abide in the form in which it has objectified itself — being pure energy, it cannot tolerate being captured in stifling concrete shapes. In man, life, with its energy thwarted by finite forms, thus presses for liberation and for realization for its vision of a better future. Life is future-oriented. Human history is the outward manifestation — or objectification — of this inner force — life.

Life's movement will never come to a standstill. As in man life becomes conscious of itself — that is, of its present needs and of its desires for the future — it forever strives for satisfaction by embodying itself in new — and hopefully more satisfying — forms. But its desires can never be fulfilled. Each concrete shape becomes a new prison.

A hunger for all kinds of satisfactions that can never be fulfilled passes from one age to the next . . . it is the nature of all finite historical forms that they are burdened with the withering of their existence [*Daseinsverkümmerung*] and with servitude — with unfulfilled longing (GS, vol. VII, 187).

Life can never reach complete fulfillment; for if life would satisfy all its desires, it would have lost its creative energy, and thus would no longer be life.

In man, life has become aware of itself, and of the limitations of each of its embodiments. Consequently, man suffers from "the tragedy of finiteness" (GS, vol. VII, 238). Sometimes, the limitations of concrete existence press so hard on the human subjects that they preclude further activity on their part; their desire to break the shackles of the present is stifled. Then history stagnates. But in most cases, life's desire within man to overcome the finiteness of existence is strong enough to urge him to go beyond the given limitations. So history moves on.

Thus, history's movement in man results from two impulses: life's dissatisfaction with each succeeding present on the one hand, and its creative urge to develop new forms of life on the other hand. Dilthey maintained that in history's great events — such as, for instance, the fall of Rome, the liberation of the Netherlands from Spanish domination, and the Revolution in France — two "forces" have been operating that together brought about these changes: a negative force caused by a people's awareness of unsatisfied needs. and a positive force caused by its creative energies pressing forward to be realized in new ideals.

Thus, Dilthey formulated a "general proposition" about the forward movement of life in human history: "tension, the feeling of insufficiency of the existing situation — that is to say, negative feeling — provides the foundation for action supported by positive feeling — the desire to reach goals" (GS, vol. VII, 165).

While such negative and positive forces live in people, most of them are not aware of them. Their existence is made conscious, and intensified, by the words and actions of those who will be later recognized as significant historical personalities. Because of the latent presence of the needs and energies in a people, leaders can find followers and direct the people's yearning for change.

Because of life's forward movement, each of life's objectifications — each concrete shape of man's collective and individual existence — represents merely a temporary balance between a stifling pressure from concrete forms and an inner desire for liberation: "As every form of historical life is finite, it contains a distribution of happy force and of restraint, of enlargement and of narrowness of life, of satisfaction and of need" (GS, vol. VII, 187). Only for a brief while can the various visible forms of historical life in the external world — political empires and epochs, institutions, works of art and thought — offer a longer, seemingly permanent shelter to life. "Only at a few points of historical life does a temporary condition of rest reign" (GS, vol. VII, 288).

Thus, every phenomenon of the historical social world, whether empire or cultural structure, is bursting with new life. Everything has an inborn tendency to change and to progress toward the future; everything is involved in a frantic attempt to leave the past and to move on. Standing still is unnatural, it is stagnation. it indicates degenerated life, decay, and approaching death.

Life has no higher authority to obey than itself. What exists at a certain point in time exists only because creative life wanted to thereby embody itself. Life could as well have taken other forms, which it would soon because life always moves forward. Historical forms and institutions are consequently arbitrary products of a spontaneous nonrational life-force; they cannot be rationally explained or justified.

Dilthey called this arbitrary nature of historical situations their "facticity" (*Faktizität*) (GS, vol. VII, 287, 289). The term facticity, meaning a "being-there," or "being-put-there-by-life," carries a connotation of life's sheer power. Life's urge to free itself from present limitation was, indeed, seen by Dilthey as a craving for power. "Every new situation has the character of being finite." The experience of such limitations produces a "will to power" (GS, vol. VII, 166). The limitations pressing upon existence express themselves in the phenomenon of domination; he maintained that power relationships can therefore never be explained away — let alone eliminated in practice — as had been vainly attempted by "idealistic" philosophers, such as Hegel and Fichte, who envisioned a utopian future (GS, vol. VII, 287). He saw in particular, the occurrence of oppressive relations between races, and the never ending struggle for space by the various peoples of the world, as expressions of life's will to power.

The suffering caused by political domination, and by the use of sheer force to enforce it, is thus founded in the nature of life itself. Concrete forms of historical existence are by nature "infected with a mutilation of life and slavery, and with unfulfilled longing, because power relations can never be eliminated from the society of psycho-physical beings" (GS, vol. VII, 187; see also vol. VII, 166).

Dilthey's conception of life reminds one of Schopenhauer's will (*Wille*) and Nietzsche's will to power (*Wille zur Macht*). Schopenhauer considered the world as the product of an irrational cosmic will — life's blind will-to-be. According to Schopenhauer, life's will-to-be and its product, the world, present illusions from which the philosopher should detach himself by means of his superior understanding. As a result of his insight into the pitiful nature of a chronically unsatiated blind instinct of life, the wise man frees himself from the will's strivings. As a person no longer entangled by the will's desires, he can look with compassion at the world, which continues so frantically to scramble for existence.[1]

Like Schopenhauer, Dilthey too longed for liberation: he wanted to free himself from the narrow concerns of everyday existence, an existence that — wrapped up as it is in its momentary passions — does not care to look further than the little moment present. But unlike Schopenhauer, he did not think it possible to take refuge beyond the world; life is not only not an illusion, but the ultimate reality.

Dilthey's conception of life reminds one therefore even more strongly of Nietzsche. Nietzche considered the world "will to power, and nothing else." In *Thus Spoke Zarathustra* Nietzsche described life as a will to power and a will to dominate and to be the master.[2]

Thus, in spite of its sufferings and unfulfilled longings, Dilthey fully embraced life. To him, life's hunger for new forms is simply the precondition for its creativity. Indeed, Dilthey was more fascinated by life's creativity and its capacity to embody itself in such an endless variety of forms than by its inherent destructiveness — or, for that matter, by the insufficiencies inherent in its present enbodiment.

Dilthey's dynamic life was a progressing energy, but not a revolutionary one; his philosophy has thus not inspired any revolutionary actions, and a brief comparison with Hegel will clarify this point. Dilthey's life is conscious of its needs and desires, but it is not critical toward itself. Whereas Hegel's mind moves on in a dialectical movement, at each moment opposing itself, Dilthey's life remains a unified force. It objectifies itself in a particular present form, then moves on to its next objectification, and so to another. The critical moment we find in Hegel's conception of mind is replaced in Dilthey's by that of uncritical life's inner needs and ideals. Criticism and conflict are not creative categories in his conception of life.

Hence, this view of life harmonized well with Dilthey's politically conservative stance. He was by no means against change, but he approved of it as continuous "historical" development — that is one which does not rupture life's flow by contradicting the present but one that prolongs and intensifies what already exists. I will come back later to Dilthey's view of historical development.

To sum up: life as Dilthey saw it is a spontaneous dynamically forward moving and conscious energy, experiencing needs and ideals, realizing itself diachronically in a succession of concrete forms — leaving behind the linear trail of its successive realizations.

After having reviewed Dilthey's dynamic conception of life as a diachronic movement from past to future, I will now turn to Dilthey's explorations of life's synchronic structure — or, as he put it, life's coherence (*Zusammenhang*).

Although historical life's products — history's artifacts, its social and cultural structures, and its events — are dispersed in linear, chronological time, they nevertheless form a coherent totality — a diachronic and synchronic temporal structure — that transcends time's successive moments. Each of life's creations somehow has its place and function in this larger temporal whole, in which past, present and future coexist.

In order to understand how Dilthey saw coherence between the discrete events of human life and history, it is necessary to first analyze his conceptions of "abstract" or natural, and "concrete" or human time.

Only man consciously experiences time; and only in human life does the awareness of time play an intrinsic role. The things of nature, by contrast, exist within time as a purely external element. Having no awareness of, or lived experience of, either past or future, nature knows no goals or purposes. The time of nature is "abstract," a mere series of discrete moments of equal value (GS, vol. VII, 72). It is Newtonian time. Not being consciously experienced, nature's time has no present, past, or future. Abstract time has, therefore, no temporal structures connecting past, present, and future.

Nature — being thus mindless and unaware of itself — rests in itself and lacks all possibility of relating to itself, or to other parts of reality. Man, by contrast, consciously experiences time not as a succession of moments, but as a web of temporal structures extending into past and future. The mind rises above the passing moments of time by retaining episodes of its past and anticipating features of its future, all on the basis of experience. Man rises above a mere natural existence by conquering time. Dilthey carefully analyzed this process.

He wrote that when one remembers an experience, memories structurally related to it crop up; then, related future events are anticipated. He illustrated this with his own experience of time, describing how he sometimes lay awake at night, worrying whether he could complete the tasks that he had set himself before his death ended all. In that dilemma, Dilthey first became aware of his situation. He then isolated what was related to his worry. He thought of his previous works, and of the situations in which they had originated; he anticipated that a great deal of work lay still before him, and he wondered whether he could accomplish it. He observed in all these related experiences a "structural coherence of consciousness" (GS, vol. VII, 139).

He was thus being "pulled back and forth," between past and future. In part, this happened unconsciously, for he described the experience as "a being-pulled, not a volition – certainly not an abstract desire for knowledge. . . ." In this way, a temporal series emerges in which "the past and the future – the possible – transcend the [present] moment filled with experience" (GS, vol. VII, 140). Although past and future are obviously not the present, they nevertheless form a synchronic whole with the present: "past and future are related to experience in a series that on the basis of these relationships becomes a totality" (GS, vol. VII, 140). Thus, he concluded that time as experienced by man – that is, concrete time – is not a series of discrete moments, but a structured totality stretching into all directions.

The structural relationships existing between experienced present and the related past and future produce the notion of ourselves as a synchronic mental structure, stretching forth in time (*Lebenszusammenhang*). Dilthey remarked that an individual's life-structure "is not a sum or total of successive moments, but a unity founded upon the relationships connecting all its parts" (GS, vol. VII, 140). Because of his ability to both remember and anticipate events, man is able to transcend the passing present's short moment, and to live, so to speak, in an enduring, or "enlarged" present that encompasses past and future. Man himself *is*, as it were, this enlarged present – this stretching through time. The passing of time is a "constant sinking of what is present into the past, and the becoming present of that what we have just expected, wanted, feared . . ." (GS, vol. VII, 72). Man experiences this passing of time as a "restless moving

on of the present, [a movement] in which the present becomes
continually past, and the future present" (GS, vol. VII, 72). In the
present, reality is actually experienced. The present is therefore
more real to him than past and future. The present is "the filling
of one moment of time with reality. The present . . . is reality, in
contrast to memory or to the images of the future, which exist
in wishing, expecting, hoping, fearing, and willing" (GS, vol.
VII, 193). Man lives always in the present. "The ship of our life
is, as it were, carried on on a constantly forward-moving
stream, and the present is always there, where we, on these waves,
live, suffer, want, and remember – in short, where we experience
the fullness of our reality" (GS, vol. VII, 72-73; see also vol. VII,
193). Thus, "the fullness of reality," or reality's "presence,"
exists all the time, while the content of this experienced reality
changes. In other words: what commonly is called the passing of
time, actually is a shifting in man's awareness of reality. Man creates
the present by consciously experiencing reality; he creates not the
moments of time, but the presence of these moments. Present
moments exist for human consciousness – and only for human
consciousness. For man, reality is larger than the actually experienced present; moreover, he himself is larger than his actually
experienced present – namely, a synchronic structure stretching
from birth to death.

Consequently, the human experience of time can be described in
the following way. The experienced present, the short moment in
which a human being actually experiences reality, does not stop
to exist for man; for him, time's moments are not really passing
moments. Man continues to experience past reality in spite of the
passage of time's moments; he holds himself, as it were, steadily
above time's stream. The short moment of present experience
is "real" in a way past and future are not; but once this short
moment has passed, it does not become "unreal," or nonexistent;
although past, it continues to belong – in its own way of having
been – to the succeeding experienced presents. The present remains
real – "present" – even if the light of actual conscious experience
is no longer focused upon the moment, and it has become past.

This means that natural-science time, that of discrete homogeneous successive moments, is alien to man's experience of reality
and of himself. It is an abstraction from his personal experience,
constructed as it is to account systematically for nature's phenomena.
Because of his consciousness, man lives a different time, he lives his
own organically structured time. Human life should accordingly be
understood on the basis of man's specific experience of time, for

the latter exerts a direct influence on the way the advances of human life and history are formed.

In order to understand the structuredness of historical life, Dilthey first analyzed the structuredness of individual life. The previous chapter already touched upon the diachronic structure of individual life by sketching Dilthey's conception of the human organism. In the act of living, this organism confronts reality, pursues goals, and acquires a soul-structure which regulates its activities. Thus, a diachronic personal life pattern, a structured life history emerges. The diachronic coherence of an individual course of life is grounded in mind's power to overcome the passing moments of natural time. Because of the mind's capacity to consciously experience, remember, and anticipate, human life occurs not as a series of discrete moments, but a structured whole.

The course of life [*Lebenslauf*] consists of parts, of experiences which have an inner relationship to each other. Every discrete experience is related to a self, of which it is a part; it is structurally connected with the other parts to form a totality. In all conscious phenomena we find structure (GS, vol. VII, 195).

Dilthey stressed that the diachronic coherence of a life history is not the result of the mind's synthesizing activity in hindsight; the coherence is inherent in the human life process itself: personal life happens in structures. The human organism is not bombarded, as it were, with events coming from the outside world that hit it one by one; the mind seeks some events, avoids others, reinterprets them. In short, the mind shapes its own life history, in the process of living. Dilthey illustrated life's diachronic structuredness by examining an autobiography.

The autobiographer does not list the events that accidentally happened to him; he describes the plan, pattern, or structure, of his life. This plan is not a product of the autobiographer's hindsight; it came about as a result of the living person's foresight, and his attempts to realize his future plans.

The same person who investigates [in hindsight] the coherence of his life in his personal history, has already formed a coherence of his life; for what he [in hindsight] experiences as valuable in his life, were goals which he has realized after having projected his life in a certain direction [Dilthey used here the word *Lebensplan*] (GS, vol. VII, 200).

In Dilthey's analysis of the human experience of time, the dynamic diachronic element is, however, deemphasized in favor of human time's synchronic structuredness — a structuredness that is perceived by mind, and by mind only. The objects experienced by the conscious mind are perceived in their presence to it. As a result the relationships that connect the objects of experience have a synchronic, or structural, character. When one considers phenomena, as Dilthey did in connection with his analysis of the human experience of time, from the perspective of the subject's lived experience — that is, consciousness — the elements that exist synchronically in the mind's field of awareness — in the present — are stressed. Where form and structure are thus emphasized, linear, diachronic temporal developments tend to be seen as irrelevant.

Consequently, Dilthey conceived of a diachronic life history as a synchronic totality dependent on a conscious subject, a "planning present" — or a "consciousness of values," as he called it. In a life history, a subject's past and future are connected with his living present to form a structural whole. A life history is thus dependent on — or created by — a conscious subject in two ways: anticipating the future in the act of living and recollecting one's experiences in hindsight. A life history is no diachronic series of disorderly events ordered from the last member onward; experience knows it to be a synchronic structure "centered around a middle to which everything exterior is related as to an interior" (GS, vol. VII, 249).[3]

Life's synchronic structure does not exist *for* an individual's mind all along during his life, an individual exists *as* this experienced unity of past and present experiences.

Dilthey's reflections on life's structure exerted an important influence on Heidegger's conception of human life as temporality. In *Being and Time* (1926), Heidegger rejects the "vulgar" notion of time as a series of discrete moments, positing that the life of an authentically living person — that is to say, a person is at all moments aware of his mortality — is a "stretching" (*Erstreckung*) between birth and death. Man (*Dasein*) does not exist merely as the sum of appearing and disappearing experiences, and neither do these experiences fill out a somehow existing framework. Man is not an existent who is "in" time. He points out that the coherence of life (Heidegger quotes Dilthey's term *Lebenszusammenhang*), is a kind of "stretching," a "constancy of existing" over a period of time, in which the self endures among the continuous change of experiences. He calls this a "stretched-stretching" of human existence within the "happening" (*Geschehen*) of life, adding that "the question of the coherence of life is the ontological problem of its happening."[4]

Dilthey, after elucidating the life history's diachronic and synchronic structural unity, used this unity as the model to explain temporal coherence in the collective history of societies, cultures, and ultimately of mankind.

The human individual is, according to Dilthey, the smallest

structural unity, the "Urzelle" (GS, vol. VII, 246) of history. Many similar structures exist, however, in the collective life of society. Empirical observation shows, he wrote, that each individual is, indeed, part of larger structures (*Zusammenhänge*), what he called "cultural systems."[5]

These cultural systems originate in the same way as the soul-structure: in them a constant and uniform will – in this case, a collective will – has objectified itself (GS, vol. V, 190).

As examples of such structural systems, he included scientific, economic, and religious organizations – as well as nations and periods. Dilthey defined them as social entities in which goal, function, and structure are united to form a whole. Because such cultural structures are created by man to fulfill a need – and in many cases actually fulfill their purpose – they belong to the realm of mind rather than to that of nature. Created in order to serve a purpose, these structures maintain a teleological character (GS, vol. VII, 49-65).

In order to explain their effectiveness, Dilthey saw such systems as history's subjects – in fact, almost like acting individuals. He referred to them, for instance, as the "ideal" or "logical" subjects of history (GS, vol. VII, 134 ff.; see also vol. VII, 283). They have a "life history" (*Lebensgeschichte*). Historiography is the historian's reflection on the course of mankind's life (GS, vol. VII, 264), just as an autobiography is the reflection of an individual subject on his own life's course.

Because he identified history with life, life with mind, and mind with the creative shaping of cultural patterns, Dilthey did not see the past as a mechanical series of chronologically occurring events, but as life's structured diachronic development. Mankind develops in the ongoing interaction between its structures – its nations, its cultural systems (GS, vol. V, 218). Universal history is, as it were, the development of mankind's mind – its super soul-structure.

By ascribing to a cultural system "a mind," as it were, with synthesizing powers comparable to those of an individual mind, Dilthey could see the histories of these systems as likewise patterned, structured and unified. The cultural systems themselves thus become entities stretching over time – collective selves, or soul-structures. Ultimately, he saw mankind as such a logical subject – in fact, as history's main actor. In other words, Dilthey explained the structuredness of human history as a whole by seeing it as mind's history.

At this point, Dilthey's analyses seem to lose their foothold in real experience. Whereas many people will readily agree with

Dilthey's phenomenological analyses of man's experience of time and with his conclusion on the temporal structuredness of human life, they will find it difficult to subscribe to his tendency to see historical collectivities, such as nations, cultures, leave alone mankind, as genuinely acting subjects. In further investigating this objection, one discovers that Dilthey's understanding of human life's structuredness led him nevertheless to many interesting historical insights, in particular concerning the structuredness of historical periods, concerning historical significance, and concerning historical development.

Historical periods are synchronic structures. As a philosopher familar with the Historical School, Dilthey had a keen eye for the limiting effects of a period's existing cultural structure on the development of its individual participants. The cultural system of a given period allows, and cultivates certain thoughts, feelings and goals for their participants, while playing down others, creating a "horizon" for their participants that they cannot transcend (GS, vol. VII, 177).

With respect to the Middle Ages, Dilthey wrote that

All the expressions of the energy characterizing the period are related to each other. . . . And as the expressions of life moving in that direction strive toward absolute values and goals, the circle in which the period's people are caught closes: because it contains also tendencies that work in the opposite direction. . . . Thus the period's total structure is immanently determined by the interconnection [*Nexus*] of its life, of its emotional world, its value-system and its practical goals (GS, vol. VII, 186).

Dilthey treated periods and nations as "structural wholes" (GS, vol. VII, 177) in which the seemingly most diverse parts are functionally related to each other. The individual is conditioned by the collective of which he is a part.

As each period has its own horizon, each is "concentrated in itself" having "its center in itself." In Dilthey's words,

the various epochs have their unity of reference [*Massstab*] concerning their way of operations in a common entity [in themselves]. The various structures of a society are organized along the same lines, evidencing similarities. Perceptual relationships, for example, evidence inner affinity. The ways of feeling, the life of the soul, and the impulses that emerge in this way are similar to each other. Consequently, the will [in one period] chooses similar goals, strives for similar goods, and finds itself bound by similar rules (GS, vol. VII, 155).

The individual human person, however creative, is therefore never completely free: he cannot escape the climate of opinion, the *Geist der Zeit*.

A common attitude toward life shapes the "mental" or cultural unity of the period; and because this attitude is expressed, or objectified, in the institutions and other social structures of the time, it shapes the period's sociological unity as well.

This common attitude which Dilthey sometimes called culture (*die Kultur eines Zeitalters*) functions in the life of the society much as the soul-structure does in the individual's:

A period's culture can be viewed as the way in which this structural coherence, stretching throughout the whole by means of the interaction between individuals, acquires an articulation of . . . [its] . . . components . . . and a connection between these components – as if [they were its] organs of perception, enjoyment and creativity, as well as a unified capacity to act (GS, vol. IV, 559).

Because of his studies about relationships connecting the different aspects of a period, Dilthey can be considered as a precursor of functionalism in cultural anthropology; historical periods as he saw them are cultures, as later understood in cultural anthropology: functionally integrated wholes, oriented toward the achievement of a goal or the realization of a value. They are based on a consensus of its participants and results in a patterned way of life. Moreover, the participants are mostly unconscious of the way in which their behavior was regulated and determined by the interlocking cultural systems of a period (GS, vol. VII, 209).

In the English-speaking world, Franz Boas was one of the first cultural anthropologists to speak of "cultures" in the plural.[6] It seems possible that Boas, who could have read the *Introduction to the Human Sciences* while still in Germany, and who had attended Dilthey's lectures at the University of Berlin, was influenced by Dilthey's conception of cultural systems.[7]

Dilthey's insight into the structural relationships connecting the various aspects of social and cultural life caused him to define the task of the historian in an interesting way; instead of reporting events, the historian should analyze the cultural systems of the past. He should, in particular, reconstruct the past's mental make-ups or cultures, "to discover in the concrete goals, values, and ways of thinking, the similarly of a common entity, that reigns over the epoch" (GS, vol. VII, 155).

In Dilthey's approach to history, the culture concept does not just serve to shield the past from present-minded judgments as had been the case with Ranke. Dilthey fully grasped the explanatory value of cultural systems for the historian; he realized also that cultural systems can function as norms enabling the historian to evaluate the actions of past actors.

In evaluating individual phenomena the historian first has to establish what the individual has done, and then judge how his actions are related to the historical context, evaluating whether they fit within the context of the time or whether they show signs of transcending the actual situation and are pointed toward the future. Such a judgment is possible because the culture – or the total historical context of the period (*das Ganze der Epoche oder des Zeitalters*) – furnishes the appropriate standard by which to evaluate the appropriateness, propriety, prematurity or creativity of a specific action (GS, vol. VII, 155).

The culture concept was also useful for Dilthey's understanding of how the historical climate – or the culture – existing at one point of time could actually shape the human behavior of the next, the next generation. This question interested Dilthey very much, preoccupied as he was by the problem of history's synchronic structure. History can condition human behavior because man lives in a shared, objectively existing cultural world, into which each person is born. In this context, we see again how much Dilthey saw the collective mind as dependent on outer circumstances. Just as the individual mind is dependent on the body and the social world, so is the collective mind dependent on the material and mental culture of which it is a part.

Dilthey's analysis of the mechanism of historical conditioning – of socialization – deserves further consideration.

Human life is not only conscious, experienced life, but expressed life as well. Some expressions, such as gestures, facial expressions, and words, vanish after having been performed. Other expressions, however, are committed to semipermanent material, as is the case with expressions contained in manuscripts, books, works of art, or institutions, such as states, churches, scientific societies. Such expressions of human life have an "objective" – that is to say, a visible, interpersonal, and enduring – existence in material objects that can be perceived by others. In such phenomena, mind has "objectified" or "externalized" itself.

As we have seen earlier, the objects in which human life and mind have embodied themselves, form collectively what Dilthey called "the external realm of the mind." He called mind that in this way embodied or externalized itself the "objective mind" – what today we call culture. The objective mind, or culture, is the aggregation of "manifold forms in which the existing commonality between individuals has objectified itself in the world of senses" (GS, vol. VII, 208). Individuals become historically conditioned in their thought and actions because they are born into a culture that outlasts the lifetime of any individual.

His conception of culture as an objectively existing environment led Dilthey to see that a culture does more than stabilizing and structuring social life: it also serves as the medium that makes communication possible between the members of a community.

In everyday life, people have to understand each other's behavior and intentions — to translate for themselves the various expressions (*Lebensäusserungen*) of other people, such as facial expressions and forms of greeting — but also such cultural expressions as the arrangement of trees in a park or chairs in a room. Because every human being has the capacity to consciously experience life and to express himself, man understands immediately that the objective cultural manifestations surrounding him are not merely "things" the way natural objects are things, but things that express, or mean, something — a form of language:

Everything in which the mind has objectified itself has something in common for the I and you. Every square planted with trees, every room with chairs, is understandable for us, because an act of planning, ordering and evaluating which we have in common [*ein Gemeinsames*] has given every square and every chair its place (GS, vol. VII, 208).

To become encultured and socialized means learning to comprehend the signs of one's culture:

A child grows up in a social order and is surrounded by the family customs which it shares with the other members, and any order given by the mother is received in the context [of this system]. Before it learns to speak, [the child] is already submerged in a medium of commonalities . . . in this way the individual orients himself in the world of the objective mind (GS, vol. VII, 208-209).

Dilthey conceived of man's cultural environment as language. Its separate elements are like words. The individual person learns the language of culture but is unaware of its underlying rules (GS, vol. VII, 209).

Dilthey was a typical transitional figure between nineteenth- and most twentieth- century history, and modern cultural anthropology. He appreciated the variety of cultures; he had an open eye for the unconscious cultural factors shaping human behavior. He even realized that at his birth man is, in contrast to the other animals, an unfinished creature that needs culture in order to live.[8] He was close to twentieth-century cultural anthropology in yet another respect: namely, in his doubts — however quickly silenced — concerning the reality of universal history — doubts that will become clear toward the end of this chapter. But he was not really a cultural anthropologist: he still believed — in the Enlightenment tradition — in history, and in the freedom of the human mind at the end of history. He did not see that to be conditioned by culture is inherent in the human condition – a condition that cannot be outgrown. To be conditioned by culture – and, thereby by the past – seemed to Dilthey a humiliating situation for a free mind – a situation that should, indeed, be overcome by a being whose pride it is to have a mind.

The culture concept influenced Dilthey's approach to historical significance. His conceptualization of historical significance is the second major feature of his approach to history.

An event's historical significance has often been "measured" by the effect it has on later events. Dilthey disagreed with this mechanistic view, stressing that an event's effectiveness depends also on how it has been experienced. As seen in chapter IV, Dilthey compared the historian with a painter. Both historian and painter single out, on the basis of their living relationships to their topic, those features that seem significant to them.

As a participant in his society, the historian articulates in his representation of the past certain features that seem significant to him – features of which society at large is also aware, be it only vaguely. The historian's representation is objectively true when in the society's actual collective life-experience the events he singles out have been experienced at the time as significant. Any authentic historian, writing on the basis of his actual life-experience – which is part of the life-experience of the age – will single out precisely those events that the society at the time had experienced as significant. This means that an event's historical significance – its effectiveness on later history – depends on its first being experienced as significant by the society; for only if that precondition is fulfilled can the event exert its effect on later events.

Thus Dilthey added to the theory of objective historical significance in terms of cause and effect the curious notion that an event has first to be subjectively experienced as significant by the community before it can ever have such an objective effect on its later history.

Dilthey distinguished two types of historical significance: subjective significance, and historical significance proper. An experience or an event pertaining to the past has a subjective significance for the person who actually has the experience. The same experience has also an historical significance if it turns out to be part of a larger history – one in which his experiences become shared with others and become part of a written record.

To explain how he saw the relation between these two kinds of significance, Dilthey pointed to the example of Luther's life. As experiences lived through by a private person called Luther, the events of Luther's life were "subjective" – historically without significance. To the extent that they were part of German or Western history, these experiences had also a historical significance. Luther's purely individual experiences died with him. They were not shared with others, not expressed in documents and other material objects, and could not be remembered by later generations; hence, they could not become incorporated into the society's culture. Consequently, they had no effect on subsequent history. But, for instance, Luther's refusal to retract his opinions at the Diet of Worms was an experience shared with many contemporaries and later generations. Thus, it became an intrinsic part of German or Western history, and had a lasting empirically verifiable or "objective" effect on subsequent events.

Viewed from Dilthey's perspective, an historically significant event is neither momentous in itself, nor is its significance a matter of a historical interpretation made in hindsight. The culture of a period – which has the same function in a society's life as the soul-structure has in individual life – determines what will be accepted as historically significant, what will have effect, and what will be forgotten.

This view of historical significance is an extreme form of idealism as it accepts as real and significant only what has been consciously experienced as such by the actors of the past themselves. One can think of many events that went almost unnoticed in their time, but that had nevertheless enormous consequences on later history, such as the invention of the plow, or the introduction of a new type of fireplace in the Middle Ages.

Nevertheless, the hypothesis of an analogy between the mental structure – the soul-structure – of an individual and the collective mind – the culture – of a society has something to recommend it. The self-image of a nation, for instance, can be considered as a regulative device that decides which events at a certain moment of its existence are considered appropriate for it, and which events are seen as "impossible" – which are, for that reason, ignored. Thomas Kuhn shows how "paradigms" function in a similar way in the history of science.[9] Claude Lévi-Strauss, to mention yet another proponent of this type of thinking, suggests that myths and rites can counteract "objectively" important events causing them to be eventually dropped from memory and robbed of historical influence.[10]

It seems equally possible that myths and rites can fulfill the opposite function, and confer significance to an event that, "objectively" considered, would not be that important; the classical example is in the reception of the Spaniards in the New World, who were seen by the Indians as previously prophesied gods. It seems likely that in the Western world there have existed (and maybe will exist) thought-structures which fulfilled similar functions.

Thus, Dilthey's conception of historical significance draws attention to the role that culture and specific mental constructs existing in culture have on the very way the past is conceptualized — not only interpreted.

Dilthey's interpretation of historical significance in terms of society's selective experiences is important for yet another reason: it reminds us of the difference between the past as experienced by participants and the image of it reconstructed in hindsight by the historian. The recognition that the culture of a period, such as the Middle Ages, is different from ours implies in fact, that people do not all experience more or less the same life, and the same history, which they subsequently interpret in different terms: because of their different cultures, people indeed experience a very different life and history which cannot, as a result, be adequately described in the common terms of our own experience. Historical understanding requires therefore translation from the "language of experience" of one period into the experiential language of the historian's own period.

After having explored Dilthey's structural conceptions of periods and cultures, and of historical significance, I will now analyze his conceptualization of historical development. In approaching this topic, Dilthey combined his structuralist insights into history's synchronic coherence with the dynamic diachronic perspective of history as a process of life's becoming. The combination of synchronic and diachronic elements led him, as we will see now, to a highly original conception of a typical historical development — a development that is neither determined by timeless laws or fixated patterns that realize themselves independently from their temporal contexts, nor ruled by accidents.

The dilemma confronting historians at the time in explaining historical events was having to choose between two models of historical development: First, the positivist model taken from the natural sciences, second, the idealist model of the humanities. The positivist model explained historical events on the basis of historical laws, or biological patterns. This naturalistic model thus reduced historical developments to closed systems following a predetermined course — systems comparable to the closed systems of organic nature.

The idealist model explained historical events as the outcome of unpredictable spontaneous human actions. This what we might call "accidentalist" model reduced historical developments to series of purely accidental happenings.[11] As we will see now, Dilthey successfully steered a middle course between these positivist naturalistic and idealist accidentalist extremes of developmental models.

Dilthey maintained, with the idealists, that in its development history follows no rules of reason, no logical patterns, no laws; he rather considered history's progression spontaneous and free. An individual is free to stop his mental development early, or to continue to grow till his death: "all theories about a progressive development in stages should be rejected" (GS, vol. VII, 244). But he did not think that history's freedom necessarily resulted in an absence of intelligible developmental patterns, with a totally accidental sequence of events.

Again, in this context, we have to recall the regulative function of the adult's soul-structure, and its formation in the course of an individual's experiences with reality. A young individual's soul-structure is frequently modified as a result of new experiences. But in growing up, the individual becomes increasingly determined by his own emergent soul-structure, which, ultimately, becomes his own personal "law." This means that after a certain point in time, the individual's development acquires a more or less steady direction. This direction does not stem from any inborn character, however. It originally was formed by cumulative experience. Once discernible, however, the soul-structure remains an important factor in the person's further development.

In Dilthey's conception of a society's historical development culture, or a society's make-up, fulfills the same regulative function for collective activities and development as the soul-structure does in individual life. In keeping with his model of the soul-structure's development, he stated that the changes in historical phenomena occur at each moment in the direction of one of a finite set of possibilities. Although the exact direction of a historical entity's development cannot be predicted, its changes constitute not an altogether arbitrary development. Dilthey compared life's developments to movements in musical compositions. At every moment, the possibilities for development are limited, but man is free to choose among these (GS, vol. VII, 221).

One of the most interesting aspects of Dilthey's "structuralism" is the fact that in his approach to history, the category of events occupies an important place. He suggested that historical events should be understood by seeing them as part of a developing diachronic structure. "Historical events become meaningful when seen as part of a structure, for as such they help to realize together with other parts the values and goals of the totality" (GS, vol. VII, 168). Historical phenomena, in other words, should be understood not only as functions of the synchronic structural context, but they should also be seen as moments of diachronical patterns of development.

Dilthey believed that actions of individuals and collectivities should be viewed as articulations of developing cultural patterns – as members of "systems of change" (*Veränderungssysteme*) (GS, vol. VII, 270), as he wrote in connection with revolutions – instead of as discrete entities adding up to form historical sequences.

The structure of a historical phenomenon shapes its future to a certain extent by limiting its possibilities for development. By the same token, it also circumscribes the extent to which past events can influence the situation of the present: the cultural structure of a period "assimilates" previous events (GS, vol. VII, 155). Thus, the cultural structure of a period – like the soul-structure of an individual – not only delineates future developments, but is retrospectively operative as well.

Dilthey's structural view of historical development throws further light on his conception of historical significance; in his opinion, an event is significant because, being experienced as such by the community, it becomes part of the cultural "soul-structure" of the society. Thus it will have an effect on later history.

The analogy between Dilthey's conception of structural change of a soul-structure and a culture explains also why he conceived of historical epochs as structures built around organizing centers rather than as linear sequences: a culture is the cultural "super soul-structure" of a society that guides its activities and determines the direction of its development.

Seen thus, history does not come about as the result of the actions of separate individuals, but as the result of changes in its cultural systems that transcend their actions. History is the continuous development of interlocking cultural structures. With this model, Dilthey avoided both the Scylla of naturalism and the Charybdis of accidentalism.

Dilthey's approach to historical development offers a useful model for the conceptualization of man's limited freedom in shaping the future. According to his model, the phenomenon of man's historical conditionedness – his conditionedness by culture – is fully recognized; the range of choices open to man in any given historical situation is shown to be limited as a result of the structured nature of historical developments. At the same time, the model leaves room for man's creativity, for he is able to use the historical or cultural elements at his disposal in new and unexpected ways.

What distinguishes Dilthey's view of individual and collective historical development from naturalistic thinkers — such as Oswald Spengler, who was equally interested in discovering patterns of historical development — is the fact that Dilthey saw the development of an individual or of a cultural system as a process of interaction between external and internal elements.[12]

Dilthey's approach to historical development has much to offer the contemporary historian. After all, the problem of the seeeming antagonism between process and structure has not yet been satisfactorily resolved in historiography. For instance, Robert A. Nisbet in *Social Change and History*[13] denounces the naturalism of much developmental thinking in history and sociology, but he substitutes a supposedly truly historical method of accounting for change by a meticulous listing of the contingent events involved. Such a method excludes theory and conceptualization in favor of story-telling. For that reason it does not satisy historians who search for a more rigorous method of explanation, even if they agree with Nisbet's argument against the use of naturalistic imagery in history. As Robert F. Berkhofer, Jr., points out in *A Behavioral Approach to Historical Analysis*, structurally oriented historians still do not know how to approach historical change.[14]

In Dilthey's model of historical change, on the other hand, a structural approach is aptly combined with concern for contingent events. Dilthey provides, moreover, a resolution for the dispute between historical objectivists and subjectivists concerning historical knowledge: he makes it clear that the significance of a historical event is neither the historian's subjective evaluation made in hindsight, nor his objective observation; rather historical significance is a function of the cultural system in which the events occurred.

This analysis of these three outstanding features of Dilthey's approach to history brings us next to Dilthey's initial insecurity concerning the question of whether there is, indeed, a total unified history of mankind, or whether mankind's history is in reality merely an amalgam of several world-views or cultures. The latter would lack the coherence he was looking for.

In the *Introduction to the Human Sciences* Dilthey stated that from the point of view of its concrete structure, history is neither a coherent totality nor a collection of discrete events. The history of mankind is composed of cultural systems, that is, of limited historical structures like nations or periods, succeeding each other continuously in time. In order to gain empirical knowledge of universal history — that is, of the structure of the total historical-social world — the historian has to analyze history into its "separate structures" (*Einzelzusammenhänge*) — like cultural systems and societies — for these are easier to survey (GS, vol. I, 110-111).

In the later *Structure of the Historical World in the Human Sciences* Dilthey repeated this point, stating that "although in the concrete course of history no law of development can be found, its analysis into separate structures opens the eye to the succession of stages . . ." (GS, vol. VII, 169). At this point, however, Dilthey came close to suggesting that perhaps there was no universal history:

> The knowledge of the significance and meaning of the historical world is often acquired . . . by observing the total direction of the process of universal history. . . . We have seen that in reality the historical process comes about in separate structures [*einzelnen Wirkungszusammenhänge*] (GS, vol. VII, 172).

By stating that history happens in separate structures, Dilthey had — without realizing it — in this passage taken a major step towards the disintegration of the Enlightenment notion of a developmental universal history, for he had begun to give up the notion that history is a continuous diachronic structure from beginning to end. Indeed, in the absence of any historical laws and any predetermined goal — rationally or religiously interpreted — history tends to become an amalgam of cultures and epochs. In such a history without mechanical laws, and without teleological patterns of development no uniform movement or direction can be distinguished. As far as his realization of history's discontinuity is concerned, Dilthey can be compared to Max Weber, Oswald Spengler, Johan Huizinga, Frederick J. Teggart, and to a more recent writer on history, Michel Foucault.

Weber — who was not only a sociologist, but also a brilliant historian — maintained that the observer creates history's meaning.[15] He called a culture a "finite cut out [*Ausschnitt*] made on the basis of man's interpretation out of the meaningless endlessness of world-happening."[16] Thus, Weber discarded objective universal history, and substituted for it man-created subjective histories. He avoided the word "history" (*Geschichte*), as he felt that that term was too much burdened with metaphysical associations. Instead, he employed terms such as "world-happening" (*Weltgeschehen*) and "innerworldly happening" (*innerweltliches Geschehen*).[17] Spengler saw history as a completely pointless succession of cultures. He saw world-history "as a picture of endless formations and transformations, of the waxing and waning of forms."[18] He ridiculed the professional historian who looks upon history "as a sort of tapeworm industriously adding unto itself one epoch after the other."[19] Instead of seeing Western history as forever progressively tending upward to presently held ideals, he considered it a historical phenomenon of limited duration, and he predicted that soon its end would be reached.[20] Huizinga moved during the years between the two World Wars toward a similar denial of progressive universal history, developing a comparative cultural history. Cultural history as Huizinga saw it had the task of describing the succession of cultural forms, and to show how they belonged to the various periods of history; it refrained from describing their succession and "growth." He no longer conceived of the past as a line, but as a "bunch of flowers," or a "cluster of circles."[21]

In the United States, Teggart pleaded in a series of essays published shortly after World War I to set aside the hypothesis of a continuous history; he urged historians to start collecting all the evidence the historian can lay hands on in order to reconstruct the past truthfully. He denounced historiography as a form of literature that has nothing to do with science. The historian with his narrative creates coherences where none exist. Teggart aimed at dissolving the coherence – and intrinsic meaning – of history.[22]

Today, the philosopher Michel Foucault draws the attention to the discontinuities in processes of historical change. He denounces the view of a continuous history as "a remnant of nineteenth-century metaphysics,"[23] and shows the "intensity of differences" between historical entities at different points of time.[24] The economy the physiocrats discussed, for example, has nothing to do with that discussed by Keynes; no continuous development connects these two conceptualizations of the economic order. In his book *The Order of Things* Foucault gives detailed descriptions of the transition from eighteenth- to nineteenth-century thought in the studies of nature, history, language and economics. At the turn of the century, he sees a sudden switch, a complete rearrangement of the material these disciplines were working with.[25] In his thought, "the theme of becoming" has been replaced by "the analysis of the transformation in their specifics."[26]

As a philosopher, Foucault is as clearly aware of the philosophical implications of this view – in particular of the challenge it poses to the Enlightenment view of man and his history – as Dilthey had been, albeit his thought tends in a direction very different from Dilthey's.[27] After this review of other writers about history who were more struck by its discontinuities than by its continuity, we must return to Dilthey.

In accordance with his view of the aimlessness of nonrational life's movement, Dilthey stated that the life of human history achieves nothing and leads to nothing. The major world-views articulated in the past still contradict each other; history has not decided among them.

The formation of world-views is determined by the will to certainty concerning the world picture, the value of life, the guidance of the will. . . . Religion as well as philosophy strives for certainty, effectiveness, domination, universal validity. But mankind has not progressed one step on this road. The struggle among world-views has at no major point been decided. History causes a selection among them, but their great types stand sovereignly, improvable and indestructible (GS, vol. VIII, 86-87).

In Dilthey's thought, the synchronic and diachronic perspectives on man and his history coexisted, albeit uneasily. The synchronic view, based on the examination of lived experience, expresses his insight into the finiteness of human existence, the insight that man forever lives in history, that he cannot emancipate himself from the conditions which the culture which happens to exist at the time impose upon him. The diachronic view based on reflective thought in hindsight expresses his hope for mankind's liberation from history, his faith in the human mind as the instrument by means of which man gradually has freed himself from his historical conditionedness.

From a twentieth-century point of view, Dilthey's faith in history's melodic structure seems unrealistically optimistic. World War I triggered a shock of great proportions to Western man's self-image. The cruel events of 1914-1918 caused many people to doubt whether the Western world was, indeed, the outcome of a progressive history. Thus, doubts were raised concerning the intellectual preconditions for this view of history: the conceptualization of mind as capable of unending progressive self-transcendence, and the continuity of historical development which makes it possible for "mind" to build upon the achievements of the previous generation. Doubts concerning historical continuity were explicitly formulated in history, philosophy of history, sociology, and anthropology.

Among the historians who questioned history's continuity have already been mentioned Weber, Spengler, Huizinga, and Teggart. Among philosophers, the doubts concerning history's continuity and progress took another form. Michael Oakeshott contended that every image of the past is created by the present, having nothing to do with a past that no longer exists. At both sides of the Atlantic such doubts in historical progress, combined with a subjectivist theory of historical knowledge, were voiced. But in spite of this handful of writers critical of the notion of continuous historical progress, most twentieth-century historiography continued, certainly in the United States, to see history in progressive terms, and to evaluate time positively as the medium in which the human mind could achieve progress.

Indeed, for many contemporary historians, the value of human life and history still lies in man's ability to transcend what is, and to create something new; that is why repetitive behavioral patterns till very recently have been considered to be not the object of history, but of sociology or cultural anthropology. Even the coryphee of the *Annales* School, Fernand Braudel, affirms the historian's traditional concern about time — although, as we will see below, he himself did more than any other historian to undermine the profession's preoccupation with time, movement and development.[28] This feeling that history's characteristic concern is with time is echoed by Leonard Krieger, who, reflecting on the difference between history and the other social sciences, remarks that history's truly distinctive mark is its concern with time and temporal processes. He calls history "the discipline working under the aegis of time."[29]

The history of historians thus has remained till very recently the expression of man's spiritual nature; linear time was the domain in which man realizes his spiritual nature, and displays his true humanity; for if man did not achieve something in history, human life would be in vain, and lack dignity. In historiography, we find the significant break between nineteenth- and twentieth-century historical method or conceptualization much later than in cultural anthropology.

Such long-lasting immunity against cultural self-doubts on the part of history may at first glance seem surprising; it follows logically, however, if the discipline's eighteenth- and nineteenth-century development as sketched above is kept in mind; it was caused, first, by the fact that historians were saddled with the burden of articulating and defending their civilization's identity and the values that supported it. Thus, historians naturally were less inclined to question these same values; thus, they remained committed in particular to the conception of man as the conqueror of time and the creator of history.

The second cause making historians immune against the Western identity crisis was caused by the narrowing of the historian's field of study to the Western world. For this was precisely the area in which history had developed in a dynamic unknown to other parts of the world; therefore historians did not feel the need for another image of man — an image in which man's ability to make history is not the hallmark of human existence and for another conceptualization of time than that of a stream making possible the human mind's progress. Given the specific nature of their area of study, with its rapid historical development, it was logical for historians to focus their attention on the new developments that seemed continually to emerge in Western history.

The idealist school in history – to which until quite recently the majority of the members of the historical profession belongs – thus continued to subscribe to the nineteenth-century Promethean image of man creating his own destiny, while the positivist school continued to adhere to the conception of history as progress resulting from operation of historical laws.[30] Dilthey's suggestion of a historiography which focuses on the analysis of past cultures was not followed.

In turning to anthropology, we observe a significant change in method and outlook early in the twentieth century – one which echoes Dilthey's doubts about history's continuity.

Traditionally, the anthropologist's object of study has been the world's so-called "unhistorical" peoples. Very much like Dilthey and the other historians of the period, the nineteenth-century anthropologists considered the absence of a positive attitude toward history among these peoples, and their seeming inability to "make history," as signs of the low place of primitive peoples in the evolutionary scale.[31]

While in the twentieth century, historians continued, by and large, to study historical developments from past to present, and to conceptualize – in spite of some protests – this development in terms of historical progress, cultural anthropologists by contrast rejected the ethnocentric conception of an evolutionary process of civilizational growth culminating in the Western world; they gave up attempts to rank cultures temporally and normatively.[32] One of the first to reject evolutionary anthropology was Franz Boas, who stressed the need for a detailed study of customs in their relationship to the total culture of a tribe,[33] before one could even begin to think about the comparative derivation of laws governing man's progressive development. During World War I, Bronislaw Malinowski developed his functionalist approach to the culture of the Trobrianders in Melanesian New Guinea. Malinowski lived with the people he described; he outlined their culture from an insider's point of view, sketching how the Trobrianders experienced reality.[34] The twentieth-century anthropological profession followed suit. It de-emphasized the diachronic perspective of history on cultures, and showed, indeed, a marked hostility toward genetic approaches. It considered each culture as unique and valuable in itself. In thus

approaching the so-called primitive cultures, the cultural anthropologists absolved them from their former "sin" of not having
history. They used two strategies to this effect, both of which can
be observed, for instance, in the work of Lévi-Strauss. First, a
counter-ideal of man is developed which de-emphasizes the ability
to make history. In *The Savage Mind*, Lévi-Strauss points out that
some peoples, although highly intelligent, simply do not *want*
history.[35]

The second strategy is to show that human creativity can take
other forms than that of making history: the unhistorical peoples
are described as equally creative, as "spiritual," and as "cultural"
(in the sense of transcending the state of nature) as we are, but as
having expressed their creativity differently. This strategy is employed
by Lévi-Strauss in his 1961 address "Race and History."[36]

Recently, however, a rapprochement between history and cultural
anthropology has been evident in historiography.[37] Uneasiness
concerning the idea of a continuous history having structure and
meaning — of a history, moreover, that for so long had been sketched
as culminating in the Western world — provides a fertile ground for
this trend.[38] The convergence between these disciplines first occurred
in the French *Annales* School, and in recent years has been rapidly
gaining ground in Europe and the United States.[39] This rapprochement between history and cultural anthropology has two facets:
first, a critique of what we may call "historical time" — the historical profession's chronological framework; second, a new interest in
non-Western cultures. The reflection on time in historiography
was started by Braudel in his now classic work *The Mediterranean
and the Mediterranean World in the Age of Philip II* (1949). Here,
Braudel distinguished between two kinds of history, "slow" and
"fast." Slow history (*histoire lente*) deals with man in his relationship to the environment. This is a history of "constant repetition,
ever recurring cycles."[40] Another form of slow history is social
history, "the history of groups, collective destinies and general
trends." Fast history is the traditional "history of events" (*histoire
événementielle*). This history occupies itself with "the emphemera
of history"[41] offering a "spectacular, but often misleading
pageant."[42] Its time is short time (*temps court*), "the most capri-
cious, the most deceptive of times."[43] Braudel considers slow
history mankind's "real" history, not only for its past, but for its
present and future as well.[44] Always and everywhere man is basically limited in his freedom to act. Not man, but the force of slow
history is the decisive factor in the course of history. Thus, Braudel
discards the Promethean image of man that has predominated in

idealist historiography since the Enlightenment. By asserting that until very recently historical progress has not been possible, he also discards the view that timeless historical laws regulate mankind's historical progress. Hardly anything "moves" in history. If there is movement, it is a movement of ups and downs, of repititions and cyclical developments rather than movement in a straight – or even meandering – line.

The historical profession in France and elsewhere has followed Braudel's example in searching for history's underlying deep structures. One of the results of this new emphasis on slow history has been the insight that Western history – except for its latest "incident," the industrial revolution – has been by far less unusual or unique than historians had thought so far. Realizing, moreover, that modern Western civilization cannot claim universality as large areas of the world continue to develop into different directions, the *Annales* School historian has acquired a fresh look upon his own past and that of others who formerly did not belong to his area of study.

André Burgière exposes in a special issue of the *Annales* School's journal, *Annales, Economies, Sociétés, Civilizations,* devoted to structuralism in history, the inadequacy of history's traditional chronological framework. Burgière contends combatively that the traditional framework suggests the existence of a time which operates as a continuous pressure which by means of devolutions or revolutions carries with it all the elements of reality. The historian's temporal frame of reference causes him to talk about other societies in terms which are, in reality, appropriate only for the Western civilization, based as it is upon its own development. But, he asks, rhetorically, can one really "measure the history of the world by means of one particular experience, by means of that accidental, or at least recent, incident [*emballement*] that the industrial revolution presents?"[45] Indeed, the historian's traditional conception of time has "made the process of growth which brought Europe a development of high temperature [and has made] the cumulative time which is its originality, the only time of history." This conception of history, "a true Procrustean bed to which one attempts to adapt the total spectrum of civilizations,"[46] justifies the imperialist attitude of the West vis-à-vis other parts of the world, but it cannot adequately explain this other world.

The trend toward an "anthropologization" of history is furthermore supported by Foucault's approach to history, who as indicated above, emphasizes the discontinuity between past and present ways of thinking and among those of historical periods among themselves.

Thus, the past does not appear less alien than cultures that have never been part of the Western world; they invite, in fact, the same methods of study as those non-Western cultures.

Thus, the realization of the nonexceptional nature of Western history combined with that of history's fundamental discontinuities are together causing the historian to look at the Western past with the eyes of a cultural anthropologist. In studying his nation's or civilization's history, the attention of the *Annales* historian is no longer focused on the events of Western history's unique development, but on such basic phenomena as demography, the environment, economic structures, kinship structures, sexual behavior, the family, magic, and ceremonies. He focuses on repetitive behavior rather than on evolutionary movements.

By the same token, the discovery for historiography of slow history has caused the historian to take a lively interest in the past of those non-Western societies that so far had belonged to the domain of anthropology. The increasing number of articles in the School's journal on non-Western cultures attests to this new cosmopolitan interest. Now the attention of the *Annales* historian is no longer focused on the "creative" actors of history and the great events they produced, the life of non-Western peoples with its slow-moving pace can enter his field of attention again. In his latest book, *Civilization and Material Life 1400-1800* (1967), Braudel, for instance, describes the human condition under the economic *ancien régime* on a world-wide scale.

This remarkable convergence between history with its diachronic perspective and cultural anthropology with its synchronic perspective we witness today indicates that for the first time since the Enlightenment, the peculiar connection between mind and history — a connection which turned the past into the development of mind — is being relinquished in historiography. Today, we are less inclined to see man as the Promethean creator of his own destiny. We feel that it is not man's calling to create history, but to creatively respond to given conditions, to make the best of what he has received in the way of natural and cultural resources. This means that the fast linear time of the industrial revolution that used to be the time of historical "human" achievements no longer represents to us the only dimension of a truly human life. Slow, repetitive, and almost motionless time also offers opportunities for a truly human existence. This unlocking of the fateful connection between mind, time and history such as we witness today in the historiography inspired by the *Annales* School makes possible again a more positive appreciation of the past's experiences: as records of genuine encounters with a varied, and challenging reality. Dilthey's hermeneutic philosophy of world-views offers a philosophical foundation for the efforts of these historians.

CHAPTER NINE

DILTHEY'S IMPORTANCE FOR THE FUTURE STUDY OF HISTORY AND CULTURE

Our exploration of Dilthey's maze has come to an end. We are about to re-enter our habitual spheres of activity. Let us at this point turn to observe its receding contours.

In looking back upon Dilthey's work as a whole, we are struck by its richness in novel ideas. Dilthey's mind was like a garden in which he cultivated side by side all kinds of ideas. This absence of a will strong enough to create order out of chaos gives his thought however, character of a maze.

In response to positivism and historicism, Dilthey developed an approach to the human world in which hermeneutic text interpretation functions as the paradigm of understanding the human world's phenomena. In this approach human behavior and cultural products are seen as autonomous sources of meaning; the process by which the student interprets their meaning has the character of a dialogue — a communicative interaction between interpreter and interpreted. Such an approach to the study of the human world is as sorely needed today in the sciences of man — history, psychology, psychiatry, sociology, cultural anthropology — as it was in Dilthey's time. Scientism and objectivism still reign in many quarters of these disciplines.

Dilthey developed moreover a conception of man which recognizes the importance of mind. With his model of man as a natural organism with limited freedom to transcend its immediate natural and cultural environment, Dilthey accounted for human existence's profound historicity: the model takes into consideration both man's conditioning by the natural and cultural environment into which he is born and his capacity to respond creatively to these circumstances on the basis of his ability to interpret in novel ways the meaning these givens have for him. However, his model of man made him see man as reality's interpreter, and philosophy as reality's interpretation.

Dilthey's philosophy of world-views elaborates the perspective of lived experience on human life. It extends the hermeneutic conception of human behavior and cultural products as texts to reality itself; it sees reality as an autonomous source of meaning — as a literary text to be interpreted. This conception of reality explains why each period and each culture have experienced and interpreted it so differently.

By being interpretations of reality, concrete life styles and cultures become in themselves comparable to works of art. They are, in effect, comparable to literary texts written in a "language" of behavior, monuments, institutions; they are comparable to works of art disclosing meanings of reality. Recording encounters with autonomous reality, these interpretations have intrinsic value.

Dilthey's hermeneutic philosophy of world-views provides the student of history and culture with a distinctive and useful theoretical framework. It offers him an opportunity for an existential encounter with actors and products of the past and the present, instead of seeing their thoughts and actions invalidated because they are determined by an age and culture that is not their own.

It understands time in analogy to space — as an open area in which man lives his interpretations of reality. By living in time, man is offered the opportunity to actualize — separately and together — meanings of reality. Instead of seeing man as a being whose dignity lies in his ability to develop, to progress, and to make history, this conception leads to a view of man whose dignity lies in having a relationship to reality, and of time as the space in which successions of generations can relate to reality.

On the basis of this conception, reality would seem to continue to generate new ways of being interpreted, and to reveal itself in different forms, in an interaction with the manifold experiences man has. The endlessness of history no longer dooms man to a hopeless search for an elusive truth, but it is a generous invitation to be receptive to reality's new self-disclosures. Philosophy — the art of interpreting reality — appears as a never-ending, exciting encounter with reality. History appears as the scene for man's ongoing playful encounters with reality. Indeed, human existence appears as a never-ending dance, with reality as man's partner.

According to Dilthey's hermeneutic perspective, it is the task of the student of history and culture to interpret the expressions of alien life experience, and — as a true Hermes-figure — to translate them into some idiom which contemporary readers raised in their own cultural environment can understand; thus is set in motion a dialogue between alien and familiar cultures. The goal of such translation is not to forge a universal language which obliterates differences, but to understand other languages, and also to gain the ability to move within these languages. In Dilthey's hermeneutic philosophy of world-views, historicism's positive aspect — its appreciation of alien cultures — is preserved, while its pitfalls — historical relativism and the idolatry of history — are largely avoided.

In his conception of individual psychological and collective historical development Dilthey combined synchronic and dia-chronic perspectives. He saw these developments as the emergence of respectively, mental and cultural structures. The forms of these structures are initially weak; they are almost completely open to their environment; gradually they acquire their specific forms; then they play an increasingly important role in determining their own future. With this model of structured, but nevertheless open personal and historical development, Dilthey shows how the elements of necessity and freedom that characterize human existence are combined in human life and history.

Alongside hermeneutic conceptions, Dilthey's thought also con-tains important elements of Enlightenment philosophy. In his philosophy of history in particular, he elaborated the diachronic Enlightenment perspective on human life. He saw history as life's progressive self-creation in which composer and musical composition together form one creative process. Dilthey interpreted its meaning in Enlightenment fashion as man's progress in mastery over himself and his natural and cultural environment.

In Dilthey's thought, the synchronic perspective on the human past as articulated in his philosophy of world-views is subordinated to the diachronic perspective on man and his history. This sub-ordination represents an important residue of the Enlightenment heritage in his thought. His philosophy of history lags behind his philosophy of world-views.

Thus, Dilthey's reflections on history and culture represent a baffling mixture of elements pointing to past and future. His view of history as a progress of the human mind seems today hopelessly *passé*; his hermeneutic approach to human behavior and cultural products, on the other hand, are a source of inspiration to many contemporary philosophers and social scientists.

Since the early twentieth century, this Enlightenment perspec-tive on human life has been de-emphasized in cultural anthropology; it continued to dominate in history until very recently. In contem-porary historiography, however, we witness a development toward a conception of the human past in which the diachronic perspective is de-emphasized.

Perhaps these wanderings through the winding alleys of Dilthey's maze will support history's development in this direction.

NOTES

CHAPTER TWO

1. Wilhelm Dilthey, "Versuch einer Analyse des Moralischen Bewuszt-seins," *Gesammelte Schriften*. Stuttgart: B. G. Teubner Verlagsgesellschaft; Göttingen: Vandenhoeck und Ruprecht, 1958 — present. 18 vols. Vol. VI, 1-26.

2. *Neue Deutsche Biographie*, ed. Historischen Kommission bei der Baveri-schen Akademie der Wissenschaften. Berlin: Dunker und Humblot, 1957, III, 723-726.

3. Leonard Krieger, *The German Idea of Freedom. History of a Political Tradition*. Chicago and London: The University of Chicago Press, 1957, p. 405.

4. Fritz Karl Ringer, *The Decline of the German Mandarins. The German Academic Community 1890-1933*. Cambridge, Mass.: Harvard University Press, 1969, pp. 7-52.

5. Ibid., p. 127.

6. See Hans-Joachim Lieber, "Geschichte und Gesellschaft im Denken Diltheys," in *Kölner Zeitschrift für Soziologie und Sozialpsychologie*, XVII (1965), 703-742.

7. Dilthey is of course referring to the main representatives of "classical" German literature: G.W. Goethe and F. Schiller.

8. Dilthey is referring to Goethe's and Schiller's *Zahme Xenien* (1796), short two-lined epigrammatical poems critical of writers outside the "classical" circle.

9. *Hermann und Dorothea* (1797) is one of Goethe's conservative reactions to the French Revolution depicting the wholesomeness of rural existence.

10. *Die Braut von Messina* (1903) is part of the German escape-literature. It is a serene idealistic tragedy consciously constructed in the tradition of clas-sical Greek drama.

11. *Der junge Dilthey. Ein Lebensbild in Briefen und Tagebüchern*. Zusam-mengestellt von Clara Misch geb. Dilthey. Stuttgart: B.G. Teubner; Göttingen: Vandenhoeck und Ruprecht, 1960, p. 237.

12. Ibid., p. 291.

13. Wilhelm Dilthey, *Briefwechsel zwischen Wilhelm Dilthey und dem Grafen Paul Yorck von Wartenburg*, 1877-1897. Halle (Saale): Verlag Max Niemeyer, 1923, p. 20.

14. H. Stuart Hughes, *Consciousness and Society: The Reorientation of European Social Thought, 1890-1930*. New York: Vintage Books, 1958, pp. 33-67, describes the decade of the 1890s as a time of revolt against positivism. On Dilthey's role, see ibid., pp. 192-200.

15. Frank Miller Turner, *Between Science and Religion. The Reaction to Scientific Naturalism in Late Victorian England*. New Haven: Yale University Press, 1974. See for the development of psychology in Germany, chapter III.

16. John Hermann Randall, Jr., *The Career of Philosophy. From the Enlightenment to the Age of Darwin.* New York and London: Columbia University Press, 1970, p. 3.

17. This approach is taken by George Lukács, *Die Zerstörung der Vernunft. Irrationalismus und Imperialismus.* Darmstadt und Neuwied: Hermann Luchterhand Verlag, 1973, pp. 100-123; and by Christopher Zöckler, *Dilthey und die Hermeneutik. Dilthey's Begründung der Hermeneutik als "Praxiswissenschaft" und die Geschichte ihrer Rezeption.*

18. See, for example, for a denial of the often cited connection between historicism and conservatism Pietro Rossi, "The Ideological Valences of Twentieth Century Historicism," *History and Theory. Studies in the Philosophy of History*, vol. XIV (1975), Beiheft 14, *Essays on Historicism*, pp. 15-30.

19. I may refer in this context to the work of the Frankfurt School. Scholars such as Herbert Marcuse and Jürgen Habermas work at a synthesis of the approaches of Marx and Freud.

20. *Briefwechsel*, p. 3.

21. Ibid., p. 8.

22. Ibid., p. 14.

23. Ibid., pp. 76, 77.

24. Ibid., p. 14.

25. Ibid.

26. As Maurice Mandelbaum has stated, historicism broadly defined is "the belief that an adequate understanding of the nature of any phenomenon and an adequate assessment of its value are to be gained through considering in terms of the place which it occupied and the role which it played within a process of development." Maurice Mandelbaum, *History, Man and Reason. A Study in Nineteenth Century Thought.* Baltimore and London: The Johns Hopkins Press, 1974, p. 42. See also: Dwight E. Lee and Robert N. Beck, "The Meaning of Historicism," *American Historical Review*, 59 (1954), 568-577; Calvin G. Rand, "Two Meanings of Historicism in the Writings of Dilthey, Troeltsch, and Meinecke," *Journal of the History of Ideas*, XXV (1964); Rolf Gruner, "Historicism: Its Rise and Decline," *Clio. An Interdisciplinary Journal of Literature, History and the Philosophy of History*, 8 (1978), 25-39. In this sense, Karl Marx and Leopold von Ranke were both historicists. In contrast to the above definition of historicism, however, nomological historians like Marx are commonly not considered historicists in the proper sense of the word. The historicists proper are the idealist historians who defend the uniqueness of historical phenomena and deny the existence of historical laws. The term historicist was coined in the late nineteenth century to designate historians who fell prey to moral scepticism and the idolatry of history. On the many difinitions of historicism, see Maurice Mandelbaum, "Historicism," *Encyclopedia of Philosophy*, IV (1972), 22-25. An historical survey of historicism is given by Carlo Antoni, *l'Historicisme*. Traduit de l'italien par Alain Dufour. Genève: Librairie Droz, 1963. German historicism is described by Georg G. Iggers, *The German Conception of History. The National Tradition of Historical Thought from Herder to the Present*. Middletown, Conn.: Wesleyan University Press, 1968.

27. Hans Meyerhoff, ed., *The Philosophy of History in Our Time: An Anthology.* Selected and with an Introduction and Commentary by Hans Meyerhoff. Garden City, N.Y.: Doubleday and Company, 1959, p. 27.

28. In his book *Natural Right and History*, Chicago: University of Chicago Press, 1953, pp. 6-8, Leo Strauss warns against the dangers of historicism: he argues that it leads inevitably to a loss of values, causing people to be uncritical toward the events of their time. The belief in natural law, on the other hand,

provides a critical standard by which to evaluate the present. Often people have felt so threatened by historicism's negative aspects — its seemingly unavoidable descent into moral scepticism, and into an uncritical acceptance of the existing world — that they have felt forced to deny the historicity of human life, and to reconstruct eternal principles and laws, such as a "law of nature," which would provide a standard by which to live and evaluate human life in past and present. But Strauss is forced to acknowledge that in our age the assertion of the actual existence of natural laws is gratuitous: natural law made sense in the teleologically ordered finite world of the Ancients. In the world as modern science has discovered it to be, it does not. The dangers of historicism are real, but I agree with Strauss that to return from fear only to an untenable concept of a hidden transcendental static reality makes no sense.

29. *Der junge Dilthey*, p. 80. For the genesis of Dilthey's thought, see also Christofer Zöckler, op. cit., pp. 19-53, and Helmut Johach, *Handlender Mensch und objecktiver Geist. Zur Theorie der Geisteswissenschaften bei Wilhelm Dilthey*. Meisenheim am Glan: Verlag Anton Hain, 1974, pp. 10-42. Johach, ibid., p. 4, is not correct in stating that especially in his later years Dilthey was aware of living in a time of crisis. From the very beginning of his philosophizing the collapse of the traditional belief-systems and the resulting uncertainty about the proper conduct of life provided the impulse to his thought.

30. Ibid., p. 81. Dilthey's rejection of philosophy in favor of history is a major example of the more general process in which history in the nineteenth century ousted philosophy as the queen of sciences. See Andrew Lees, *Revolution and Reflection. Intellectual Change in Germany during the 50's*. The Hague: Martinus Nijhoff, 1974, p. 33.

31. *Der junge Dilthey*, p. 80.

32. Ibid., p. 93.

33. Ibid., pp. 93, 94.

34. Ibid., p. 120.

35. Ibid., p. 140.

36. Ibid.

37. Ibid. and p. 142.

38. Ibid., p. 146. Dilthey may have been influenced by Schleiermacher in this regard. In his 1799 book *On Religion: Speeches to its Cultural Despisers* (translated by John Oman. New York: Harper and Brothers, 1958, p. 213), Schleiermacher wrote that "multiplicity is necessary for the complete manifestation of religion; and that religion is "an endlessly progressive work of the Spirit that reveals Himself in all human history" (p. 214). Religion as a whole can be present only "when all different views of every relation [to God] are actually given," which is not possible except "in an endless number of different forms" (p. 218). Each person understands his relation to God in a different way (p. 217), and a religion arises by a selection of "some one of the great relations of mankind in the world to the Highest Being," and by making it "religion's center, and by referring all the other [relations] to it" (p. 223). The form of a religion thus "depends entirely on what relation develops in a person as fundamental feeling and middlepoint of all religions" (p. 224). The nature and variety of religious truths are partial disclosures of religion (p. 229).

In Schleiermacher, Dilthey found also the transfer of God away from Heaven and into the soul of the individual, which made it possible for him to make the human mind the focus of his interest. Schleiermacher wrote that he often wondered "whether you would not be led to religion simply by giving heed to the . . . way in which the Deity builds up, from all that has otherwise been developed in man, that part of the soul in which He specially swells, manifests His immediate operation, and mirrors himself, and thus makes his sanctuary . . . (ibid.).

39. *Der junge Dilthey*, p. 120.

40. Ibid., p. 141.

41. See, for instance, GS, vol. V, 152. On Dilthey's faith in science, see Hans-Georg Gadamer, *Wahrheit und Methode. Grundzüge einer Philosophischen Hermeneutik*. Tübingen: J.C.B. Mohr (Paul Siebeck), 1972, pp. 224-226.

42. *Der junge Dilthey*, pp. 243, 283.

43. In 1971, Wilhelm von Humboldt had stated likewise that lifeless physical nature only could be explained in terms of uniform principles and laws; by contrast, the phenomena of living nature required an intuitive experiencing of their "idea," or essence. Georg G. Iggers, *The German Conception of History*, p. 51.

44. The controversy concerning the proper method of understanding the world of man, in particular history, has been revived by William Dray, *Laws and Explanation in History*. London: Oxford University Press, 1957. His book is a reaction against Carl G. Hempel, "The Function of General Laws in History," first published in 1942, reprinted in *Theories of History*, ed. Patrick Gardiner. New York: The Free Press; London: Collier-McMillan, 1969, pp. 344-356.

45. Dilthey was the first to use the term in the plural. While Hegelians had used the term *Geistwissenschaft* − by which they referred to the science or philosophy of Mind − Johann Gustav Droysen had used the term *Geisteswissenschaften*, but only casually; he preferred the expression *Wissenschaft der Geschichte*. Rudolf A. Makkreel, *Dilthey. Philosopher of the Human Studies*. Princeton: Princeton University Press, 1975, p. 36. With the plural, *Geisteswissenschaften*, Dilthey expressed his abandonment of the hope that one science could embrace all of human life, and thus the traditional aspiration of the metaphysicians to establish an absolute philosophical or scientific system. With the translation of *Geisteswissenschaften* by *human sciences*, the positivistic − in the sense of empiricist − intentions behind Dilthey's conception of the *Geisteswissenschaften* are acknowledged; I prefer therefore this translation over the common English translation *human studies*.

46. Because Dilthey's source material came from Western civilization, he did not occupy himself with the material available on "primitive" cultures. Dilthey made only fleeting references to non-Western civilization, although in an 1868 review of Adolf Bastian's book *The Anthropologist and Ethnologist as Traveller*, he acknowledged that history, ethnology and anthropology present much material for a philosophy which conceives of itself as the empirical study of human life (GS, vol. XI, 207).

47. H. Holborn, "Wilhelm Dilthey and the Critique of Historical Reason," in *Journal of the History of Ideas*, XI (1950), 97.

48. Immanuel Kant, *On History*. Indianapolis and New York: The Bobbs-Merrill Company, 1963, p. 12.

49. Hellmut Diwald does not see the persistent positivist tendencies of Dilthey's thought. He stresses Dilthey's relativistic position, in particular in regard to historical knowledge (Hellmut Diwald, *Wilhelm Dilthey. Erkenntnistheorie und Philosophie der Geschichte*. Göttingen, Berlin, Frankfurt: Musterschmidt, 1963, p. 108). Better in this respect is Jürgen Habermas, *Knowledge and Human Interests*, translated by Jeremy J. Shapiro. Boston: Beacon Press, 1968, pp. 179-181.

50. Pierre Bayle, *Historical and Critical Dictionary. Selections*, translated by Richard H. Popkin. Indianapolis and New York: The Bobbs-Merrill Company, 1965, p. xxiv.

51. However, the similarity of Dilthey's enterprise to that of Hume's may be judged from a passage of the *Treatise on Human Nature* (1729-1740): "We must therefore glean up our experiments in this science from a cautious observation of human life, and take them as they appear in the common course of the world, by men's behavior in company, in affairs, and in their pleasures. Where experiments of this kind are judiciously collected and compared, we may hope to establish on them a science which will not be inferior in certainty and will be much superior in utility to any other of human comprehension." Quoted in Norton and Popkin, eds., *David Hume: Philosophical Historian*. Indianapolis, New York, Kansas City: The Bobbs-Merrill Company, 1965, p. xxxviii.

52. Georg G. Iggers, *The German Conception of History*, pp. 124-174.

53. He was, however, much encouraged by the publication of Edmund Husserl's *Logical Investigations* (1900-1901), for he perceived in Husserl's phenomenological method a congenial attempt to protect philosophy as a scientific enterprise vis-à-vis psychologism and positivism. See below, chapter V.

54. After Dilthey's death, his works, including some hitherto unpublished essays, were published together in the eighteen volumes of the *Collected Writings* (Gesammelte Schriften), which is still in progress. A bibliography of his works and of the secondary literature about the various aspects of Dilthey's thought is provided by Ulrich Hermann, *Bibliographie Wilhelm Dilthey. Quellen und Literatur*. Weinheim, Berlin and Basel: Verlag Julius Belz, 1968.

CHAPTER THREE

1. In his novel *Nausea*, Jean-Paul Sartre made the same point: one can only know a sequence of events to be an "adventure" after it is over. Jean-Paul Sartre, *Nausea*. Translated by Lloyd Alexander. Introduction by Hayden Carruth. New York: New Directions Publishing Corporation, 1964, pp. 39-40.

2. I prefer. with Walter Kaufmann. the translation *Overman* for the German *Übermensch*. See Walter Kaufmann, *Thus Spoke Zarathustra*. Translated with a preface by Walter Kaufmann. New York: The Viking Press, 1968, p. 12 and passim.

3. These concepts will be more fully explicated in chapter VIII.

4. This point has forcefully been made by Carl Becker in his essay "Everyman His Own Historian," in *Everyman His Own Historian. Essays on History and Politics*. Chicago: Quadrangle Books, 1966, pp. 233-256.

5. See for the pronineteenth century tradition of historiography: Günther Pflug, "The Development of Historical Method in the Eighteenth Century," in *History and Theory. Studies in the Philosophy of History, Beiheft 11, Enlightenment Historiography: Three German Studies*, 1971, pp. 1-23.

6. See Frances Yates, *The Art of Memory*. Chicago: University of Chicago Press, 1966. Reinhold Niebuhr, *Faith and History: A Comparison of Christian and Modern Views of History*. New York: Charles Scribner's Sons, 1949, p. 18, states that neither mysticism nor classical rationalism were interested in memory.

7. Lord Bolingbroke, *Historical Writings*, ed. with an introduction by Isaac Kramnick. Chicago and London: University of Chicago Press, 1972, p. 71.

8. Ibid., p. 72.

9. Ibid., pp. 81-82.

10. Johann Gottfried von Herder, *Reflections on the Philosophy of Mankind*. Abridged and with an introduction by Frank E. Manuel. Chicago and London: The University of Chicago Press, 1968, p. 5.

11. Ibid., p. 164.

12. Ibid., p. 86.

13. Ibid., pp. 217-218.

14. Georg Wilhelm Friedrich Hegel, *The Phenomenology of Mind*. Translated with an introduction and notes by J.B. Baillie. New York and Evanston: Harper and Row, Publishers, 1967, p. 221.

15. Ibid., p. 22.

16. This feeling was first formulated around 1700 in connection with the modern literature of Charles Perrault in the famous "Quarrel of the Ancients." Soon the view that eighteenth-century man was achieving more than the Ancients spread from literature to scientific thought. On the genesis of the idea of progress, see John Bagnell Bury, *The Idea of Progress; an Inquiry into its Origin and Growth*. London: MacMillan and Co., 1921; Sidney Pollard, *The Idea of Progress: History and Society*. Middlesex, England: Penguin Books, 1971; Paul Hazard, *La Crise de la Conscience Européenne (1680-1735)*, 3 vols. Paris: Boivin et Cie, 1935.

17. Turgot, *Oeuvres et Documents le Concernant*, ed. G. Schelle. Paris, 1913, pp. 214-215.

18. Bolingbroke, op. cit., pp. 81-82.

19. Ibid., p. 83.

20. *The Works of Voltaire*, 22 vols., eds. Smolell and Fleming. New York, 1901, XIX, 269.

21. Sergio Moravia, *Beobachtende Vernunft. Philosophie und Anthropologie in der Aufklärung*. München: Carl Hanser Verlag, 1973.

22. Hegel on "old" peoples, *The Philosophy of History*. New York: Dover Publications, 1956, pp. 74-75; on non-Western peoples, ibid., pp. 61, 63, 105, 112-172.

23. Ibid., p. 73.

24. Ibid., p. 63.

25. Hans Meyerhoff, *Time in Literature*. Berkeley and Los Angeles: University of California Press, 1955, p. 95. See on the connection between history and time in the nineteenth century, Heinz Angermeier, *Geschichte oder Gegenwart. Reflektionen über das Verhältnis von Zeit und Geist*. München: Verlag C. H. Becker, 1974.

26. Hegel, *The Philosophy of History*, p. 77.

27. Ibid.

28. In a similar fashion, Søren Kierkegaard in his book *Stages on Life's Way* distinguishes memory as remembrance of inessential matters external to the personality — in our terminology "outer" memory — from recollection which is reflection on the subject's essential life experiences. (Søren Kierkegaard, *Stages on Life's Way. Studies by Sundry Persons*. Translated by Walter Lowrie, D.D. Princeton: Princeton University Press, 1945, p. 29.) Recollection is difficult, whereas "the labor of a memory is light" (ibid., p. 32).

29. Hegel describes mind in its final stage as a "self-comprehending totality" to which the totality of its past is present (op. cit., p. 78). About India which he sees as not having emancipated itself from nature and therefore as unable to make history, he writes: "Where that iron bondage of distinctions derived from nature [the social castes] prevails, the connection of society is nothing but wild arbitrariness — transcient activity — or rather the play of violent

emotions without any goal of advancement or development. Therefore no intelligent reminiscence, no object for Mnemosuny presents itself . . ." (*The Philosophy of History*, p. 62).

30. Nietzsche, *Thus Spoke Zarathustra*, p. 86.

31. Ibid., p. 39.

32. Ilse N. Bulhof, *Apollos Wiederkehr. Eine Untersuchung der Rolle des Kreises in Nietzsches Denken über Geschichte und Zeit*. The Hague: Martinus Nijhoff, 1969, pp. 146-148.

33. F.W. Nietzsche, *On the Genealogy of Morals*, translated by Walter Kaufmann and R. J. Hollingdale. New York: Random House, 1969.

34. Ibid., p. 48.

35. Ibid.

36. Ibid., p. 59. Nietzsche does neither slight nor condemn knowledge of the past; he rejects only historical knowledge that does not "feed" the present for the sake of the future. Alien, useless, and troublesome elements of the past should be forgotten; but what belongs to the true self has to be remembered. See Bulhof, *Apollos Wiederkehr*, passim.

37. Meyerhoff, *Time in Literature*, pp. 26-54.

38. Michael Foucault, *The Order of Things. An Archeology of the Human Sciences*. New York: Vintage Books, 1970, pp. 78-166.

CHAPTER FOUR

1. Georg Misch (1923 Preface to GS, vol. V, ix) and Bernard Groethuysen (1926 Preface to GS, vol. VII, viii) see a change in Dilthey's thought from a psychological to a hermeneutic orientation during the years 1905-1911. More recently, commentators have emphasized the continuity in Dilthey's thought. See Makkreel, op. cit., p. 295, and Johach, op. cit., p. 130. Before Dilthey, Johann Gustav Droysen had also looked upon the historical world as a field of expressions requiring interpretation. But in his interpretation method he was closer to the philological than to the theological hermeneutical method. As Gadamer puts it, "Das historische Verstehen erweist sich als eine Art Philologie im Groszen." Op. cit., p. 322.

2. For the history of philological text interpretation, see Joachim Wach. *Das Verstehen, Grundzüge einer Geschichte der Hermeneutischen Theorie* im 19. *Jahrhundert*, I-III. Hildesheim: Georg Olms Verlagsbuchhandlung, 1966. Gadamer, op. cit., pp. 318-322. Benjamin W. Dwight, *Modern Philology: Its Discoveries, History, and Influence*. New York: Charles Scribner, 1864.

3. Familiarity with hermeneutic principles is still greatest in theological, in particular Protestant, circles. The word hermeneutics is, for instance, listed neither in *The Encyclopedia of Philosophy*, ed. Paul Edwards. London: Collier MacMillan Publishers, 1967, nor in *Philosophical Dictionary*, Walter Brugger, editor of the original German edition, Kenneth Baker, translator and editor of the American edition. Spokane, Wash.: Gonzaga University Press, 1972. Theological hermeneutics received a new impulse from Karl Barth's resumption of the ancient approach to the Bible as a source of revelation rather than as an object of critical historical investigation. The hermeneutic movement Barth inspired is known as the "New Hermeneutic." (See James M. Robinson, op. cit., pp. 1-147.)

During the nineteenth century, hermeneutics became also influential in literary studies. During the twentieth century it became important in philosophical studies as well. Martin Heidegger made hermeneutics the focal point of philosophy as a whole, by seeing philosophy as the interpretation of Being. Hans-Georg Gadamer and Paul Ricoeur are the most authoritative representatives of philosophical hermeneutics today. The theologian Schleiermacher applied the principles of the art of understanding the Bible to the interpretation of the literary and philosophical texts of classical antiquity. Schleiermacher represents a first step in the transition from the theological to a nontheological hermeneutics.

4. For the history of the type of hermeutics used in theology see Richard E. Palmer, *Hermeneutics. Interpretation Theory in Schleiermacher, Heidegger and Gadamer.* Evanston: Northwestern University Press, 1969, pp. 12-32; Klaus Weimann, *Historische Einleitung zur Literaturwissenschaftlichen Hermeneutik.* Tubingen: J.C.B. Mohr (Paul Siebeck), 1975; James M. Robinson, "The New Hermeneutic," in *The New Hermeneutic,* ed. James M. Robinson and John D. Cobb, Jr. New York, Evanston and London: Harper and Row, Publishers, 1974. Joachim Wach, op. cit.; Gadamer, op. cit., pp. 162-185. See also Dilthey, GS, vol. II, 110-129, 322.

5. Wach, op. cit., p. 167.

6. Palmer, op. cit., p. 14.

7. It is in this context highly significant that in his lengthy historical survey of philology from the earliest times till 1860, when he was writing, Benjamin W. Dwight mentions only in passing that the philologist "has the high office of interpreting the voice of God, in the Holy Scriptures, to the world, so it is his grand function to interpret man to himself, and to unroll at his feet the scroll of the past as it actually has been rolled up together in the gradual development of human life and action" (Benjamin W. Dwight, op. cit., pp. 171-172).

8. For a further explication of the forms of elementary and higher understanding, see chapter VIII.

9. Dilthey referred to the example of a judicial system as it exists at a certain time and place to refute the interpretation of his thought as psychologistic: "the understanding of mind (*Geist*) is not psychological knowledge. It is a going at (*Rückgang auf*) a mental form that has its own particular structure and laws" (GS, vol. VII, 85). He pointed out that the historian has to go "behind" the evidence's visible attributes (lawbooks, judges, processes) and to proceed to their origin, the collective will — the "force of the community" that shapes these outer forms.

Dilthey added that other authors besides himself have referred to this "force" as "spirit" (*Geist*), for instance, in referring to the "spirit" of Roman law. Dilthey did not specify what he meant be expressions such as "the life of the spirit," or "the spirit of the time." The word that approximates best Dilthey's notion of "spirit" is "culture"; *geistiges Leben* or the *Geist der Zeit* mean "cultural life" or the "culture of a period." See also below, chapter VIII.

10. Jürgen Habermas, *Knowledge and Human Interests.* Boston: Beacon Press, 1971, p. 176.

11. *Der junge Dilthey*, p. 152.

12. This aspect of Dilthey's approach to the past has been further elaborated by Hans-Georg Gadamer, who calls upon the historian to listen to the voices of the past, and to allow themselves to be told something by them (Hans-Georg Gadamer, op. cit., pp. 342-344).

13. This will be more fully explained in the next chapter.

14. René Wellek points out that the term was first used by Kant, *A History of Modern Criticism: 1750-1950. The Later Nineteenth Century.* New Haven and London: Yale University Press, 1965, p. 332.

15. Barthold Georg Niebuhr (1776-1831), author of the famous *Roman History*, knew political life from his experience as a statesman in the service of the King of Denmark, and as a financial expert and an ambassador serving the Prussian monarchy.

16. I will come back to this point in chapter VIII.

17. H. Diwald, op. cit., overlooks this aspect of Dilthey's theory of historical knowledge; he only states that Dilthey stressed the movement of history.

18. David E. Linge makes the same point in a different way: he states that for Dilthey "historical understanding occurs only insofar as the knower breaks the immediate and formative influence of history upon him and stands purged of all prejudices" (David E. Linge, "Dilthey and Gadamer. Two theories of Historical Understanding," in *American Academy of Religion*, XLI (1973), 546). The historian has to be alienated from the past in order to know it (ibid., p. 544). Other statements corroborate the inferences that Dilthey viewed the past as an object existing independently from the observer. He underlined, for instance, the solid objectlike nature of the past by stating that "in observing the past we ourselves behave passively; [the past] is the unalterable — man, conditioned by it, tries in vain to change it in his dreams" (GS, vol. 193).

Dilthey wrote that, because the future has not yet materialized, man can behave actively. It still offers endless possibilities for shaping it (GS, vol. VII, 193). The movement of time is the process in which future potentialities are made concrete in present, and subsequently, past reality. He assumed that llfe is immutably fixed after it has become this present, congealed, as it were, forever after. Life is thus literally a process of solidification out of fluid future life.

19. On truth in literature, see Meyerhoff, *Time in Literature*, pp. 121-136; Gadamer, op. cit., pp. 77-157.

20. Dilthey's hermeneutic view of art moves art into the vicinity of philosophy — if philosophy is understood as an attempt to understand reality. During the same period, philosophy and some of the sciences studying man, such as psychiatry and psychology, moved into the vicinity of art, in particular to literary art. This can be seen in existentialist philosophers such as Nietzsche, Karl Jaspers, Gabriel Marcel, Albert Camus and Jean-Paul Sartre, and in scientists such as Freud, Jaspers, Helmuth Plessner, F.J.J. Buytendijk and Michael Polyani. During the same time, the gap between theology and philosophy was somewhat narrowed in the philosophy of Heidegger.

21. Dilthey's conception of art is similar to that presented by Hans Meyerhoff in *Time in Literature*, pp. 121-136.

22. It would seem that Dilthey's personal experience of works of art and philosophy — that is the experience of their lasting challenge to be responded to — gave Dilthey an idea of historical evidence in general as somehow revealing truth — just as the experience of art opened Gadamer's eyes for the lasting truth value of the products of the past.

23. Dilthey's conception of historical knowledge reminds one of Nietzsche's in the latter's *Use and Abuse of History*. For Nietzsche, the "real value of history lies in inventing ingenious variations on a probably commonplace theme, in raising a popular melody to a universal symbol and showing what a world of depth, power and beauty exists in it" (F.W. Nietzsche, *The Use and Abuse of History*. Translated by Adrian Collins with an introduction by Julius Kraft. Indianapolis and New York: The Bobbs-Merrill Company, 1957, p. 39). Nietzsche commented that for the writing of history "a great artistic faculty, a

creative vision from a height, the loving study of the data of experience, the free elaborating upon a given type" is necessary (ibid.). For the historian, an attitude of "cold detachment" is not required – a detachment that merely copies the past, but an attitude of truthfulness that does "justice" to it (ibid., pp. 34-40, 53) by truthfully separating the essential from the inessential. Nietzsche added that history is therefore written "by the man of experience and character" – the person to whom life has disclosed itself in its depths, and who is consequently able to see the depths in other lives.

24. The categories developed by Dilthey for the study of life will be further explicated in chapter VIII.

25. The constructivist position is analyzed by Jack W. Meiland, *Skepticism and Historical Knowledge*. New York: Random House, 1965.

26. In order to further clarify Dilthey's view of hermeneutic historical understanding it might be useful to compare it with the theory of historical knowledge formulated by Robin George Collingwood. Collingwood's interest in the philosophy of history started with his realization of the difficulties in translating the philosophical texts of classical antiquity. The classical writers, he realized, did not talk in a different language about the same things as we do – such as motion and energy – they talk about altogether different things. Most of his colleagues, he felt, were not even aware of the fact that their own vocabulary was highly historical (Robin George Collingwood, *An Autobiography*. London: Oxford University Press, 1951, p. 650). In order to understand the meaning of the text written in the past, Collingwood in his well-known book *The Idea of History* advocated like Dilthey a theory of understanding history by re-experiencing. But Collingwood's interest in history is much narrower than Dilthey's: he conceived of the past and its events as the conscious products of past individuals (R.G. Collingwood, *The Idea of History*. London, Oxford, New York: Oxford University Press, 1968, p. 213). By contrast, Dilthey occupied himself extensively with collectivities and social and cultural structures. Collingwood maintained that the course of history can be best understood by focusing on the motivations of past actors: "historical knowledge is the knowledge of what mind has done in the past, and at the same time it is the redoing of this, the perpetuating of past actors in the present" (ibid., p. 218). Thus, Collingwood called historical knowledge "the reenactment of past thought in the historian's own mind" (ibid., p. 215). Collingwood stressed that only rational thoughts can be reenacted and hence known by the historian. Emotional experiences such as the feeling of triumph of Archimedes or the bitterness of Marius cannot be recaptured as they were experienced at the time; only rational thought is "not wholly entangled in the flow of experience" (ibid., p. 296). Seen from Collingwood's perspective, historical knowledge is limited to the rational understanding by the historian of acts that are conceived of as conscious and rational responses to situations on the part of actors. Dilthey, on the other hand, stressed, first, that historical knowledge, as all knowledge, is a matter of the whole person of the knower, and not only of his reason; second, that historical knowledge is not confined to knowing rational thoughts of past actors, but is oriented toward the totality of past human experience; and third, that historical actors are not totally conscious of what they intend and achieve with their acts.

Another significant difference is that Collingwood was interested in the past because it represents the cultural inheritance received by the present; he saw historical knowledge as a taking possession by the historian and his generation of his society's culture (ibid., p. 226). Dilthey, on the other hand, was fascinated mostly by the different ways in which people have given form to their humanity; he was interested in the past that had escaped the present.

A further point of difference is the fact that Collingwood completely gave up the ideal of objective historical knowledge. He quite happily stressed that history is only an "imaginary picture" (ibid., p. 245) of the past, "created" by the historian on the basis of the necessarily scanty evidence, and existing only in the historian's head. Dilthey's efforts were, on the other hand, directed towards securing objective knowledge of a past that still existed in an unconscious latent form in man's fixed expressions.

27. On the Greek roots of the visual model of knowledge, see Habermas, op. cit., pp. 301-303.

28. Habermas, op. cit., p. 180.

29. In *Philosophical Fragments*, Kierkegaard describes how in the "Moment" God reveals himself as the "Teacher" of a message which the learner, man, does not have in himself. He stresses that man cannot recollect Truth, that is, God, but that he has to be taught (Søren Kierkegaard, *Philosophical Fragments, or Fragments of Philosophy*. Translated by David Swenson, new introduction and commentary by Niels Thulstrup, translation revised and commentary translated by Howard V. Hong. Princeton, N.J.: Princeton University Press, 1974).

CHAPTER FIVE

1. The best introduction to the metaphysical dimension of Dilthey's work to date is still Otto Bollnow, *Dilthey. Eine Einführung in seine Philosophie.* Stuttgart, Berlin, Köln, Mainz: Kohlhammer, 1967.

2. Hugo Dormagen, O.M.I., "Wilhelm Diltheys Konzeption der Geschichtlichpsychischen Struktur der menschlichen Erkenntnis," in *Scholastik, Vierteljahrsschrift für Theologie und Philosophie*, XXIX (1954), 363-386.

3. Heidegger further developed Dilthey's concept of mood (*Gemütsverfassung*). In *Being and Time* he calls mood (*die Stimmung, das Gestimmtsein*) a fundamental feature of human life (*Existential*). Man (*Dasein*) is always "in a mood" (*je schon immer gestimmt*). (Martin Heidegger, *Sein und Zeit*. Tübingen: Max Niemeyer Verlag, 1963, p. 134.) It is a sign of man's finitude, his "thrownness" (*Geworfenheit*) (ibid., p. 143).

4. Peter Krausser sees in Dilthey's theory of knowledge an anticipation of contemporary cybernetic theories: the human organism is an open system with a feedback mechanism. "Dilthey's Revolution in the Theory of Scientific Inquiry and Rational Behavior," *Review of Metaphysics*, XXII (1968), 262-280; *Kritik der endlichen Vernunft: Diltheys Revolution der allgemeinen Wissenschafts- und Handlungstheorie*. Frankfurt am Main: Suhrkamp, 1968.

5. Thomas S. Kuhn's *The Structure of Scientific Revolutions*. 2nd ed., enlarged. Chicago and London: The University of Chicago Press, 1970) revolutionized the traditional conception of the history of science as a progressive, unilinear and rational development of scientific knowledge. Kuhn drew the attention to the discontinuities in the history of science.

6. The human organism's relationship to the world is a "living" one, because it is an actually experienced relationship, and it changes with the occurrence of new experiences. Dilthey sometimes used the word *Lebendigkeit* instead of consciousness: world-views "express the aspect of aliveness [*Lebendigkeit*] in relation to the world they confront." Because philosophical systems originate in structured lived experience, he called them both "functions

of our mental structure," and "functions of aliveness" (*Lebendigkeit*) (GS, vol. VIII, 8).

7. Dilthey's conception of the personality structure will be further explicated in chapter VII.

8. In chapter VII we will be shown that world-views are, as it were, the personality structures of societies.

9. In contemporary cultural anthropological literature a distinction is made between ethos, which refers to the tone, character and quality of the life of a people, and world-view, which refers to the picture a people has of the way things are. The ethos is rendered intellectually acceptable by the world-view, as the latter shows a world to which the ethos corresponds; the world-view is rendered emotionally convincing by being an image of an experienced reality. Dilthey's usage of the term world-view covers both ethos and world-view in the sense of intellectual images of reality. With the term world-view of an historical epoch, its culture is designated (Clifford Geertz, *The Interpretations of Cultures. Selected Essays*, New York: Basic Books, Publishers, 1973, p. 89).

10. Warren and Wellek, *Theory of Literature*. New York: Harcourt, Brace and World, 1970, p. 151.

11. Ibid., pp. 156-157.

12. Ibid., p. 156.

13. Gadamer explains his concept of effective history, op. cit., pp. 284-290.

14. William Empson, *Seven Types of Ambiguity*. Middlesex, England: Penguin Books, n.d., p. 255.

15. Ibid.

16. Ibid., p. 256.

17. Ibid., p. 245.

18. Ibid.

19. In a similar way, Schleiermacher had studied religions "with the same relevant care that one devotes to the curiosities of nature" (Friedrich Ernst Daniel Schleiermacher, *On Religion: Speeches to its Cultural Despisers*, Translated by John Oman. New York: Harper and Brothers, 1958, p. 229). Oswald Spengler likewise considered philosophies living things, but his conception is more naturalistic than Dilthey's. The difference between Dilthey and Spengler will be further discussed in chapter VIII.

20. Empson, op. cit., p. 247, states that the modern reader when confronted with a literary work needs "a fair equilibrium or fairly strong defenses." This reminds one of Dilthey's ideal of sovereignty toward life.

21. Quoted by Lionel Gossman, "August Thierry and the Liberal Tradition of Historiography," *History and Theory. Studies in the Philosophy of History*, XV (1976), Beiheft 15, p. 38.

22. Wolf Lepenies, *Das Ende der Naturgeschichte. Wandel kultureller Selbstverständlichkeiten in den Wissenschaften des 18. und 19. Jahrhunderts*. München, Wien: Carl Hanser Verlag, 1976, p. 118.

23. Ibid.

24. *The Marx-Engels Reader*. Edited by Robert C. Tucker. New York: W. W. Norton and Company, 1972, p. 5.

25. Ibid., p. 70.

26. See Bernard Delfgaauw, *The Young Marx*. Translated by Franklin Schütz and Martin Redfern, with a letter from Karl Marx to his father translated by William Glenn-Doeppel. Westminster, Md., New York, Glen Rock, N.J., Amsterdam, Toronto: Newman Press, 1967, p. 59.

27. Dilthey became acquainted with Husserl through his Berlin colleague in psychology, Carl Stumpf. Husserl had studied with Stumpf at the University of Halle (Herbert Spiegelberg, *Phenomenology and Psychiatry. A Historical Introduction*. Evanston: Northwestern University Press, 1972, p. 33). Husserl visited Dilthey in Berlin in 1905 (ibid., p. 250). On Husserl's influence on Dilthey, see Gadamer, op. cit., p. 212; Michael Ermarth, *Wilhelm Dilthey: The Critique of Historical Reason*. Chicago and London: The University of Chicago Press, 1978, pp. 201-209. Rudolf R. Makkreel, op. cit., pp. 274-279.

28. Walter Biemel, "Einleitende Bemerkungen zum Briefwechsel Dilthey-Husserl," *Man and World. An International Philosophical Review*, I (1968), 434-437.

29. Edmund Husserl, *Logische Untersuchungen. Zweiter Band. Untersuchungen zur Phaenomenologie und Theorie der Erkenntnis*. I Teil. Halle a.d. S.: Max Niemeyer, 1913, p. 16.

30. Ibid., p. 11.

31. Ibid., p. 91.

32. Ibid., p. 4. In German, the definition of logical judgment is "die identische Aussagebedeutung welche eine ist gegenüber den mannigfaltigen, descriptive sehr unterschiedenen Urteilserlebnissen."

33. Ibid., p. 8.

34. Ibid., p. 11.

35. Ibid., p. 19.

36. Ibid., p. 31.

37. Ibid., pp. 61-62.

38. Ibid., p. 94.

39. Ibid., p. 99.

40. Ibid., p. 100.

41. Ibid.

42. Jacques Derrida, *La voix et le phénomène. Introduction au problème du signe dans la phénomenologie de Husserl* (Paris: Presses Universitaires de France, 1967) gives a penetrating analysis of Husserl's conception of meaning. He points out that the cartesian duality of mind and matter is present in the way Husserl separates the concrete material sign and the origin of its meaning in a speaker's consciousness (ibid., p. 91).

43. Gadamer, op. cit., p. 343.

44. Ibid., p. 261.

45. Ibid., p. 262.

46. Ibid., p. 295.

47. Ibid., p. 253.

48. Habermas, op. cit., p. 213.

49. Ibid., pp.

50. The promise of the ideas of Gadamer and Habermas for the study of non-Western cultures will be the topic of a separate study.

51. This will be shown in chapter VIII.

52. Clifford Geertz, *The Interpretation of Cultures. Selected Essays* (New York: Basic Books, 1973), p. 10.

53. This will be described in more detail in chapter VIII.

54. Habermas' project for a new theory of communication is referred to by Dieter Heinrich, *Zwei Reden. Aus Anlass des Hegelpreises*. Frankfurt a.M.: Suhrkampf Verlag, 1974, p. 20. Earlier indications for this project can be found in Habermas' essay "Vorbereitende Bemerkungen zu einer Theorie der Kommunikativen Kompetenz," in Jürgen Habermas und Niklas Luhman,

Theorie der Gesellschaft oder Sozialtechnologie – was leistet die System-forschung? Frankfurt a.M.: Suhrkampf Verlag, 1971, pp. 101-142.

CHAPTER SIX

1. Niebuhr, op. cit., pp. 1-6, 66-69. See also Karl Löwith, *From Hegel zu Nietzsche. The Revolution in Nineteenth-Century Thought.* Translated from the German by David E. Green. New York, Chicago, San Francisco: Holt, Rinehart and Winston, 1964, Part I.

2. On the distinction between speculative and critical philosophy of history see W. H. Walsh, op. cit., pp. 15-29.

3. On the cyclical conception of non-Christian classical antiquity, see Frank E. Manuel, *Shapes of Philosophical History.* Stanford, Calif.: Stanford University Press, 1967, pp. 1-10; Niebuhr, op. cit., pp. 38-41. Most commentators agree with J.B. Bury, op. cit., pp. 7-20, that the idea of progress – and thus of a continuous history – was absent in non-christian classical antiquity. See also R. G. Collingwood, op. cit., pp. 14-45. The exception is Robert A. Nisbet, *Social Change and History. Aspects of the Western Theory of Development.* New York: Oxford University Press, 1969, pp. 15-62.

4. Manuel, op. cit., pp. 25-32. Karl Löwith, *Meaning in History*, Chicago and London: The University of Chicago Press, 1949, pp. 160-174. Niebuhr, op. cit., pp. 20-29.

5. Manuel, op. cit., pp. 46-70.

6. Since Hegel, the term history is commonly reserved for continuous developmental processes. Hegel stated, for instance, that India has no history because it does not evidence development (Hegel, *The Philosophy of History*, p. 62). In Robert L. Heilbroner's book *The Future as History*, the word history in the title means a continuous process of development with an identifiable direction (Robert L. Heilbroner, *The Future as History. The historic currents of our time and the direction which they are taking America.* New York: Harper and Row, Publishers, 1968).

7. Manuel, op. cit., pp. 174-190.

8. Henri de Lubac, *Exégèse Médiévale. Les Quatre Sens de L'Ecriture.* 2 vols. Paris: Aubier, 1959. The number of the Bible's meanings varied during the Middle Ages. Beryl Smalley (*The Study of the Bible in the Middle Ages.* Oxford: The Clarendon Press, 1941, p. 27) mentions an interpreter who discerns seven meanings. The tradition according to which the Bible has a literal and one or more spiritual meanings goes back to the Greek and Latin Fathers of the Church. See on this tradition and its development in the Middle Ages, Smalley, op. cit.

9. De Lubac, I, 384-438.

10. See Ilse N. Bulhof, "Experiencing Nature: A Comparison between Early Medieval and Modern Encounters with Nature," *Diogenes*, 81 (1973), 27-43, in particular pp. 36-39.

11. Voltaire does not specifically state that his conception of history is at odds with the traditional Christian one, but it is clearly implied by his inclusion of the history of the Egyptians, Chinese and Indian civilizations, and his scorn for Jewish history as the supposed nerve of universal history. See, for instance, *Voltaire's Philosophical Dictionary.* Unabridged and unexpurgated, with special introduction by William F. Fleming. 10 vols. Paris, London, New York, Chicago: E. R. Dumont, 1901, VI, article *History*, pp. 68-70.

12. Günther Pflug, "The Development of Historical Method in the Eighteenth

Century," *History and Theory. Studies in the Philosophy of History*, Beiheft 11 (1971), *Enlightenment Historiography: Three German Studies*, pp. 1-23, in particular pp. 17-23.

13. The ways in which a speculative philosophy of history is smuggled into historical narratives is admirably explained by Hayden White, *Metahistory: The Historical Imagination in Nineteenth-Century Europe*. Baltimore and London: The Johns Hopkins University Press, 1973.

14. Weber's position is more fully explicated in chapter VIII.

15. The only exception was, of course, Nietzsche. Reacting against the Christian roots of linear history, Nietzsche reintroduced the concept of cyclical history in the form of an "Eternal Recurrence of the Same."

16. On Ranke's view on history, see G. P. Gooch, *History and Historians in the Nineteenth Century*. With a new introduction by the author. Boston: Beacon Press, 1959, pp. 72-98; Georg G. Iggers, *The German Conception of History*, pp. 63-90; Leonard Krieger, *Ranke: The Meaning of History*. Chicago and London: The University of Chicago Press, 1977.

17. St. Augustine, *The Confessions*. Translated, with an introduction and notes, by John K. Ryan. Garden City, N.Y.: Image Books, 1960, pp. 301-302, 303.

18. This point will be more fully explicated in chapter VIII.

19. This point will be more fully explicated in chapter VII.

20. Heidegger was a student of Husserl, and in his first major work, *Being and Time*, he uses the phenomenological method. In his philosophical conceptions he was, however, as much, if not more so, influenced by Dilthey, in particular by the latter's views of the historicity of human life and of the temporality of human existence.

21. Heidegger states this as follows: "Wie aber, wenn das Ausbleiben dieses Bezugs (zum Sein) und die Vergessenheit dieses Ausbleibens von weither das moderne Weltalter bestimmten? Wie, wenn das Ausbleiben des Seins den Menschen immer ausschlieszlicher nur dem Seienden überliesze. . . ?" (Martin Heidegger, *Was ist Metaphysik?* Antrittsvorlesung 1929. Frankfort a.M.: Vittorio Klostermann, 1965, p. 18. ". . . das westentliche Denken (ist) ein Ereignis des Seins" (ibid., p. 47). Thinking has to obey being's voice (ibid., p. 50). See on Heidegger's conception of the modern age and its relationship to Being's hiding from man: Thomas Langan, *The Meaning of Heidegger: a critical study of an existentialist phenomenology*. New York: Columbia University Press, 1959, pp. 168-175.

22. Man has to take upon him "die Wachterschaft des Seins" (ibid., p. 49).

23. In a lecture given during a course in 1935, Heidegger expresses faith in the "inner truth and greatness" of National Socialism (*Einführung in die Metaphysi'*. Tübingen: Max Niemeyer Verlag, 1957, p. 152). In a 1966 interview with the German newsweekly *Der Spiegel*, Heidegger discusses the circumstances which surrounded his controversial acceptance of the presidency of the University of Freiburg in 1933 and the opinion on National Socialism just quoted. He admits that he believed National Socialism to represent a "national awakening" ("Only a God can save us now." An interview with Martin Heidegger. Translated by David Schendler. *Graduate Faculty Philosophy Journal*, 6 (1977), pp. 5-28, p. 9). Heidegger was indeed very much the victim of German historicism's philosophy of value, believing that truths and values are manifested in certain persons and institutions which have developed historically.

24. Jean-Paul Sartre, *Nausea*. Translated from the French by Lloyd Alexander. Introduction by Hayden Carruth. 8th French edition 1938. New York: New Directions Publishing Company, 1964, p. 22.

25. Ibid., p. 32.

26. Ibid., p. 33.

27. Ibid., p. 37.

28. Jean-Paul Sartre, *L'Etre et le Néant. Essai d'ontologie phénoménologique*. Paris: Editions Gallimard, 1943, p. 719.

29. Paul Ricoeur, "Existence et Herméneutique," *Dialogue. Canadian Philosophical Review*, IV (1965-1966), 1-25.

30. An example of this attitude of demystifying hermeneutic interpretators of exegetic hermeneutic interpreters is Habermas' criticism of Gadamar. Habermas accuses Gadamer of idealizing the tradition. He states that what becomes permanent — fixed in a work — is therefore not yet true: the work can have been created under various kinds of pressure (Jürgen Habermas, "Der Universalitätsanspruch der Hermeneutik" (1970). *Kultur und Kritik. Verstreute Aufsätze*. Frankfort a.M.: Suhrkampf Verlag, 1973, pp. 264-301, p. 229). Gadamer, on the other hand, reproaches demystifying hermeneutic interpreters such as Habermas to falsely oppose reason to tradition and authority. He states that "reflection is not always and unavoidably a step toward dissolving prior convictions. Authority is not always wrong" (Hans-Georg Gadamer, "On the Scope and Function of Hermeneutical Reflection," *Continuum*, VIII (1970), 77-95, p. 88). Richoeur, op. cit., occupies a middle ground between these two positions. He warns that the works of the tradition can harbor elements of repression that need to be discovered, but that they also can speak truth.

CHAPTER SEVEN

1. Wilhelm Hehlmann, op. cit., pp. 117-124.

2. Stephen Strasser, *The Soul in Metaphysical and Empirical Psychology*. Pittsburgh, Pa.: Duquesne University, 1962, p. 36.

3. Wilhelm Hehlmann, op. cit., pp. 117-124.

4. A.A. Roback, *History of Psychology and Psychiatry*. New York: Philosophical Library, 1961, pp. 59-60. Wilhelm Hehlmann, op. cit., pp. 215-216.

5. Hehlmann, op. cit., p. 168.

6. On positivism in psychology see Wilhelm Hehlmann, op. cit., pp. 144-149. A later form of positivism in the study of man is presented by John Stuart Mill. In contrast to Comte, Mill recognized the specific character of man, but he felt that man could nevertheless be studied by means of the same methods as the rest of nature. In psychology, he accepted the associationist point of view according to which psychic occurrences follow each other according to fixed rules.

7. F.W. Nietzsche, *Thus Spoke Zarathustra*, p. 34.

8. Hehlmann, op. cit., p. 177.

9. The fact that the representatives of this school were almost without exception humanist philosophers may make us surmise a certain nostalgia of this school for forms of society in which cultural and/or "spiritual" values were still respected. A certain measure of conservative political engagement of these philosopher-psychologists might therefore be expected, but the correspondence between political position and scientific theory has to be studied in great detail before statements to this effect can be made.

10. Dilthey's claim that "psychology" is a fundamental discipline for the human sciences has caused much confusion; the statement suggested to many readers that Dilthey was a representative of psychologism — that is, the tendency to explain history "psychologically" on the basis of the historical actors' subjective motivations. Because Dilthey, however, understood "psy-

chology" as the general science of the human embodied or finite mind – and not as the science of the individual mind – this is a misunderstanding of his position, as will become clearer in the remainder of this chapter.

11. I have translated *geistiges Leben* as "mental life" because it corresponds with the common use of language ("mental health," "mental institutions," etc.). "Mental" is derived from mind, but it should be remembered that for Dilthey "the life of the mind" (*Geist*) comprises more than the activities of reason: it includes willing and feeling; it is, indeed, "psychic life" in a broad sense.

12. Michael Polanyi introduced the term personal knowledge in his book *Personal Knowledge: Toward a Post-Critical Philosophy*. Chicago, Ill.: The University of Chicago Press, 1958. He here describes the personal element in knowledge in the following words: "Tacit assent and intellectual passions, the sharing of an idiom and of a cultural heritage, affiliation to a life-minded community: such are the impulses which shape our vision of the nature of things on which we rely for our mastery of things. No intelligence, however critical or original, can operate outside such a fiduciary framework" (op. cit., p. 266).

13. The conception of the mind's creativity further clarifies Dilthey's notion of *Verstehen*. Because the mind links experienced events with other experienced events, any experience always affects the experiencing subject's mind as a whole: each "discrete occurrence is at the time of experience supported by the totality of the soul's life" (GS, vol. V, 172). *Verstehen* begins, as it were, at the other end of the process by which reality is experienced and interpreted: by the finished product of the ordering mind – after mind has made its connections and expressed them in behavior, or fixed them in a product. Confronted with a gesture, an action, an artifact, an institution, the scholar puts himself in its creator's place, and thus discovers the structural coherences in that particular object of investigation based as they are upon the totality of its creator's world. *Verstehen* is the finding of such connections; it is seeing the object of investigation in the context of the creator's world.

14. Peter Krausser has sketched Dilthey's model of the way in which man acquires knowledge in his article "Dilthey's Revolution in the Theory of the Structure of Scientific Inquiry," *Review of Metaphysics*, 22 (1969), 262-280. Krausser states that this model is in particular apt to function as a "science of science," a theory of the scientific processes of inquiry (op. cit., p. 280). In the introductory paragraph of the article he seems to suggest that Dilthey himself was not quite aware of the implications of his theory. I think Dilthey was quite aware of its consequences for the human sciences, but not for its consequences for the natural sciences. The application of Dilthey's model of knowledge to the natural sciences has become possible after the publication of Kuhn's *The Structure of Scientific Revolutions*.

15. These ideas served as an important stimulus to Helmuth Plessner and Frederik Jacobus Johannes Buytendijk who each studied the interrelations between man and his body as forming a structural whole. Plessner stated as his goal to overcome Cartesian dualism by means of "a hermeneutic, that is, a science of expression, of understanding of expressions and possibilities of understanding – which is not limited . . . to the area of language" (Helmuth Plessner, *Die Stufen des Organischen und der Mensch. Einleitung in die philosophische Anthropologie*. Berlin und Leipzig: Walter de Gruyter, 1928, p. 23). He was particularly interested in bodily expressions, such as laughing and crying.

16. On the notion of man's unfinishedness at birth, see below, chapter VIII.

17. See Jacques Kornberg, "Wilhelm Dilthey on the Self and History: Some Theoretical Roots of Geistesgeschichte," in *Central European History*, V, no. 3 (1892), 295-317.

18. *Der junge Dilthey*, p. 117.

19. Dilthey attributed the rise of the individual to the dissolution of the social-political characteristic of the *anciene régime*, the decline of traditional religion, and the freedom of the individual to shape a private sphere of life and world-view had also contributed to the rise of the autonomous person. In this context Dilthey compares the contemporary flowering of appreciation for the individual with similar developments at other historical periods of transition, such as the time of the Sophists, of the late Roman Empire, and of the Italian Renaissance. In each of these periods, social ties loosened, while the individual person gained in importance.

20. Nietzsche, *The Genealogy of Morals*, p. 59.

21. Ibid.

22. Karl Löwitz, "Max Weber und Karl Marx," in *Archiv für Sozialwissenschaften und Sozialpolitik*, no. 67 (1955), 212.

23. See also Günter Abramowski, *Das Geschichtsbild Max Webers. Universalgeschichte am Leitfaden des okzidentalen Rationalisierungsprozesses*. Stuttgart, Ernst Klett Verlag, 1966, pp. 161-163.

24. Sigmund Freud, *A General Introduction to Psychoanalysis*, translated by Joan Riviere. New York: Pocket Books, 1963, p. 442.

25. Ibid., p. 441.

26. Dilthey elaborated on this theme in his essay "Dichterische Einbildungskraft und Wahnsinn," GS, vol. VI, 90-103. See in particular p. 93. In *Moses and Monotheism*, Freud drew attention to the similarity of symbols in religion, dreams and insanity. See also his Tenth Lecture on "Symbolism in Dreams," in his *General Introduction to Psychoanalysis*, in particular pp. 172-177.

27. Heinrich Rickert, *Kulturwissenschaft und Naturwissenschaft*, 7th ed. Tübingen: J.C.B. Mohr, 1926, p. 26.

28. Ibid., pp. x, xi.

29. Hermann Ebbinghaus, *Über erklärende und beschreibende Psychologie*, in *Zeitschrift für Psychologie und Physiologie der Sinnesorgane*, IX (1896), 161-205.

30. In spite of its emphasis on experimental research, Wundt's approach to psychology has nevertheless nonmechanistic aspects. It focuses, for instance, on the person's creative synthesis of experience and on the function of emotions and will in human life (see Helhmann, op. cit., pp. 177-179). But Dilthey did not recognize these new elements. He assumed, on the contrary, that Wundt's version of scientific psychology was as detrimental to the understanding of the mind's creativity as its older versions. We must remember at this point that at the University of Basel, Dilthey became acquainted with those older forms of scientific psychology, physiology and biology, for at that time Wundt's laboratory had not yet been founded.

31. Karl Jaspers, "Kausale und Verständliche Zussammenhänge zwischen Schicksal und Psychose bei der Dementia Praecox," reprinted in *Gesammelte Schriften zur Psychopathologie*. Berlin: Springer, 1963.

32. Karl Jaspers, *Allgemeine Psychopathologie*, translated by J. Hoenig and M.W. Hamilton. Chicago: The University of Chicago Press, 1963. On Dilthey's influence on Jaspers, see Spiegelberg, op. cit., pp. 182, 186.

33. On Dilthey's influence on psychology, see Wilhelm Hehlmann, op. cit., pp. 258-262; Spiegelberg, op. cit., pp. 134 and 217.

34. Dilthey's importance for sociology has been pointed out by Carlo Antoni, *From History to Sociology, The Transition in German Historical Thought*, translated by Hayden V. White. Detroit: Wayne State University Press, 1959, pp. 1-39. Johach, op. cit., pp. 4-9, points out that Dilthey's importance for sociology has not sufficiently been appreciated so far. His book attempts to remedy this situation.

35. Abraham H. Maslow, *The Psychology of Science. A Reconnaissance.* Chicago: Henry Regnery Company, 1966, pp. 3-4.

36. Ludwig von Bertalanffy, "System, Symbol and the Image of Man (Man's Immediate Socio-Ecological World)," in *The Interface between Psychiatry and Anthropology*, ed. Iiago Goldston, M.D. London: Butterworth's; New York: Brunner, Mazel Publishers, 1971, p. 104.

37. Ibid., p. 109.

38. Ibid., p. 111.

39. Ibid., p. 116.

40. Ibid., p. 117.

41. Oliver Sacks, *Awakenings*. Garden City, N.Y.: Doubleday and Company, 1974. Following Leibnitz, Sacks calls the nonmechanical or nonchemical approach "metaphysical" (p. xiii) — an unfortunate term, bound to scare off many scientists. See, for instance, R. H. van den Hoofdakker, *Een pil voor Doornroosje. Essays over een Wetenschappelijke Psychiatrie*. Amsterdam: van Gennep, 1976, pp. 71-87.

CHAPTER EIGHT

1. Arthur Schopenhauer, *Die Welt als Wille und Vorstellung. Sämtliche Werke*. Wiesbaden: F.A. Brockhaus, 1961, I, 442-446. See pp. 174-182 for a description of the will and how the world is its objectivation.

2. Nietzsche, *Thus Spoke Zarathustra*, pp. 114-116.

3. Ilse N. Bulhof, "Structure and Change in Wilhelm Dilthey's Philosophy of History." *History and Theory: Studies in the Philosophy of History*, XV (1976), 2.

4. Martin Heidegger, *Sein und Zeit*, pp. 372-377.

5. H.N. Tuttle, *Wilhelm Dilthey's Philosophy of Historical Understanding. A Critical Analysis*. Leiden, 1966, has pointed out the importance of systems in Dilthey's historical thought. Dilthey's morphological orientation is studied by Frithjof Rodi, *Morphologie und Hermeneutik. Zur Methode von Diltheys Aesthetik*. Stuttgart, Berlin, Köln, Mainz: Kohlhammer, 1969.

6. George W. Stocking, *Race, Culture and Evolution. Essays in the History of Anthropology*. New York and London: The Free Press, 1968, p. 203. He mentions, however, that Boas' use of the term cultures was not consistent (p. 231), and that the term cultures was regularly used only by his students (p. 203).

7. It is interesting in this respect that Ruth Benedict refers to Dilthey's conception of culture as integrated wholes in her book *Patterns of Culture*. New York: The New American Library of World Literature, 1953, p. 47.

8. Michael Landmann, *Philosophische Anthropologie. Menschliche Selbstdeutung in Geschichte und Gegenwart*. Berlin: Walter de Gruyter, 1955, pp. 249-250, argues that although the romantic philosophies of history which genuinely appreciated the plurality of cultures, they still lacked the anthropological element: "Das Fundament zu ihr liefert erst unser heutiges Bild vom

Menschen als des ursprünglich Unvollendeten und sich daher notwendig in immer wieder neuen und anderen Kulturschöpfungen Vollendenden" (ibid.,pp. 249-250). Dilthey was one of the first to see man as fundamentally unfinished at birth.

9. Thomas S. Kuhn, op. cit., p. 37, writes that paradigms provide criteria for choosing problems that can be assumed to have solutions. He then continues: "to a great extent these are the only problems that the community will admit as scientific. . . . Other problems are rejected as metaphysical, as the concern of another discipline, or sometimes as just too problematic to be worth the time." This suggests that during a paradigm "heyday," facts that do not fit its expectations are not taken seriously as scientific facts and consequently are ignored by the scientific community. It would be interesting to investigage the psychological and biological conditions necessary for the "awareness of anomaly" (ibid., p. 52) that precedes paradigm change.

10. Claude Lévi-Strauss, The Savage Mind. Chicago: The University of Chicago Press, 1970, pp. 66-74. It may be interesting to quote Lévi-Strauss on the influence of myths and rites on social systems. Lévi-Strauss writes that demographic evolution can shatter the social structure but that "if the structural orientation survives the shock it has, after each upheaval, several means of re-establishing a system, which may not be identical with the earlier one but is at least formally of the same type." The structural orientation will continue through the myths and rites, "so as to maintain new structural solutions along approximately the same lines as the previous structure," as if the structure were a motor with a feedback device. The result will be "a compromise between the old state of affairs and the confusion brought in from outside." Lévi-Strauss mentions as a possible example of such a structural adjustment of the historical process the legends of the Osage Indians (pp. 68-69).

11. For a short description of the positivist and idealist positions in historical explanations, see William Dray, Philosophy of History. Englewood Cliffs, N.J.: Prentice Hall, 1964, pp. 4-20.

12. Frithjof Rodi, op. cit., pp. 46-52, distinguishes two kinds of morphological structures: closed organic structures and open historical ones. Peter Krausser, "Diltheys Philosophische Anthropologie," in Journal of the History of Philosophy, I (1963), 212, characterizes the structural relationship between the human organism and its environment as "ein System mit Rückkopplung und Selbstregulation," "ein dynamisch stabiles System."

13. Robert A. Nisbet, Social Change and History. Aspects of the Western Theory of Development. New York: Oxford University Press, 1969, pp. 3-11.

14. Robert F. Berkhofer, Jr., A Behavioral Approach to Historical Analysis. New York: The Free Press; London: Collier-MacMillan Limited, 1969, p. 268.

15. Max Weber, "Die Objektivität socialwissenschaftlicher und socialpolitischer Erkenntnis" (1904), Gesammelte Aufsätze zur Wissenschafslehre. Tübingen: J.C.B. Mohr (Paul Siebeck), 1973, p. 54.

16. Ibid., p. 180.

17. W.J. Mommsen, "Universalgeschichtliches und politisches Denken bei Max Weber," Historische Zeitschrift, 201 (1960), 569). Mommsen writes that according to Weber science knew nothing of a world ordered by God and thus somehow having an ethical orientation (p. 562).

18. Oswald Spengler, The Decline of the West. An abridged edition by Helmut Werner. English abridged edition prepared by Arthur Helps from the translation by Charles Francis Atkinson. New York: The Modern Library, 1962, p. 18.

19. Ibid.

20. Ibid., p. 30.

21. Johan Huizinga, "De Taak der Cultuurgeschiedenis," *Verzamelde Werken*, 9 vols. Haarlem: H.D. Tjeenk Willink en Zoon, 1950, VII, 35-95, in particular pp. 56-90. See on Huizinga's conception of cultural history, Ilse N. Bulhof, "Johan Huizinga, Ethnographer of the Past: An Analysis of Johan Huizinga's Approach to History," *Clio. An interdisciplinary Journal of Literature, History and the Philosophy of History*, IV (1975), 201-225.

22. Frederick J. Teggart, *Theory and Processes of History*. Gloucester, Mass.: Peter Smith, 1972, in particular the essays "The Aims of the Academic Historian," "National History and World-History," and "The Logical Implications of Historical Narrative." This list of those who felt uncomfortable with the idea of knowable coherent history is by no means complete. Raymond Aron, Lucien Febvre, Charles Beard and Carl Becker might also have been mentioned in this context.

23. Michel Foucault, "History, Discourse and Discontinuity," *Salmagundi. A Quarterly of the Humanities and the Social Sciences*, 18 (1972), 225-248, 240.

24. Ibid., p. 229.

25. Michel Foucault, *The Order of Things*, p. xxii.

26. Michel Foucault, "History, Discourse and Discontinuity, p. 230. See also *The Order of Things*, p. xii.

27. See his chapter "Man and His Doubles," in *The Order of Things*, in particular p. 310.

28. Fernand Braudel, "Histoire et Sociologie," *Traité de Sociologie*, ed. G. Gurvitch. Paris: Presses Universitaires de France, 1958,I, 83-98. On p. 95, Braudel writes: "pour l'historien, tout commence, tout finit par le temps, un temps mathématique et démiurge, dont il serait facile de sourire, temps comme extérieur aux hommes, qui les pousse, les contraint, emporte leurs temps particuliers aux couleurs diverses; le temps impérieux du monde."

29. Leonard Krieger, "The Horizons of History," *American Historical Review*, LXIII (1957), 71.

30. For these two historical schools, see note 11 of this chapter.

31. On evolutionary anthropology, see Fred W. Voget, "Progress, Science, History and Evolution in Eighteenth and Twentieth Century Anthropology," *Journal of the History of the Behavioral Sciences*, 3 (1968), 132-155.

32. On the development of the culture concept in cultural anthropology, see Fred W. Voget, "Man and Culture: An Essay in Changing Anthropological Interpretation," *American Anthropologist*, 61 (1961), 943-965.

33. George Stocking, "Franz Boas and the Culture Concept in Historical Perspective," *Race, Culture and Evolution. Essays in the History of Anthropology*. New York: The Free Press; London: Collier-MacMillan, 1968, p. 210.

34. Bronislaw Malinowski, *Argonauts of the Western Pacific. An Account of Native Enterprise and Adventure in the Archipelagoes of Melanesian New Guinea*. New York: E.P. Dutton, 1961. First published in 1922.

35. Claude Lévi-Strauss, *The Savage Mind*, chapter VIII, in particular p. 234.

36. Claude Lévi-Strauss, *Race et L'Histoire*. UNESCO: Editions Gonthier, 1961, pp. 44-50.

37. See on this convergence, F. Furet, "L'histoire et l'homme sauvage," and Jacques LeGoff, "L'historien et l'homme quotidien," *Méthodologie de l'histoire et des sciences humaines. Mélanges en l'honneur de Fernand Braudel*. Toulouse: Edouart Privat, Editeur, 1972, pp. 227-243, 233-243; Wolf Lepenies, "History

and Anthropology. An Historical Appraisal of the Current Contact between the Disciplines," *Social Science Information Bulletin*, 15 (1976), 287-306; Keith Thomas, "History and Anthropology," *Past and Present*, no. 24 (1963), 3-24.

38. Odo Marquand, *Schwierigkeiten mit der Geschichtsphilosophie. Aufsätze.* Frankfurt a.M.: Suhrkampf Verlag, 1973, pp. 138-144, describes several ways in which anthropology has functioned as the means to escape the traditional philosophy of history.

39. On the *Annales* School, see J.H. Hexter, "Fernand Braudel and the Monde Braudellien," *The Journal of Modern History*, 44 (1972), 480-540. The other articles of the issue are also devoted to the *Annales* School. Furthermore, see Traian Stoianowich, *French Historical Method. The Annales Paradigm.* With a foreword by Fernand Braudel. Ithaca and London: Cornell University Press, 1976; Georg G. Iggers, *New Directions in European Historiography.* With a contribution by Norman Baker. Middletown, Conn.: Wesleyan University Press, 1975, pp. 43-80.

40. Fernand Braudel, *The Mediterranean and the Mediterranean World at the Age of Philip II.* 2 vols. New York, Evanston, San Francisco: Harper and Row, Publishers, 1975, p. 20.

41. Ibid., p. 901.

42. Ibid., p. 903.

43. Fernand Braudel, "Histoire et Sciences Sociales. La Longue Durée," *Annales. Sociétés, Economies, Civilizations,* 26 (1958), 728.

44. Fernand Braudel, *The Mediterranean*, p. 122.

45. André Burgière, "Présentation," *Annales, Economies, Sociétés, Civilizations*, special issue entitled *Histoire et Structure*, 1971, pp. i-vii, p. iv.

46. Ibid.

BIBLIOGRAPHY

I. WORKS BY WILHELM DILTHEY

Wilhelm Dilthey. *Gesammelte Schriften*. 18 vols. Stuttgart: B.G. Teubner Verlagsgesellschaft; Göttingen: Vandenhoeck und Ruprecht 1958 – present.
— *Briefwechsel zwischen Wilhelm Dilthey und dem Grafen Paul Yorck von Wartenburg, 1877-1897*. Halle (Saale): Verlag Max Niemeyer, 1923.
Misch (née Dilthey), Clara. *Der junge Dilthey. Ein Lebensbild in Briefen und Tagebüchern*. Stuttgart: B.G. Teubner; Gottingen: Vandenhoeck und Ruprecht, 1960.

II. ENGLISH TRANSLATIONS OF DILTHEY'S WRITINGS

Descriptive Psychology and Historical Understanding. Translated by Richard M. Zaner and Kenneth Heiges, with an introduction by Rudolph Makkreel. The Hague: Martinus Nijhoff, 1976.
"The Dream." Translated by William Kluback, *Wilhelm Dilthey's Philosophy of History*. New York: Columbia University Press, 1956, pp. 103-109.
The Essence of Philosophy. Translated by Stephen A. Emery and William T. Emery. New York: AMS Press, 1969. *Gesammelte Schriften*, vol. V, 339-416.
Patterns and Meaning in History: Thoughts on History and Society. Translator unacknowledged. H.P. Rickman, ed. New York: Harper and Row, 1962. Fragments from *Gesammelte Schriften*, vol. VII.
"The Rise of Hermeneutics." Translated by Frederik Jameson In *New Literary Theory: A Journal of Theory and Interpretation*, III (1972), 229-244. *Gesammelte Schriften*, vol. V, 317-331.

III. BIBLIOGRAPHY OF SOURCES AND SECONDARY LITERATURE

Bibliographie Wilhelm Dilthey. Quellen und Literatur. Weinheim, Berlin und Basel: Verlag Julius Belz, 1968. Edited by Ulrich Herrmann.

IV. SECONDARY LITERATURE

Abramowski, Günther. *Das Geschichtsbild Max Webers. Universalgeschichte am Leitfaden des okzidentalen Rationalisierungsprozesses*. Stuttgart: Ernst Klett Verlag, 1966.
Angermeier, Heinz. *Geschichte oder Gegenwart. Reflexionen über das Verhältnis von Zeit und Geist*. München: Verlag C.H. Becker, 1974.
Antoni, Carlo. *From History to Sociology. The Transition in German Historical Thought*. Translated by Hayden V. White. Detroit: Wayne State University Press, 1959.

Augustine, St. *The Confessions*. Translated, with an introduction and notes, by John K. Ryan. Garden City, N.Y.: Image Books, 1960.

Bayle, Pierre. *Historical and Critical Dictionary. Selections*. Translated by Richard H. Popkin. Indianapolis and New York: The Bobbs-Merrill Company, 1965.

Benedict, Ruth. *Patterns of Culture*. The New American Library of World Literature. New York, 1953.

Bergstraesser, A. "Wilhelm Dilthey and Max Weber: An Empirical Approach to Historical Analysis." *Ethics. An International Journal of Social, Political and Legal Philosophy*, 62 (1947), 92-110.

Berkhofer, Robert F. Jr. *A Behavioral Approach to Historical Analysis*. New York: The Free Press; London: Collier-MacMillan, 1969.

Bertalanffy, Ludwig von. "System, Symbol and the Image of Man (Man's Immediate Ecological World)." *The Interface between Psychiatry and Anthropology*, ed. Iago Goldston, M.D. London: Butterworths; New York: Brunner/Mazel, Publishers, 1971, pp. 88-119.

Biemel, Walter. "Einleitende Bemerkungen zum Briefwechsel Dilthey-Husserl." *Man and World. An International Philosophical Review*, 1 (1968), 428-446.

Bolingbroke, Lord. *Historical Writings*. Edited with an introduction by Isaac Kramnick. Chicago and London: University of Chicago Press, 1972.

Bollnow, Otto F. *Dilthey. Eine Einführung in seine Philosophie*. Stuttgart, Berlin, Köln, Mainz: Kohlhammer, 1967.

Braudel, Fernand. *Capitalism and Material Life 1400-1800*. Translated by Miriam Kochan. New York, Evanston, San Francisco, London: 1973.

– *The Mediterranean World in the Age of Philip II*. 2 vols. Translated by Sîan Reynolds. New York, Evanston, San Francisco: Harper and Row, Publishers, 1975.

Bulhof, Ilse N. *Appollos Wiederkehr. Eine Untersuchung der Rolle des Kreises in Nietzsches Denken über Geschichte und Zeit*. The Hague: Martinus Nijhoff, 1976.

– "Johan Huizinga, Ethnographer of the Past: An Analysis of Johan Huizinga's Approach to History." *Clio. An Interdisciplinary Journal of Literature, History and the Philosophy of History*, 4 (1975), 201-225.

– "Structure and Change in Wilhelm Dilthey's Philosophy of History." *History and Theory. Studies in the Philosophy of History*, 15 (1976), pp. 21-32.

– "Fernand Braudel's cosmopolitan Orientation to History." *Clio. An Interdisciplinary Journal of Literature, History and the Philosophy of History*, 9 (1980), forthcoming.

Burgière, André. "Présentation." *Annales. Economies, Sociétés, Civilizations. Histoire et Structure*, 1971, pp. i-vii.

Bury, J.B. *The Idea of Progress. An Inquiry into its Growth and Origin*. New York: Dover Publications, 1955.

Collingwood, R.G. *An Autobiography*. London: Oxford University Press, 1951.

– *The Idea of History*. London, Oxford, New York: Oxford University Press, 1968.

Delfgaauw, Bernard. *The Young Marx*. Translated by Franklin Schütz and Martin Redfern, with a letter from Karl Marx to his father translated by William Glenn-Doeppel. Westminster, Md., New York, N.Y., Glen Rock, N.J., Amsterdam, Toronto: Newman Press, 1967.

Diwald, Hellmut. *Wilhelm Dilthey. Erkennistheorie und Philosophie der Geschichte*. Göttingen, Berlin, Frankfurt: Musterschmidt, 1963.

Donoso, A. "Wilhelm Dilthey's Contributions to the Philosophy of History." *Philosophy Today*, 12 (1968), 151-163.
Dormagen, Hugo, O.M.I. "Wilhelm Diltheys Konzeption der geschichtlich-psychischen Struktur der menslichen Erkenntnis." *Scholastik. Vierteljahrschrift für Theologie und Philosophie*, 29 (1954), 363-383.
Dray, William H. *Philosophy of History*. Englewood Cliffs, N.J.: Prentice Hall, 1964.
Droysen, Johann Gustav. *Outline of the Principles of History*. Translated by E. Benjamin Andrews. Boston: Ginn and Company, 1897.
Dwight, Benjamin W. *Modern Philology: Its Discoveries, History and Influence*. New York: Charles Scribner, 1864.
Ebbinghaus, Hermann, "Über Erklärende und Beschreibende Psychologie." *Zeitschrift für Psychologie und Physiologie*, 9 (1895), 161-205.
Ebeling, Gerhard. "The Significance of the Critical-Historical Method for Church and Theology in Protestantism." Ebeling, Gerhard, *Word and Faith*. Translated by James W. Leitch. Philadelphia: Fortress Press, 1963, pp. 17-62.
Ermarth, Michael, *Wilhelm Dilthey: The Critique of Historical Reason*. Chicago and London: The University of Chicago Press, 1978, pp. 201-209.
Fain, Haskell. *Between Philosophy and History. The Resurrection of Speculative History within the Analytic Tradition*. Princeton: Princeton University Press, 1970.
Foucault, Michel. "History, Discourse, and Discontinuity." *Salmagundi: Quarterly of the Humanities and the Social Sciences*, 20 (1972), 225-248.
– *The Order of Things. An Archeology of the Human Sciences*. New York: Vintage Books, 1973.
Freud, Sigmund. *A General Introduction to Psychoanalysis*. Translated by Joan Rivière. New York: Pocket Books, 1963.
Furet, François, and Legoff, Jacques. "L'historien et l'homme sauvage." *Méthodologie de l'histoire et des sciences humaines. Mélanges en l'honneur de Fernand Braudel*. Toulouse: Deouart Privat, Editeur, 1972.
Gadamer, Hans-Georg. "Hermeneutik und Historismus." *Wahrheit und Methode*, pp. 477-515.
– "Hermeneutics and Social Science." *Cultural Hermeneutics*, 1 (1975), 307-316.
– "On the Scope and Function of Hermeneutic Reflection." *Continuum*, 8 (1970), 77-95.
– *Wahrheit und Methode. Grundzüge einer Philosophischen Hermeneutik*. Tübingen: J.C.B. Mohr, 1972.
Geertz, Clifford. *The Interpretation of Cultures. Selected Essays*. New York: Basic Books, 1973.
Gooch, G. P. *History and Historians in the Nineteenth Century*. With a new introduction by the author. Boston: Beacon Press, 1959.
Gruner, Rolf. "Historicism: Its Rise and Decline." *Clio. An Interdisciplinary Journal of Literature, History and the Philosophy of History*, 8 (1978), 25-39.
Habermas, Jürgen. *Knowledge and Human Interests*. Translated by Jeremy J. Shapiro. Boston: Beacon Press, 1971.
Habermas, Jürgen and Niklas Luhman. *Theorie der Gesellschaft oder Sozialtechnologie–was leistet die Systemforschung?* Frankfurt a.M.: Suhrkampf Verlag, 1971.
Hegel, Georg Wilhelm Friedrich. *Grundlinien der Philosophie des Rechts*. Mit den von Gans redigierten Zusätzen aus Hegels Vorlesungen neu herausgegeben

von Georg Lasson. *Sämtliche Werke* herausgegeben von Georg Lasson, Band VI. Leipzig: Verlag von Felix Meiner, 1930.
— *The Phenomenology of Mind.* Translated by J.B. Baillie. New York and Evanston: Harper and Row, Publishers, 1967.
— *The Philosophy of History.* Translated by J. Sibree. New York: Dover Publications, 1956.
Hehlmann, Wilhelm. *Geschichte der Psychologie.* Stuttgart: Alfred Kroner Verlag, 1967.
Heidegger, Martin. "Only a God can Save us Now, An Interview with Martin Heidegger." Translated by David Schendler. *Graduate Philosophy Journal*, 6 (1977), 5-28.
— *Sein und Zeit.* Tübingen: Max Niemeyer Verlag, 1963.
— *Was ist Metaphysik?* Frankfort a.M.: Vittorio Klostermann, 1965.
Heinrich, Dieter. *Zwei Reden. Aus Anlasz des Hegelpreises.* Frankfurt a.M.: Suhrkampf Verlag, 1974.
Herder, Gottfried von. *Reflections on the Philosophy of the History of Mankind.* Abridged and with an introduction by Frank E. Manuel. Chicago and London: The University of Chicago Press, 1968.
Hexter, J.H. "Fernand Braude and the Monde Braudellien." *The Journal of Modern History*, 44 (1972).
Hirsch, Eric Donald, Jr. *Validity in Interpretation.* New Haven: Yale University Press, 1967.
Hodges, Herbert Arthur. *The Philosophy of Wilhelm Dilthey.* London: Routledge and Paul, 1952.
Holborn, Hajo. "Wilhelm Dilthey and the Critique of Historical Reason." *Journal of the History of Ideas*, 12 (1950), 93-119.
Horkheimer, Max. "The Relation between Psychology and Sociology in the Work of Wilhelm Dilthey." *Studies in Philosophy and Social Science*, 8 (1939), 430-443.
Hughes, H. Stuart. *Consciousness and Society. The reorientation of European Social Thought, 1890-1930.* New York: Vintage Books, 1958.
Huizinga, Johan. "De Taak der Cultuurgeschiedenis," *Verzamelde Werken.* 9 vols. Haarlem: H. Tjeenk Willink en Zoon, 1950, VII, 35-90.
Hume, David. *David Hume: Philosophical Historian.* Editors David Pate Norton and Richard N. Popkin. Indianapolis, New York and Kansas City: Bobbs-Merrill Company, 1965.
Husserl, Edmund. *Logische Untersuchungen.* Erster Band. *Prolegomena zur Reinen Logik.* Edited by Elmar Holenstein. The Hague: Martinus Nijhoff, 1975. Zweiter Band. *Untersuchungen zur Phänomenologie und Theorie der Erkenntnis.* I Teil. Halle a.S.: Max Niemeyer, 1913.
Hyppolite, Jean. *Studies on Marx and Hegel.* Edited and translated by John O'Neill. New York, Evanston, San Francisco, London: Harper and Row, Publishers, 1969.
Iggers, Georg G. *The German Conception of History. The National Tradition of Historical Thought from Herder to the Present.* Middletown, Conn.: Wesleyan University Press, 1969.
— *New Directions in European Historiography.* Middletown, Conn.: Wesleyan University Press, 1975.
Jaspers, Karl. *General Psychopathology.* Translated by J. Hoenig and M.W. Hamikon. Chicago: The University of Chicago Press, 1963.
— "Kausale und Verständliche Zusammenhänge zwischen Schicksal und Psychose bei der Dementia Praecox." Reprinted in *Gesammelte Schriften zur Psychopathologie.* Berlin: Springer, 1963.

Johach, Helmut. *Handlender Mensch und Objektiver Geist. Zur Theorie der Geisteswissenschaften bei Wilhelm Dilthey.* Meisenheim am Glan, Verlag Anton Hain, 1974.

Kant, Immanuel. *On History.* Edited, with an introduction, by Lewis White Beck. Translated by Lewis White Beck, Robert E. Anchor and Emil L Falckenheim. Indianapolis and New York: The Bobbs-Merrill Company, 1963.

Kierkegaard, Søren. *Philosophical Fragments.* Originally translated and introduced by David Swenson. New introduction and commentary by Niels Thulstrup. Translation revised and commentary translated by Howard V. Hong. Princeton: Princeton University Press, 1974.

– *Stages on Life's Way. Studies by Sundry Persons.* Translated by Walter Lowrie, D.D. Princeton: Princeton University Press, 1945.

Kluback, William. *Dilthey's Philosophy of History.* New York: Columbia University Press, 1956.

Kornberg, Jacques. "Wilhelm Dilthey on the Self and History. Some Theoretical Roots of Geistesgeschichte." *Central European History*, 5 (1972), 295-317.

Krausser, Peter. "Dilthey's Philosophische Anthropologie." *Journal of the History of Philosophy*, 1 (1963), 211-221.

– "Dilthey's Revolution in the Theory of the Structure of Scientific Inquiry and Rational Behavior." *The Review of Metaphysics*, 22 (1968), 262-280.

– *Kritik der endlichen Vernunft: Diltheys Revolution der Allgemeinen Wissenschafts- und Handlungstheorie.* Frankfurt a.M.: Suhrkamp, 1968.

Krieger, Leonard. *The German Idea of Freedom. History of a Political Tradition.* Chicago and London: The University of Chicago Press, 1957.

– *Ranke: The Meaning of History.* Chicago and London: The University of Chicago Press, 1977.

Kuhn, Thomas S. *The Structure of Scientific Revolutions.* 2nd ed., enlarged. Chicago and London: The University of Chicago Press, 1970.

Landmann, Michael, *Philosophische Anthropologie. Menschliche Selbstdeutung in Geschichte und Gegenwart.* Berlin: Walter de Gruyter, 1955.

Lee, Dwight E., and Robert N. Beck. "The Meaning of 'Historicism.'" *American Historical Review*, 59 (1954), 568-577.

Lees, Andrew. *Revolution and Reflection. Intellectual Change in Germany during the 50's* The Hague: Martinus Nijhoff, 1974.

Lepenies, Wolf. *Das Ende der Naturgeschichte. Wandel kultureller Selbstverständlichkeiten in den Wissenschaften des 18. Jahrhunderts.* München, Wien: Carl Hansen Verlag, 1976.

– "History and Anthropology: A Historical Appraisal of the Current Contact between the Disciplines." *Social Science Information*, 15 (1976), 287-306.

Lévi-Strauss, Claude. *The Savage Mind.* Chicago: The University of Chicago Press, 1970. Translated from the French.

Lieber, Hans-Joachim. "Geschichte und Gesellschaft im Denken Diltheys." *Kölner Zeitschrift für Soziologie und Sozialpsychologie*, 17 (1965), 703-742.

Linge, David E. "Dilthey and Gadamer: Two Theories of Historical Understanding." *Journal of the American Academy of Religion*, 61 (1973), 536-553.

Löwith, Karl. "Max Weber und Karl Marx." *Archiv für Sozialwissenschaften und Sozialpolitik*, 67 (1955), 175-214.

– *From Hegel to Nietzsche. The Revolution in Nineteenth-Century Thought.* Translated from the German by David E. Green. New York, Chicago, San Francisco: Holt, Rhinehart and Winston, 1964.

— *Meaning in History*. Chicago and London: The University of Chicago Press, 1970.

Lubac, Henri de. *Exégèse Médiévale. Les Quatre Sens de l'Ecriture*. 3 vols. Paris: Aubier, 1959.

Lukacs, Georg. *Die Zerstörung der Vernunft. Irrationalismus und Imperialismus*. Darmstadt und Neuwied: Herman Luchterhand Verlag, 1973.

Makkreel, Rudolf A. *Dilthey: Philosopher of the Human Studies*. Princeton: Princeton University Press, 1975.

Mandelbaum, Maurice. "Historicism." *Encyclopedia of Philosophy*, 1972, IV, 22-25.

— *History, Man and Reason. A Study in Nineteenth-Century Thought*. Baltimore and London: The John Hopkins Press, 1974.

Manuel, Frank E. *Shapes of Philosophical History*. Stanford: Stanford University Press, 1967.

Marquard, Odo. *Schwierigkeiten mit der Geschichtsphilosophie. Aufsätze*. Frankfurt a.M.: Suhrkampf Verlag, 1973.

Marx, Karl. *The Marx-Engels Reader*. Edited by Robert C. Tucker. New York: W. W. Norton and Company, 1972.

Mazlow, Abraham H. *The Psychology of Science. A Reconnaissance*. Chicago: Henry Regnery Company, 1966.

Meyerhoff, Hans. *Time in Literature*. Berkeley and Los Angeles: University of California Press, 1960.

Mommsen, Wolfgang J. *Die Geschichtswissenschaft jenseits des Historismus*. Düsseldorf: Drosteverlag, 1971.

— "Universalgeschichtliches und politisches Denken bei Max Weber." *Historische Zeitschrift*, 101 (1960), 557-585.

Moravia, Sergio. *Beobachtende Vernunft. Philosophie und Anthropologie in der Aufkläring*. München: Carl Hanser Verlag, 1973.

Nietzsche, Friedrich Wilhelm. *Beyond Good and Evil. Prelude to a Philosophy of the Future*. Translated, with commentary by Walter Kaufmann. New York: Random House, 1966.

— *On the Genealogy of Morals*. Translated by Walter Kaufmann and H. J. Hollingdale. New York: Random House, 1969.

— *Thus Spoke Zarathustra*. Translated and with a preface by Walter Kaufmann. New York: The Viking Press, 1966.

— *The Use and Abuse of History*. Translated by Adrian Collins with an introduction by Julius Kraft. Indianapolis and New York: The Bobbs-Merrill Company, 1957.

Nisbet, Robert A. *Social Change and History. Aspects of the Western Theory of Development*. New York: Oxford University Press, 1969.

Palmer, Richard E. *Hermeneutics: Interpretation Theory in Schleiermacher, Dilthey, Heidegger and Gadamer*. Evanston: Northwestern University Press, 1969.

Pflug, Günther. "The Development of Historical Method in the Eighteenth Century." *History and Theory. Studies in the Philosophy of History*. Beiheft II, 1971, pp. 1-24.

Polanyi, Michael. *Personal Knowledge: Toward a Post-Critical Philosophy*. Chicago: The University of Chicago Press, 1958.

Rand, Calvin C. "Two Meanings of Historicism in the Writings of Dilthey, Troeltsch and Meinecke." *Journal of the History of Ideas*, 25 (1964), 503-518.

Randall, John Hermann, Jr. *The Career of Philosophy*. 2 vols. New York and London: Columbia University Press, 1970.

Reill, Peter Hanns. *The German Enlightenment and the Rise of Historicism*. Berkeley, Los Angeles, London: The University of California Press, 1975.

Rickert, Heinrich. *Kulturwissenschaft und Naturwissenschaft*. Tübingen: J.C.B. Mohr, 1926.

Ricoeur, Paul. "Existence et herméneutique." *Dialogue*, 4 (1965-1966), 1-25.

— *De l'interprétation: essai sur Freud*. Paris: Editions du Seuil, 1965.

Ringer, Fritz Karl. *The Decline of the German Mandarins; the German Academic Community, 1890-1933*. Cambridge, Mass.: Harvard University Press, 1969.

Roback, A.A. *History of Psychology and Psychiatry*. New York: Philosophical Library, 1961.

Robinson, James M. "The New Hermeneutik." *The New Hermeneutic*, ed. James M. Robinson and John B. Cobb, Jr. New York, Evanston and London: Harper and Row, Publishers, 1964, pp. 1-147.

Rodi, Frithjof. *Morphologie und Hermeneutik. Zur Methode von Diltheys Aesthetik*. Stuttgart, Berlin, Köln, Mainz: Kohlhammer, 1969.

Rossi, Pietro. "The Ideological Valences of Twentieth Century Historicism." *History and Theory. Studies in the Philosophy of History*, 14 (1975), Beiheft 14, *Essays on Historicism*, pp. 15-30.

Sacks, Oliver W. *Awakenings*. Garden City, N.Y.: Doubleday and Company, 1974.

Sartre, Jean-Paul. *L'être et le néant. Essai d'ontologie phénoménologique*. Paris: Librairie Gallimard, 1943.

— *Nausea*. Translated by Lloyd Alexander. New York: New Directions Publishing Corp., 1964.

Schleiermacher, Friedrich Ernst Daniel. *On Religion: Speeches to its Cultural Despisers*. Translated by John Oman. New York: Harper and Brothers, 1958.

Schopenhauer, Arthur. *Die Welt als Wille und Vorstellung. Sämtliche Werke*. Wiesbaden: F. A. Brockhaus, 1961, vol. I.

Schulin, Ernst, ed. *Universalgeschichte*. Köln: Kiepenheuer und Witsch, 1974.

Spiegelberg, Herbert. *Phenomenology and Psychiatry: A Historical Introduction*. Evanston: Northwestern University Press, 1972.

Spengler, Oswald. *The Decline of the West*. An abridged edition by Helmut Werner. English abridged edition prepared by Arthur Helps from the translation by Charles Francis Atkinson. New York: The Modern Library, 1962.

Spitz, Lewis W. "Natural Law and the Theory of History in Herder." *Journal of the History of Ideas*, 16 (1953), 453-475.

Stocking, George W. *Race, Culture, and Evolution. Essays in the History of Anthropology*. New York and London: The Free Press, 1968.

Stoianowich, Trainan. *French Historical Method: The Annales Paradigm*. With a foreword by Fernand Braudel. Ithaca and New York: Cornell University Press, 1976.

Strasser, Stephen. *The Soul in Metaphysical and Empirical Psychology*. Pittsburgh, Pa.: Duqesne University, 1962.

Strauss, Leo. *Natural Right and History*. Chicago: The University of Chicago Press, 1953.

Suter, Jean François. *Philosophie et histoire dans Wilhelm Dilthey; Essai sur le problème de l'historicisme*. Basel: Verlag für Recht und Gesellschaft, 1960.

Teggart, Frederick J. *Theory and Processes of History*. Gloucester, Mass.: Peter Smith, 1972.

Toliver, Harold. *Animate Illusions. Explanations of Narrative Structures.* Lincoln, Neb.: University of Nebraska Press, 1974.

Troeltsch, Ernst. *Der Historismus und Seine Probleme.* Tübingen: J.C.B. Mohr, 1922.

Turner, Frank Miller. *Between Science and Religion. The Reaction against Scientific Naturalism in Late Victorian England.* New Haven: Yale University Press, 1974.

Tuttle, Howard Nelson. *Wilhelm Dilthey's Philosophy of Historical Understanding. A Critical Analysis.* Leiden: E. J. Brill, 1969.

Voltaire, François-Marie Arouet. *The Works of Voltaire.* 22 vols. Editors Schmollell and Fleming. New York, 1901.

Wach, Joachim. *Das Verstehen. Grundzüge einer Geschichte der Hermeneutischen Theorie im 19, Jahrhundert, I-III.* Hildesheim: Georg Olms Verlagsbuchhandlung, 1966.

Walsh, W.H. *Philosophy of History. An Introduction.* New York and Evanston: Harper and Row, Publishers, 1967.

Weber, Max. "Die Objectivität socialwissenschaftlicher und social-politischer Erkenntnis" (1904). *Gesammelte Aufsätze zur Wissenschaftslehre.* Tübingen: J.C.B. Mohr (Paul Siebeck), 1973.

— *The Protestant Ethic and the Spirit of Capitalism.* Translated by Talcott Parsons. London: Allen and Unwin, 1948.

Weimann, Klaus, *Historische Einleitung zur literaturwissenschaftlichen Hermeneutik.* Tübingen: J.C.B. Mohr (Paul Siebeck), 1975.

Wellek, René. *A History of Modern Criticism, 1750-1950. The Late Nineteenth Century.* New Haven and London: Yale University Press, 1965.

Wellek, René and Austin Warren. *Theory of Literature.* New York: Harcourt, Brace and World, 1970.

White, Hayden. *Metahistory. The Historical Imagination in Nineteenth-Century Europe.* Baltimore and London: The Johns Hopkins University Press, 1973.

Yates, Francis. *The Art of Memory.* Chicago: The University of Chicago Press, 1966.

Zöckler, Christofer. *Dilthey und die Hermeneutik. Diltheys Begründung der Hermeneutik als "Praxiswissenschaft" und die Geschichte ihrer Rezeption.* Stuttgart: J.B. Metzlersche Verlag, 1975.

INDEX

and identity, 53; and reason, 41; as conquest over time, 50, 51; field of, 74; Freud on, 52; function of, 43; Hegel on, 33, 34, 48, 50; in autobiography, 36; in personal life, 37, 52, 121; "inner", 42, 43, 45, 50, 52, 54, 179; – knowledge, 142; memorized knowledge, 41; Nietzsche on, 50, 51; "outer", 42, 43, 45, 46; stability of – images, 142; storage in, 143

Meta-philosophy. *See* philosophy of world-views

Meyerhoff, Hans: 49, 204n

Michelet, Jules: 114

Mill, John Stuart: 18, 20, 211n

Mind: 8; active nature of, 143; connection between – and history, 191; creative nature of, 15, 212n; Dilthey's conception of, 81-82, 141; Dilthey's philosophy of, 163; emancipation of – from nature, tradition, 162; finite, 29, 136, 144, 163, 212n; Dilthey's psychology of the finite –, 136; history of, 163; objective, 56; sovereign over itself, 158; Hegel on. *See* Hegel, on mind

Misch, Georg: 202n

Mommsen, Wolfgang W.: 215n

Montaigne: 141

Niebuhr, Bartold: 70, 204n

Nietzsche, Friedrich Wilhelm: 5, 6, 14, 20, 39, 134, 167, 202n, 204n, 205n, 210n; on memory, 50-51; on the autonomous individual, 156-157; on meaning in history, 130

Nihilism: 115

Nisbet, Robert A.: 183, 209n

Oakeshott, Michael: 186

"The Origin of Hermeneutics" (*Die Entstehung der Hermeneutik*): 55

Pareto, Vilfredo: 94

Pascal, Blaise: 141

Peoples, non-Western. See cultures, non-Western

Periods (of the past) (of history): 3, 5, 43, 46, 47, 163, 190; become cultures of the past, 175

Personality, – development. *See* development, personal. – structure. *See* structure, personality –

Philology: 27, 58

Philological: approach, 3, 57; interest, 57; interpretation, 58. – Hermeneutics. *See* hermeneutics, philological

Philologist: 3, 56, 57

Philosopher: comparable to literary critic, 86-88; social function of, 86, 88

Philosophy: as empirical science of mental phenomena, 24, 25; Dilthey's meta-, 80-94; goal of, 90; history of. 22, 24; originates in life itself, 86; scope of Dilthey's, 86

Philosophy of history: 40, 110-115, 116, 117, 163, 164, 195; Dilthey on, 109, 110, 117

Philosophy of world-views: and cultural anthropology, 107, 192; and experience, 84-85; and its continuation by Gadamer, 105; and its continuation by Habermas, 104; and its synchronic perspective on life, 121; and the "anthropologization" of history, 5; and the conflict with Dilthey's philosophy of history, 109; and the human sciences, 87, 90; and the intrinsic meaning of individual cultures, 110; and the Promethean view of man, 103; as artistic view of reality, 103; as exegetic hermeneutics, 129; as meta-philosophy, 80, 90, 93; as philosophy for the age, 89; considers reality as text, 4, 7; Dilthey's project of the, 23, 164, 193, 194, 195; overcomes psychologism, 145; types of, 92

Plato: 16, 59, 60, 106

Platonic: 74

Plessner, Helmuth: 160, 204n, 212n

"Poetic Imagination: Elements for a Poetic" (*Die Einbildungskraft des Dichters: Bausteine für eine Poetik*): 76, 87

Polyani, Michael: 142, 147, 204n, 212n

Positivism: challenge of, 10, 17-18, 25; Comte's, 134; contrast to idealism, 16; conception of knowledge, 77; Dilthey's affinity to, 2, 24, 25; Dilthey's struggle against, 30, 98, 193; denies soul, 132; human sciences as an attack on, 7, 14; Husserl's attack on, 95; idealist reaction against, 15; in psychology, 211n; negative effects of, 21

Positivistic: in the sense of "empirical", 23; – belief in historical laws, 114; conception of historical development, 180-181; conception of man, 15, 142-143; conception of reality and objects, 146; neglect of man's moral nature, 17; world-view, 23

Post-historical: 94, 103, 108

Post-history: 109

Present age: Dilthey's evaluation of the, 12, 14, 20, 88

Date Due

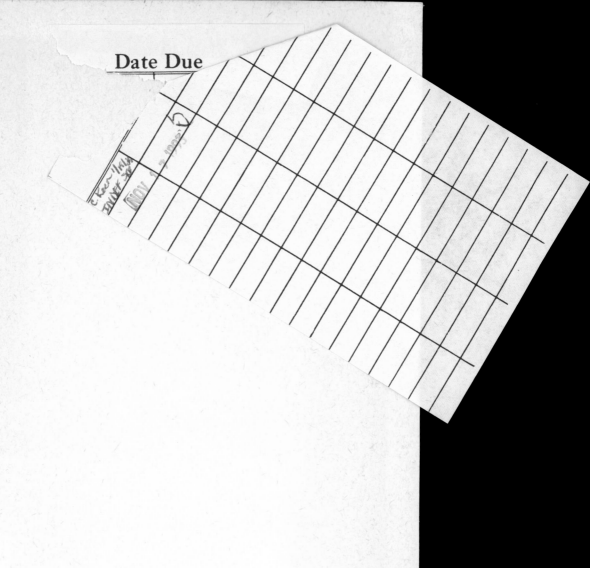